Thomas J. Hutchinson

Summer Holidays in Brittany

Thomas J. Hutchinson

Summer Holidays in Brittany

ISBN/EAN: 9783337288600

Printed in Europe, USA, Canada, Australia, Japan

Cover: Foto ©Andreas Hilbeck / pixelio.de

More available books at **www.hansebooks.com**

SUMMER HOLIDAYS

IN

BRITTANY.

BY

THOMAS J. HUTCHINSON,

VICE-PRESIDENT D'HONNEUR DE L'INSTITUT D'AFRIQUE, PARIS ;
HONORARY MEMBER OF THE LIVERPOOL LITERARY AND PHILOSOPHICAL SOCIETY ;
SOCIO ESTRANJERO DE LA SOCIEDAD PALEONTOLOGICA DE BUENOS AIRES, &c., &c.
AUTHOR OF "IMPRESSIONS OF WESTERN AFRICA ;"
"BUENOS AYRES AND ARGENTINE GLEANINGS ;" "THE PARANA," &c.
"TWO YEARS IN PERU," &c., &c.

WITH MAP AND ILLUSTRATIONS.

LONDON :
SAMPSON LOW, MARSTON, SEARLE, & RIVINGTON
CROWN BUILDINGS, 188, FLEET STREET.
1876.

All rights reserved.

LONDON:
GILBERT AND RIVINGTON, PRINTERS,
ST. JOHN'S SQUARE.

"CŒLUM, NON ANIMUM MUTANT."
HORACE, Epis. xi.

TO

MRS. S. C. HALL,

AS A TRIFLING TRIBUTE

FOR THE MANY PLEASANT HOURS ENJOYED,

AND WEARISOME ONES ASSUAGED,

—WHEN ON FOREIGN SERVICE,—

IN PERUSING HER TRUTHFUL DELINEATIONS OF

IRISH CHARACTER,

This Work

IS RESPECTFULLY DEDICATED,

BY HER ADMIRING FELLOW-COUNTRYMAN, AND

OBEDIENT, HUMBLE SERVANT,

THE AUTHOR.

PREFACE.

Y preface shall be very brief,—and only to make a couple of explanations.

FIRST—That a portion of the contents of this volume has appeared during the past Summer in the "*Liverpool Weekly Albion,*" under the title of "*Holiday Letters from France.*" But all the materials from these letters have been revised. Some of them are omitted altogether—others, where amalgamated with this, are curtailed—whilst occasionally more has been added from my note-book. The whole has been re-written, and corrected, where needful.

SECOND—That in spite of the Guides, Tours, Rambles, and Itineraries already published, with

PREFACE.   vii

reference to Brittany, there are still highways and bye-ways in that historic land, about which little or nothing is known to the outside world.

I therefore trust that the account of some of these in the following pages will prove of sufficient interest to justify me in presenting them to the public.

BALLINESCAR LODGE.
    CURRACLOE, WEXFORD,
        March 1, 1876.

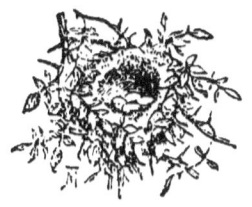

CONTENTS.

CHAPTER I.

London to Brittany in seventeen hours—Roadstead of St. Malo—Chateaubriand—The ubiquitous Gendarme—Classic pose—Irreproachable uniform—Hôtel de la Paz—Ramble through the city—St. Maclou—The Alethians—Pell-mell of streets—Cathedral—Deficiency of light—Military all over—Disagreeable odours—Hotel without baths—Sanitary motto—St. Servan—Dinard—Old town and new—Ancient priory   1

CHAPTER II.

Starting from St. Malo—To Dol and Rennes—Projected railway to Brest from St. Malo—Resemblance of Dol to Chester—St. Samson—St. Michael's Jump—Rennes—Capital of Bretagne—Solemn and serious—Great fire of 1720—Distracting regularity of architecture—Ancient name of Candate—Traces of Roman occupation—Battle of St. Aubin de Cormier—Treaty of the Orchard—Drowsiness and education — Mordelaise Gate — Obliterated inscription—Museums—From Rennes to Redon .   11

CHAPTER III.

Préparez vos billets, s'il vous plait!—Breton white caps on platform—Pilgrimage to St. Anne d'Auray—Comfortable Hôtel de Bretagne—Cheery aspect of Redon—St. Conwoion—Dolmens, Menhirs, and tumuli of Druids—Church of St. Sauveur—Square tower—Sparrows and swallows—

CONTENTS. ix

Taking time by the forelock—Human chattering at railway bureau—Passengers in pens—Clatter of talk—That blessed baby—Double squint—Crammed to convulsions—Appeals of Corkscrew glances—Juvenile Breton martyrdom—Pernicious feeding of children in France—Vannes—Capital of Venetians—Naval battle in Conclusum Bay—Scene at St. Anne station—Gendarmes again—Dress of Bretons—Embroidered clothes—Quaker's cut of garments   18

CHAPTER IV.

Omnibuses and beggars—Mediocrity of hotels—Shop element near the shrine—Stalactite-looking bread—Miraculous fountain—Seven cups of water, and seven sous—The Scala Sancta—Congregation of 20,000—The church of St. Anne—Shelves of the Renaissance—The Carmelite Friars—Devotion of the Bretons to their patron Saint—*Ex voto* offerings—Crown of emeralds—Thanksgiving for birth of Louis XIV.—Visit of Queen Henrietta Maria—Napoleon III. at St. Anne—Offerings of ships' models—Story of 700 sailors from Vannes—Rich offerings—First discovery of statue—Yves Nicolazic—Early pilgrimages—Simple faith of the Breton people—200,000 visitors in one year—Pilgrimage from Granville in Normandy—On foot to St. Anne for 180 miles—Burning of ancient statue—Steadfast devotion of Bretons   31

CHAPTER V.

Round and about Auray—Curious rocking-stone—Horse named Bismarck—How it was made by the coachman to travel—Valley of Tre-Auray—La Chartreuse—Battle of Auray in 1364—College of St. Michael—Erected on account of a vow—St. Bruno, founder of La Chartreuse—The precious liqueur—Damage done by Revolution in 1793—Austere lives of Carthusian monks—Dispersion of goods and chattels—*Les Sœurs de la Sagesse*—Deaf and dumb porter—Invention of substitute for bell—Monument of Quiberon—952 martyrs—"*Droits de la cou-*

CONTENTS.

ronne"—History of St. Bruno—Carved oak in Chapel— Umbrageous tree—"*Champ des Martyrs*"—*Ilie cecidcrunt*—Valley of Kerso—Poor Bismarck. . . . 47

CHAPTER VI.

The city of Auray—Likeness to Chester and to Dol— Sleepy town—Antiquity of Cathedral and of Château— Hôtel de Ville—Chapel of Cordeliers—Gloomy castle of Treulan—Inhabited by bats or toads—Bismarck *en route* for Carnac—Barren and savage country—Village of Carnac, with nothing to speak of like a street—Church of St. Corneille—Church of St. Michael—Built on Druidical tumulus—Explorations in 1862—Dolmens found—Mr. Milne's diggings in the Roman Villa—What he has turned out—Avenues of large stones—Stretching to Kerlescan and Plouharnel—Sonorous stone masses—15,000 in sixteenth century—Modern Vandalism—Guesses about the monuments—Dolmen at Corcoro—Oyster parks—The Baron de Wolbock—Enormous profit—Curious grottoes— Old town of Locmariaker—Visit of London Anthropologists—Analogies of Archaic Anthropology between Bombay and Carnac—*Embarras des richesses* about Auray . 59

CHAPTER VII.

A trip to Basse Bretagne—Red petticoats in the fields—From Auray to Landernau—Junction to Pontivy and St. Brieuc —Pretty view of Hennebont—Ships amongst the houses— Lorient and the river Scorff—Large water basins—Old East Indian company—Gestel and Guidel—Limits of Morbihan and Finisterre—Dolmens and Menhirs—Quimperle—*L'Arcadie* de Basse Bretagne—Mail phaeton— Where are the letter-bags—Abbey of St. Croix—St. Gurloës—Cure of the gout—Galloping madly—Charming country—Vile huts of peasants—Fancy ploughing by pigs —Church of St. Fiacre—Dirty town of Faouet—Church of St. Barbe and the "Pardón"—Apparition round the corner—The *gendarme* again—Spurs and white gloves— Fibrous apples and old men of same class—Capot and

coif—Gourin—The Black Mountains—Château de Kerbiguet—More Dolmens and Menhirs—To Scaer and
through the Landes 71

CHAPTER VIII.

One of the conscripts—Talk about past and future German
wars—Bannalec to Redon—St. Gildas des Bois—Pont-
Château—Savenay Junction—"Sillon de Bretagne"—
"La Grande Brière"—Salt making at Guerande—Isolation still existing—*Égalité et Fraternité*—Stand-offishness
in the church—Varieties of dialect—To Donges, and
across the Loire—Druidical remnants at Donges—Old
priory—Paimbœuf—Relation to the Sea—Derivation of
name—Formation of sand-banks blocking up the Loire—
Change of scene—The *Quenouille* and *fuseau*—Ugly Duc
de Guesclin—From Paimbœuf—Architecture of churches
—Through St. Brenin, St. Père Retz, and La Plaine to
Préfailles—Pornic and Kirouard 88

CHAPTER IX.

Nooks and corners of Brittany—Topographical position of
Préfailles—Outside of Mrs. Grundy's territory—" Deportment," and "the proprieties"—Geographical divisions of
France—Noirmoutier and the Pillar Rock—Away, over
the Bay of Biscay, oh !—London to Préfailles in twenty-
four hours—*Ménage* at Hôtel des Voyageurs—"La
Source"—The Chalybeate well—Pleasant and homely
scene at the spring—Varieties of company—Analysis of
Source water—Gasifying it—Good only when drunk at the
fountain—Other hotels—Lodgings of entire cottages or of
chambers—Artistic grouping of houses—"*Établissement
Hydrothérapique*"—Breton English—Ancient use of Préfailles chalybeate—No paradise for the Artist at Préfailles
—Tranquil beauty everywhere 99

CHAPTER X.

What about the sea-bath ?—The season at Préfailles—On the
strand and amongst the dressing-boxes—The Marquee—

xii   CONTENTS.

                                                      PAGE
Traditional night-caps—Flopping up and down—*Le Baigneur*—On the bank to St. Gildas—Quadrupeds of Préfailles—Jerusalem pony—*Comment s'appelle-t-il?*—Varieties of titles—Classical, historical, and mythological—Sexual difference not regarded—Chatty little market-place—"*Dam Oui*" or "*Dam Non*"—Derivation—*Emotion* at arrival of fish-boat—Breton coif—Increase of kid-gloveology—Ozone and wild camomile—Agreeable recollections—General hybernation—Close of bathing season—Melancholy ocean—*Au revoir* to Préfailles   .   .   . 113

CHAPTER XI.

Picnic to Noirmoutier—Beautiful morning—"*Le paradis des ânes*"—Charming programme - General success of impromptu pleasure parties—Terrific whistling of steamer's pipe—Delay of getting passengers on board—Doubts of the propriety of such a trip before breakfast—"They *do not* manage these things better in France"—At the island—Tediousness of going on shore—Clamour at the hotel—Hurrying to and fro—Is it a fire, or a revolution?—No breakfast for anybody — Frantic gabble — Improvised cookery—Foray on bread-basket—"*Poulet pour trois*"—Scrap of liver and shaving of leg—Asses and mules—Progress to capital of island—Aspirations for oysters—Château—Church and *Paludiers*—Dirty water in the streets—Bad smells—Double *morale* 121

CHAPTER XII.

Préfailles to Nantes—Three different routes—Beauty of the old city—Hide-and-go-seek style of architecture—The Château—Cathedral—The railway station—Early foundation of Nantes—At what epoch?—Primitive Christian teaching and martyrdom here—Anne de Bretagne—Famous prisoners in the Château—Visit to Cathedral—Begun in Fifteenth Century and not yet finished—Deficient in harmony of proportions—Reign of Terror in Nantes—The Noyades, or Republican marriages—Narrative by one of the *employés*—Knocking the victims on the head—*Le*

CONTENTS. xiii

PAGE

mariage civique—Five girls sent for execution with their mother—Motherly feelings of fisherwoman—Reward for Carrier—Clisson and its Inquisition memories—*Tivoli de l'Occident* 133

CHAPTER XIII.

Departments in Brittany—Château Villegontier—Hospitality of Baron d'Arthuys—Candé—A considerable barony - The Feudal period—A mother-in-law in these days—Fête at Candé—The town in its normal state—Grand names of hotels—Dead-and-alive commerce—Squealing of young pigs—Melancholy-looking shops—Comfortable farmhouses—Elegant châteaux—Cattle Show and Agricultural Exhibition—Merry-go-rounds—Monsieur de Falloux—Philanthropic Frenchmen—Les Prix de Vertu—Dr. Letort's speech—Anne Tessier—Her history—"God's ladies and gentlemen"—The prize for filial piety well earned . 143

CHAPTER XIV.

Disregard of punctuality—"*Tout de suite*" not always "right away!"—Waiting for historic cavalcade—Champ des Foires—Site of Old Priory—Musty, mediæval-looking Candé—Three gendarmes—Splendid fellows—Horses well trained—Noble Crusader smoking a meerschaum—Pages and equerries sucking çigaritas—François I. and Jean IV. of Brittany—Mounted trumpeters—Gaulois chief and soldiers—"Char d'Agriculture"—Franks—"Char des Fleurs"—"Char de l'Industrie"—Perfect order and discipline of cavalcade—Doubtless due to presence of the Ubiquitous—Illuminations at night—Music and jollification at Prairie de la Porte—Source of paying expenses—Menhirs—Bourg d'Iré—Segré—Laval 152

CHAPTER XV.

Visit to Angers—The second capital of England in the Plantagenet period—Originally peopled by Andes tribe—Their chief Dumnacus—Roman curia—Dispute between Francs and Saxons—Expulsion of Roman paganism—The first Bishop Defensor—Visitandine Nunnery, now a barracks

—Cathedral on the site of a temple of Apollo—Tradition
of foundation—Solemn light inside—Chief attractive features—Presentation by King René—The Logis Barrault
—Tower of St. Aubin—Museums and Library—Awe-
inspiring cocked-hats—Sculptor David—Ruins of Toussaint Abbey—By moonlight—Effects of age on ruins—
Place de Railliement and Theatre—Château and its
gloomy aspect—Birthplace of King René—His statue in
the Place du Château 164

CHAPTER XVI.

Disagreeable water of the Maine—Waterworks at Pont de Cé
—Holiday town—The bridges of Angers—First bridge in
sixth century—Those made by Foulques Nerva III. and
Henry II.—223 soldiers killed by falling of Suspension
Bridge in 1850—Doutre side of the river—"*École des Arts
et des Métiers*"—Abbey de Ronceray—Hôtel Dieu of
Henry II.—Churches of St. James and La Trinité—Comfort and luxury in King Henry's Hospital—Granary and
caves cut in the rock—Now used as a brewery—The Mall
and its pleasures—Cleanliness of Angers city—Interesting
objects of antiquity—Great field for explorers . . . 178

CHAPTER XVII.

Sablé and its marble quarries—Château of Duchesse de Chartreuse—The river Sarthe—To the Abbey of Solesmes—
Famous for works of Art—Gracious courtesy—Accommodation for strangers—Thorn from our Saviour's Crown a
relic here—Anachronisms and anomalies—Statue of St.
Peter—Beautifully carved stalls—The Sepulture of Christ
—Sepulture of Blessed Virgin—Crowning of the Virgin in
Heaven—Christ amongst the Doctors—Figures of sublime
Majesty—Divine aspect of the Saviour—King René
lowering the winding-sheet—Prior Jean Bougler doing
like office with that of the Virgin—Soldiers' faces
battered and smashed—Figures of Luther and Calvin
representing the Doctors in the Temple—Foundation
of Abbey in eleventh century—Strange reading during
dinner—Château Juigné 187

CHAPTER XVIII.

To Notre Dame du Chêne—Miraculous statue of A.D. 1494—Charming prospect—Valley of Sarthe—Shops at the Church door—Scaffolding around the building—*Ex voto* offerings and bannerets—Ancient traditions—Of wild pigeons as of starry lights—Statue placed in an oak-tree—Miracle subsequently occurring—Crick in the neck—Other prodigies—Oak held in veneration after it fell down—Preservative against thunder and lightning—Large pilgrimages in 1515—Results of the Calvin heresy—The Huguenots laying the country waste—Sablé pillaged—Farms despoliated—Monasteries destroyed—Pilgrimages suspended—New miracles—Reign of Terror here—Sale of Church of Notre Dame—Purchaser broke his leg—Statue concealed by Mayor of Vion—Restoration in 1866—New chapel and new wonders—Latest of those in October 1874 . 198

CHAPTER XIX.

Pardóns and pilgrimages in Brittany—Universality of the ceremonies—Half fair, half festival—Hereditary sentiment in religious devotions—Statues and fountains—Guingamp—Wrestling matches, and Armorican bagpipes—Martyrdom of St. Lawrence—Muscular Christianity—Old Breton costume—The *Bragou-bras*—*Pardón des Oiseaux*—*Danse Macabre*—Mixture of Druidical with Christian ruins—*St. Jean du Doigt*—Legend of Notre Dame de Folgoët—The idiot Salaun—The *Ave Maria* lily—Highest Druidical Menhir—Strange superstition connected with it—Pagan cemetery—Bread turned into stones—Setting dogs at the Virgin—Punishment for this offence—Church of St. Herbot—Showers of oxen tails and horns thrown in as offerings—*Les Vies des Saints de Bretagne*—Canonized in the hearts of the people 209

CHAPTER XX.

Cathedral of St. Pol—Deep religious feeling—Seriousness and sincerity *versus* Irreligion and impiety—From Quimper to Vannes—So-called "trashy" legend—Nature's

xvi   *CONTENTS.*

PAGE

nobility—*Les prix de Vertu*—The locksmith of Rennes—His wonderful charities—Madame Besnard—Remarkable self-denial—Rescuing unfortunates—In the field of battle—Madlle. Prudhomme—Nursing the cancer patient—Cancer developed in the Nurse—Stinted resources—Marie Grosbois of Paimbœuf—Noble sacrifice to self-imposed duty—Rosin Cherin, the sempstress—Supporting three families by her needlework—Great privations—Assiduous industry—The Paris locksmith—Extraordinary filial piety—Yearly prizes through French Academy—M. Montyon and philanthropic confrères—Such deeds need to be exalted—High-souled development—Deficiency in organic laws   .   .   . 223

LIST OF ILLUSTRATIONS.

St. Malo	*Frontispiece*
Part of Vannes with Cathedral	*To face* 27
Interior of Church of St. Anne d'Auray .	. 32
Breton Peasantry passing a Cross	. 35
Valley of Tre-Auray	. 49
Druidical Menhirs at Carnac	. 65
Interior of a Breton Peasant's House (Morbihan) .	. 78
Saint Fiacre Church	. 80
Inside of a Breton Cabin near Faouet . .	. 82
Ancient Breton House at Quimper . . .	. 84
Wandering Musicians in Lower Brittany . .	. 85
Pardon Dance at Larmoor	. 209
Breton Peasant Costumes of the Bragou-Bras . .	. 213

SUMMER HOLIDAYS IN BRITTANY.

CHAPTER I.

London to Brittany in seventeen hours—Roadstead of St. Malo—Chateaubriand—The ubiquitous gendarme—Classic pose—Irreproachable uniform—Hôtel de la Paz—Ramble through the city—St. Maclou—The Alethians—Pell-mell of streets—Cathedral—Deficiency of light—Military all over—Disagreeable odours—Hotels without baths—Sanitary motto—St. Servan—Dinard—Old town and new—Ancient priory.

FROM Waterloo station, by any train to correspond with one of the commodious and well-arranged steamers, carrying her Majesty's mails to St. Malo, we can run over from London to Brittany in about seventeen hours.

So, after selecting a fine evening for the crossing, and taking our tickets at the terminus on the Surrey side, we get through the journey bravely. In rough weather there are nasty breezes, and a rolling sea in the neighbourhood of the Jersey and Alderney Islands. The average voyage from Southampton to St. Malo is fourteen hours: and with people, (of whom the world holds a large number,) that have an unconquerable proclivity to sea-sickness, it is always expedient, if possible, to choose calm weather for the traverse.

As morning comes on, and we go up to deck, we find the steamer in perfectly smooth water, in a bay that washes part of the coast of Normandy as well as Brittany, and into which flows the river Rance. We are in the roadstead of St. Malo, gliding on between the charming bathing place of Dinard on the right, and on the left the city, with its frowning forts, batteries, and big walls. At the entrance here on a rocky islet, called the Grand-Bey, is the grave of Chateaubriand, to whose memory, all the world knows, a statue was erected in the course of last summer, in front of the house where he was born—now part of the Hôtel de France in the principal Plaza. It appears that the desire to be interred here was expressed by the author of "*Le Génie du Christianisme*," in a letter to the Mayor of St. Malo in the year 1828. We can see nothing of the tomb except the iron railings as the steamer passes by. But I am told by the chief steward, that there is no inscription on the simple stone—that the waves wash over it in stormy weather—and that it is much visited by pilgrims, when the water is low, and the sea is smooth.

Rounding a corner, now at diminished speed, we get alongside of a quay, which abuts from a grim, dungeon-like wall. " Haul in ! " here and there—" let go hawser ! "—" stop her ! "

The usual accessories to the arrival of a steamer in any part of the world, with the ordinary crowd close to the gangway ! No ? " Hardly the *common* crowd on this occasion," I hear a reproachful voice observing. For looking upwards I see a figure there, such as will be before me on every arrival or departure of mine as long as I am in France, and whether my journeys are made by steam-boat, railroad, or *diligence!* The ubiquitous and irrepressible *gendarme!* Although in the middle of the throng, not bending himself in the smallest possible degree from his normal *pose* of a classic statue. With cocked-hat, white cotton gloves, silver cord in festoons on his left breast, yellow belt, light blue trowsers, dark blue coat, spurs and sword ! He is the same wherever you meet him. On the boulevards at Paris—at a country railway station—in a little village where they know nothing of steamboats or railways—through the *bourgs* of Basse Bretagne—under shadow of the Black Mountains. The cocked-hat, white gloves, spurs, and sword are out in all weathers. I have often wished to penetrate the mystery of whence he comes, or whither he goes, after the passengers depart? He is never absent from his post on arrival or gathering of travellers, or any other class of multitude.

But as I have not, at any time, seen him enter, or make exit through door of a railway station, (though invariably recognizing him among the group on the platform,) I am almost inclined to believe he has some magic way of coming and going, like the fiends that start up and fall down through the stage in a Christmas pantomime. Of course not with their vulgar flash, noise, and clatter. A stranger, at first sight, must find it difficult to believe he is only a policeman. For common sense puts in a protest against the possibility of that majestic cocked-hat, falling during a scuffle into the gutter: or those spotless gloves employed in hauling along a draggle-tailed party in petticoats, such as our force is occasionally obliged to patronize in Wapping, St. Giles's, the New

Cut, or down Whitechapel way. Policeman
indeed! Shame on the comparison! As you see
him when you land from, or enter, a steamer, get
out of or go into a railway carriage, or a diligence
from one village to another,—in fact wherever
is a gathering, be it ever so small,—he appears
the concentration of universal and official administration. Telling to the world in every gleam
of his buttons, his silver cord and epaulettes, as
in every rattle of his spurs and sword, "I am
France." Yet if a rambler going through the
interior of the country arrives late at night, either
at diligence office or railway station, and is in want
of direction to a good hotel, I would advise him,
before going outside the gates amongst the
touters, to ask the guidance of the *gendarme*, who
is as certain to be there as the platform itself.
This is invariably given without the slightest
appearance of interest, or of any *emotion*, tending
to derange that military and imposing *tout-en-
semble*. But the traveller may be satisfied that
it is always trustworthy.

We, however, are not needful of such inquiries.
Therefore, after giving up our tickets, and having
our luggage examined, we proceed in an omnibus
through one of the dungeon-looking gates to
the Hôtel de la Paz. There is a large number

of excellent hotels at St. Malo, of which that just mentioned is our favourite.

After breakfast we set out for a ramble through the old city. Very old it must be considered too—in spite of its few new houses, and other modern improvements. For so far back as the sixth century, Adolphe Joanne tells us,[1] on this granite isle lived an old cenobite, named Aaron, who was Abbé of a Monastery here at the period. Into that convent he received at the time mentioned Malo, or Maclou, a Welsh bishop (*Evêque Cambrien*) who succeeded Aaron in A.D. 545, and afterwards became bishop of the Alethians, whom he had converted to Christianity. The Alethians were people of the city of Aleth—which to-day is called St. Servan—on the same side of the river Rance, but higher up than St. Malo. In the twelfth century Jean de la Grille transferred (A.D. 1144) the episcopal seat to the island of Aaron, which then got the name of " St. Malo of the island."

There is a large field in St. Malo for archæological study, if our holiday rovers are inclined thereto, with the knowledge that they have to work for themselves.

[1] "Guide de Bretagne." Par Adolphe Joanne. Paris: Hachette & Co, 1874. Page 97.

The Museum, which is installed in a dependence on the Hôtel de Ville, has only pictures, statues, and a large collection of ornithological specimens in it. A search after any records of the epochs when Paganism flourished in Aleth, and the Armorican cities set up separate governments, would be futile. The district of Aleth is reputed to have been one of the last refuges of Druidism. But we cannot find any traces of even the Gallo-Roman period. So we must take St Malo as it is.

" A pell-mell of streets and alleys," as Joanne describes it, "with a decided parsimony everywhere of space and light." An equally decided parsimony I might add—in the summer time at least—"of pure air and sweet smells." Not far from our hotel is the Cathedral. This appears quite a busy part of the town. But as we enter the side door of the sacred edifice we go in out of a street, where the holy building is so crowded and hustled up with shops, that at a distance of ten yards from the door, we see people buying cabbages at a greengrocer's counter. I can tell nothing of the exterior aspect of the pile, as from the passage here whence we go in being so narrow, it gives me a crick in the neck to look upwards. Inside its chiefest characteristic is deficiency of light. It was therefore next to impossible to have a good view of three fine marble statues that are here—one representing Faith—another, St. Benoit, and the third, St. Maur. These were formerly the property of the convent of English Benedictines'—most probably in the period of the Plantagenet dynasty. Besides these are several paintings. Amongst them St. Malo preaching to the Druids, by Monsieur Duveau. Behind the grand altar, too, are preserved the remains of St. Celestin.

The earliest church built on the spot, which is the highest point of the island, was burned down by the soldiers of Charlemagne in A.D. 811. On the foundations of that was erected the chapel of St. Vincent in the ninth century by Bishop Helocur; and the different fortunes through which it went since the first cathedral was built here in the twelfth century cannot be discussed by a holiday seeker.

The Château—the Fort de la Cité—the Fort Royal, La Conchée, Harbourg Island, La Varde, and some others—together with the towers, batteries, citadels, ramparts, high walls, and huge gates, proclaim St. Malo to be military all over. Of the gates there are five. Going through the narrow and tortuous streets of the city for any distance, we find it difficult to be impressed with the balmy atmosphere, which in rural districts and by the seaside is one of the chief charms of France. Here, as at Angers and Nantes—even in some portions of Paris—I could not escape the disagreeably ammoniacal odour, which, by the peculiarity of its nastiness, leaves no doubt of the source whence it comes. I may add, that the English tourist will not be very long in this country—and I believe it to be the same over much of the Continent—before he is made to feel the discomfort of hotels without baths, and with badly arranged W.C.'s. As I mention my having put up at the Hôtel de la Paz, I must in justice say that with regard to the latter point it is very well regulated. But here, as elsewhere, no bath can be got in the house. I trust mawkish prudery will not object to the record of my experience that "Reform your W.C.'s" ought to be impressed on the proprietors of nine out of every ten hotels to be found in France.

To St. Servan—the site of Aleth—the traveller may take a trip whilst he is at St. Malo. Either by steamer or diligence, and for a few sous, this journey can be made. It is only about three quarters of a mile from St. Malo, and is quite close to what is considered the embouchure of the river Rance. Although there may probably be some relics of the old Roman occupation, or of the time of the Druids, we are told that no buildings exist here of a period anterior to the reign of Louis XIV.

If, however, time can be spared, I should recommend a run across the bay to Dinard, taking one of the steamers, reputed to ply every half-hour. You can get a first-class ticket for five sous, or a second-class return for the same price, the distance being three miles.

Dinard possesses two towns, the Old and the New. The principal attractive feature of the Old is in the ruins of a priory, founded in A.D. 1321, by the brothers Oliver and Geoffry de Montfort. I believe it has been transformed into private dwellings. The vault-roofed chapel, partly destroyed, contains the well-preserved tombs of its founders.

The new town of Dinard, which has a Protestant church amongst its buildings, is the fashionable bathing-place, and owns some elegantly constructed mansions, châteaux, and villas.

In the neighbourhood are the villages of St. Enogat, St. Lunaire, and St. Briac. On the roads around Dinard are many walks perfectly shaded overhead by umbrageous foliage; and several picturesque views are to be had from the high cliffs.

CHAPTER II.

Starting from St. Malo—To Dol and Rennes—Projected railway to Brest from St. Malo—Resemblance of Dol to Chester—St. Samson—St. Michael's Jump—Rennes—Capital of Bretagne—Solemn and serious—Great fire of 1720—Distracting regularity of architecture—Ancient name of Candate—Traces of Roman occupation—Battle of St. Aubin de Cormier—Treaty of the Orchard—Drowsiness and education—Mordelaise Gate—Obliterated inscription—Museums—From Rennes to Redon.

EFORE starting from the station at St. Malo, I would advise the excursionist to provide himself with one of the railway guides—"*L'Indicateur Général*"—which can be bought at the bookstall for about twelve sous, or sixpence. This is applicable to all France—has very good maps of the lines—is an excellent index to correspondence of trains one with another, and to many people is more easily understood than the itineraries of Cook or Bradshaw.

From St. Malo to Rennes is a journey of

sixty-five miles. At Dol, the third stopping-place, there is a line of railway projected, that when finished, will bring the traveller, after passing Dinan, along the coast by St. Brieuc, Guingamp, Morlaix, and Landernau to Brest. At present from Dol to St. Brieuc the district is accessible only by diligences or mail *calèches*. But from Rennes passengers can go *viâ* St. Brieuc per rail to Brest. A much larger tract of country may, however, be embraced by the journey I am about to take—past Dol, Rennes, Redon, Vannes, Auray, Lorient, and Quimperle, whence back by rail to Nantes and Angers. My rambles through such parts of Brittany as I have visited during three months of last year are comprised within the larger portion of the peninsula that extends westward of a straight line drawn from St. Malo to Nantes.

Dol de Bretagne, its orthodox name, is a very curious old town, and well worthy of a visit by lovers of the antique and picturesque. Many of its ancient houses, particularly in *La Grande Rue*, have their gable-ends to the street, and are marked by the projection of the first story, so as to allow a passage underneath. This last is fronted by pillars with various forms of capitals. These dwellings date from the twelfth century, and are on the same models as those of Auray to be visited hereafter, as of our own old city of Chester, when I saw it thirty years ago. Although Dol has only a little over 4000 inhabitants, it owns a Cathedral dedicated to St. Samson, who is reputed to have come hither from England. This is a building of many epoch-stages, yet begun so late as the thirteenth century. Its predecessor was burned down in A.D. 1203. The church of Notre-Dame-sous-Dol is now used as a corn-market. On the extensive moors northward of the town is another village with 2000 inhabitants, and bearing the name of a hill close by. This is Mount Dol. It is said to have been a sacred place of the Druids in old times. At the top of the granite rock here, about 150 feet high, is a fountain that never dries up, and believed to have resulted from the imprint of the Archangel St. Michael's foot, when he made a bound, from this Dol to the rock which bears his name in the bay between St. Malo and Granville. The latter may be seen on any map to the northeast of St. Malo. When one thinks of the distance of this jump, we must dread that the Saints of our time have degenerated in their acrobatics.

At the sixth station farther on, we turn out on the platform of Rennes, the capital of Bretagne, in the olden times. The Villaine river, cutting the town in two, is met at the corner of the Mall by a canal, which is formed out of the waters of the Rance and Ille. The territory of which Rennes is now the capital, is simply the department of Ille et Villaine. No longer a metropolitan city, it nevertheless retains much of its ancient grandeur, whilst being one of the most solemn and serious places it is possible to conceive,—solemn and serious even to grimness and melancholy. I find it difficult to avoid regretting, that the whole city, instead of a considerable part, was not burned in the great fire of 1720, which lasted for seven days. There is a distracting regularity in the architecture of all the houses that have been built since that fire. Gloomily monotonous in their sombre colours of granite and sandstone, with a persistent aspect, even in the bright sunshine, as if they were all in mourning. In its primitive days Rennes bore the name of Candate. It was the capital town of the Redones, one of the peoples of Armorica when the Romans came here, and the latter changed its title to that which it now bears, as more appropriate, in regard of the tribe whose chief town it was at the period. Traces of Roman occupation have been dug up and are treasured in its Museum. Medals of Nero, of Aurelian, and of many others from the City of the Seven Hills, were excavated when they were laying the foundations of the station. After expulsion of the Romans, Rennes was held by the Franks up to the reign of Charles the Bald, A.D. 840. He was conquered by Nomenoë, who took in A.D. 843, the title of King of the Bretons. The kingdom was, however, soon dismembered by the quarrels of Counts Pasquiten and Gurvaud. From them commenced the terrible civil strifes, including the wars of succession, that went on till the marriage of Anne of Brittany with Louis XII. A.D. 1501, which united the Breton territory to the crown of France. Near to Rennes was fought the great battle of St. Aubin de Cormier, A.D. 1488, when Brittany lost its independence. In the succeeding year was ratified at Redon what is called the Treaty of the Orchard, between Francis II. and Charles VIII., the latter being the first husband of the celebrated Anne de Bretagne.

The quiet and silence, amounting almost to a perpetuity of drowsiness, that pervade the streets of Rennes, are given as reasons for its being the central focus of civil, military, and ecclesiastical education. Besides its Cathedral—dedicated to St. Peter—and many churches, some of which have been destroyed, and rebuilt over and over again, it has a number of schools and barracks. The only thing approaching to a château or fort which we find here is the Mordelaise Gate, which stands between the Cathedral and the Place des Lices. It is supported on each side by a large tower with slits for shooting through. By this gate the Dukes of Bretagne, and the bishops always made their solemn or triumphal entries. But there is something of the grotesque about it, with all that stateliness. For on the left as you come out of the Cathedral and in one of the projecting elbows of the tower, is a stone with an inscription on it. This is said to be taken from some very old monument, and to have on it the date A. D. 238. Although the words are now almost illegible—the stone is so placed that the letters appear upside down. One must therefore stand on his head to decipher them.

The several museums—of painting, sculpture, and antiquities—in the Palace of the University are open to the stranger at any time on presenting his card at the *conciergerie*. The public are admitted from noon to 4 p.m. on Thursdays and Sundays.

Within the city walls as well as round the suburbs are many interesting places to visit.

But if the holiday-seeker desires to stay here for a few days, he can buy for a franc at the bookstall in the station a guide to the city and its surroundings.

From Rennes to Redon there are half a dozen stoppages of the train, and the journey generally occupies two hours. In this transit we cross the river Villaine twice or three times, so tortuous is its course. Through the country as we go along, there is little noticeable save the rurality of fields, farms, and houses.

CHAPTER III.

Préparez vos billets, s'il vous plait!—Breton white caps on platform—Pilgrimage to St. Anne d'Auray—Comfortable Hôtel de Bretagne—Cheery aspect of Redon—St. Conwoion—Dolmens, Menhirs, and tumuli of Druids—Church of St. Sauveur—Square tower—Sparrows and swallows—Taking time by the forelock—Human chattering at railway bureau—Passengers in pens—Clatter of talk—That blessed baby—Double squint—Crammed to convulsions—Appeals of Corkscrew glances—Juvenile Breton martyrdom—Pernicious feeding of children in France—Vannes—Capital of Venetians—Naval battle in Conclusum Bay—Scene at St. Anne station—Gendarmes again—Dress of Bretons—Embroidered clothes—Quaker's cut of garments.

"PREPAREZ *vos billets, s'il vous plait!—Préparez vos billets, s'il vous plait!*"—each syllable drawled out in a monotonous chant, as the man in uniform strolled along by the side of the carriages on our stopping at the ticket-collecting place outside of Redon. Such a contrast as it was to the lively—" Tickets ready—tickets, tickets please; ALL tickets ready!"—which was spoken so rapidly a few days back at Southampton. But the vision

I had seen at the landing-place in St. Malo had prepared me for this. So I began to feel myself on my way to naturalization.

As soon as we had got to the platform I observed a large number of clergymen, and a greater quantity still of white-capped Breton women. Mingled up with them were several old men—thin, slender curls hanging from heads covered with broad-brimmed, low-crowned hats, and stand-up collars to their coats. They were just arriving by a train which had come in at the same time as ours,—although from another direction. For Redon is an extensive junction station.

Anxious to know what was the occasion of such a presence, one of the porters, in reply to my inquiry, informed me that next morning, 26th July, would be the feast of St. Anne d'Auray, and that these were pilgrims on their way thither. So fellow-rambler (who was my wife) and self at once made up our minds to pay a visit to the shrine. As the train by which we had come did not go farther that night than Redon we had to stay for the first on the day succeeding. Within ten yards of the station, in fact, across the street from the outside gate, is the clean and comfortable Hôtel de Bretagne, where we put up, and at which the charges are very moderate.

When I rose up next morning very early, I was much pleased with the cheery aspect of everything here;—an impression that I cannot account for, but which I have always felt on my subsequent visits to Redon. This is more inexplicable, when one comes to think of its antiquity. In the early ages the town bore the name of Rotho or Rothomun. Here an abbey was founded in the ninth century by a saint, with the peculiarly Breton name of Conwoion. Even before that period it was inhabited by the Romans, of whose presence relics have been turned out on the banks of the Villaine. This is the river, of which we made acquaintance at Rennes, crossed on our rail journey yesterday, and that flowing to the eastern side of the town, empties itself into the sea near Penestin. But these relics of the Romans, or of the middle-age saint are new things, compared to what the traveller can see, if he visits the Cromlechs, Dolmens, Menhirs, and tumuli of the Druids (?), Celts (?), Gaels (?), or Kymri (?) which are to be found in plenty around Cojoux, St. Just, Treal, and Cresiolan—all within a carriage drive of Redon. Even so near as Renac, barely nine miles distant, many of these can be seen.

Only a few minutes in the early morning could

be available for me to look about, as we had to start by the 6 a.m. train, which goes on to Brest, and frequently takes passengers who have come by the night-trains from Nantes. Not far from the hotel, down to the left, and in a spacious open plot, on which the railway works are creeping in, is a grand square tower of great height and massive architecture. This, though belonging to the neighbouring church of St Sauveur, is perfectly detached from the latter. It seems to have been the belfry and clock-tower. The church itself dates from the end of the twelfth century. Many of the carved stone figures, that were on corners and elbows of this tower, are battered and disfigured. The doorway of entrance to the steps mounting up to the clock is rotten and decayed. An aspect of lifelessness pervades the whole, church and tower included, —save from the chirupping of sparrows and the twittering of some swallows, that seemed to mock me as I went into the sacred building. A scream from one of the engines at the station added emphasis to the chatter of the birds.

A solemn edifice it is! with exqusitely carved pulpit, lofty arches, very spacious nave and transept, colossal pillars, oaken doors of great strength and magnitude. I walked round behind the grand altar, past the monuments of the many great men, who are buried here;—amongst them, François Ier, Duc de Bretagne. All these have their inscriptions defaced and mutilated— not so much (I am informed) by the hand of time, as by the profanity of visitors. As I came out, a luggage-train was passing in front, and within a few yards of the tower. Again the engine whistled, whilst the sparrows and swallows were as active as ever, and the sun was brightly coming up. Opposite to me was the Post-Office, whilst some short distance to the right, and behind a boulevard was a Mansion-House-looking building with the word "Tribunal" in golden letters above its peristyle. But hark! there is the first bell, announcing the train by which we are to start for St. Anne. And although I bought this morning one of those guides of "Redon and its Environs," I am afraid the engine will not wait till I can make use of it. Even my reflections about the anomalies and incompatibilities of the church, tower, sparrows, swallows, locomotive, and the sunshine are nipped in the bud by the ringing of that bell. I had begun to ask myself, "If I were a few days resident in that old tower, or amongst the forgotten dead in the venerable church, and listening to the engine screeching, or to the sparrows and swallows in their joyful chirruping? But *cui bono?* Perhaps I may finish it in the train as we go along!

At the station we found a large gathering of people, the white Breton cap, as on yester-evening, being in the ascendant.[1] The greater number of these consisted of passengers and pilgrims, who had just arrived by two trains, one from Nantes, the other from Rennes. A much larger crowd than that here now, had gone in two specials to St. Anne's on the previous day, which was the eve of the feast. In matters of this kind, if in no other, the French, Italians, and Spaniards invariably "take time by the forelock," their grand festivities, processions, and rejoicings being commenced after mid-day preceding the actual *die de fiesta*. In South America I remember Good Friday is always commemorated by the burning of Pontius Pilate in effigy, the crossing of ship's yards, the half-masting of flags, and other signs of mourning begun as soon as the clock strikes twelve on Holy Thursday.

---

[1] I may here mention, that besides the 26th of July, the feast-day of St. Anne, there is a pilgrimage made to this shrine at Pentecost, that of St. Louis, and all the feasts of the Blessed Virgin.

On an occasion like this the *bureau* of the railway, both inside and out is such a Babel of human chattering as is not to be heard in many parts of the world. Redon is a junction; and when a train comes in, passengers are expected to get off the platform as soon as they can. Then they have to wait with the other new-comers till tickets are given out at about twenty minutes before the next train starts. Furnished with the *billet*, you are admitted into a square pen—first, second, or third as the case may be—where though looking out on the platform, you are locked in till six or seven minutes before starting time. Such an arrangement as shutting people out from the platform of a railway station would hardly be tolerated in England. But it suits admirably here. In France, and especially in the summer time, the tourist who wishes to observe all he can, should not confine himself to one class of carriage. I sometimes went in the first—occasionally in the second—but more frequently, on account of its superior coolness, in the third. In the last named, on an occurrence like the pilgrimage to St. Anne d'Auray, you can see the Breton peasantry in their most interesting peculiarities.

We had some difficulty in getting two places

amongst the third class—for which I had taken tickets—and as soon as we were seated all possibility of continuing the reflections, alluded to in my last chapter, completely vanished. Nine-tenths of the passengers in the large waggon were females. The clatter of talk was fearful. The idea of "a voice ever soft, gentle, and low—an excellent thing in woman," does not yet seem much developed amongst the fair sex in those parts of Brittany through which I have travelled. It is, however, nearly as bad with the conflicting sex—if that be a consolation. For almost every man talks—be it at a *table d'hôte*, or in the streets, with a voice as loud, and shrieky as if he were making a speech or delivering a sermon. Yet this gabble soon faded into insignificance, in sight of a horror that I observed in the next compartment to ours, and directly in front. A woman having on her lap a baby, with a most hideous squint in both eyes! During the whole of our two hours' journey from Redon to St. Anne, and for what I know many hours before—the mother not only kept up her share in the general palaver, but stuffed "that blessèd baby" in a way that was horrible to look at. She crammed him first with a lump of bread, that she had moistened in her mouth; then with a piece of green apple. To which succeeded some hard-boiled egg. On the first occasion I saw this series of doses repeated four times in the order enumerated—all the items being masticated by the mother previous to pressing them into the infant's mouth. The child begins to wriggle! Perhaps some of those corkscrew glances at his parent's face were an appeal to her mercy. If so, they utterly failed in their aim. For she, with a face beaming in the most perfect happiness and contentment, as of a consciousness that she was giving him gratification, administered a drink from her breast. Only a moment's pause to arrange her clothes! The wriggling is suppressed! But he is again hove down on his back across her knees, and once more he is charged with bread—apple—and hard egg! Over and over still, the like doses were shoved in as unremittingly as the fireman put coals into the engine-stove; till I began to wonder—not that the baby had a double squint, but, that, with the constant heaping up of what must form concrete on its little stomach, and the uninterrupted physical exertion of deglutition, the eyes of that juvenile Breton had not long ago screwed themselves out in early training for martyrdom.

A propos of this occurrence, I hope my comments

PART OF VANNES, WITH CATHEDRAL.

Page 27.

will be taken in the same good spirit as they are intended. No more mistaken system can be followed than that of making very young children eat or drink food that is not fit for them. I speak of it here because I observe more of it in France than in England. French parents may be assured that nothing will tend so much to the degeneracy of their race as feeding of the kind that I have just described. Or that other equally pernicious practice, whereof I regret to have seen many examples, of allowing young children under eight years of age to take *vin ordinaire* at their meals. The plain physiological fact should be known, that the mucous membrane of the stomach, in a child of such tender years, has not the faculty properly to assimilate condiment of this description. Hence it remains in the system, and is sure to lay the foundation of some organic disease.

Stopping for a short time at the intermediate stations of Malansac, Elven, and Vannes, very few passengers come in, except at the last-named, where several clergymen join us. Vannes is a celebrated old town, famous in the ecclesiastical history of France. There is an excellent view of it from the train, as the line runs along a lofty viaduct in passing the spot. Like most of the old cities in Brittany its streets are irregular and confused in their mal-arrangement. It is said to have been the capital of the Veneti in the old Celtic period, of having colonized the Adriatic as well as given its name to Venice. This city was at the head of the Armorican Confederation, and resisted Cæsar when he came to achieve the conquest of Gaul. Record exists of a naval battle with a fleet of Venetians thirty-seven years B.C. in the Conclusum Sea, which now bears the title of the Bay of Morbihan. It is distant only fourteen miles from Vannes. During the wars of succession in Brittany this place was besieged four times in A.D. 1432. It was frequently the residence of the Breton kings. Here was married the Comte d'Etampes to Margaret of Brittany, and from this marriage was born the famous Anne de Bretagne. Its cathedral dedicated to St. Peter, burned by the Normans in the tenth century, was begun to be rebuilt in the eleventh, and finished only in the eighteenth. It is a very fine edifice, but the different styles of architecture of the various ages can be scarcely said to harmonize. There are besides nearly a dozen chapels in the city, although its inhabitants number little over 14,000. An archæological Museum is here, in which exists a good collection, chiefly of Gallo-Roman remains, arms, pottery, coins, and bronze statues. Several pleasant promenades are about. The walking in which, planted as they are with oak and poplar shades, is very refreshing after a visit to the antiquities of the Museum.

The scene on our arrival at the St. Anne station would be an excellent subject for a companion to the celebrated picture of Frith's. Some thousands, who had concluded their pilgrimage the day before, were on the platform, and their efforts to get into the carriages before the others came out gave rise to an increase of talking, that subdued the engine screech into a whisper. But there was no rudeness amongst the crowd, and the courtesy on the part of the officials was as perfect as could be in such a cabal. It was, no doubt, aided by the presence of three or four *gendarmes*, whose lofty cocked-hats towered over the surging multitude. These members of the ubiquitous, occasionally out of the crowd, and in bold relief, offered a glaring contrast to the Breton peasant or farmer: the latter, with his broad-brimmed and low-crowned hat, long hair, stand-up coat collar, and richly embroidered waistcoat; the former already described. The Bretons of this class have a difference of costume and dialect in every department, and in some parts of Basse Bretagne they do not understand the French language. Some of the younger men wear their jackets, and jacket-frocks (that go barely down to the hips), worked in gold, silver, and silken threads. These patterns are generally of a religious type, several representing the Holy Sacrament, others a chalice, and mostly done on the middle of the back. On the waistcoats a row of bright buttons, sewn closely together, runs up on each side. These are their holiday suits no doubt. Many of them have garlands of a bunch of wheat, or head of Indian corn in the hat. Such stand-up collars to the coats, together with the broad-brimmed head covering, and the long caps of the women, seem to me to have been the models of the Quakers' dress. Can it be that William Penn came to Brittany to search for simplicity of costume?

CHAPTER IV.

Omnibuses and beggars—Mediocrity of hotels—Shop element near the shrine—Stalactite-looking bread—Miraculous fountain—Seven cups of water, and seven sous—The Scala Sancta—Congregation of 20,000—The church of St. Anne—Shelves of the Renaissance—The Carmelite Friars—Devotion of the Bretons to their patron Saint—*Ex voto* offerings—Crown of emeralds—Thanksgiving for birth of Louis XIV.—Visit of Queen Henrietta Maria—Napoleon III. at St. Anne—Offerings of ships' models—Story of 700 sailors from Vannes—Rich offerings—First discovery of statue—Yves Nicolazic—Early pilgrimages—Simple faith of the Breton people—200,000 visitors in one year—Pilgrimage from Granville in Normandy—On foot to St. Anne for 180 miles—Burning of ancient statue—Steadfast devotion of Bretons.

FOUR or five omnibuses are at the station; the distance up to the village, chapel, and hotels being about three quarters of a mile. The crowd of walkers going to and returning from the shrine is very numerous. On both sides the road is literally lined with beggars;—the lame, the blind, and the halt,—on crutches, and with distorted limbs exposed. Each hotel has its omnibus, to and from, every departure or arrival of a train. We find Theuff's Hôtel de France, the Hotel of the Golden Lion, Hôtel des Postes, Hôtel de St. Anne, and a few lesser ones. The charges are not very high, neither is the *menu* very good. But as no one comes here for luxurious eating, this can scarcely be objected to. In the small streets, quite close to the chapel, numerous stalls are put up on which are exposed rosaries, small statues, crucifixes, pictures, books of the history about the pilgrimage with its many miracles, and other religious mementoes. With these are likewise pears, grapes, and similar fruits in season. You observe women, hawking about in baskets a kind of dark brown bread, apparently half-baked, and such stalactite-looking cakes as I never saw elsewhere. It was not the black bread, or *galette* of Brittany made from the *blé noir*, which is quite a relishable condiment. Out of curiosity, I took a piece of both bread and cake in my hand to look at them. But unless in case of threatened famine from shipwreck I should not attempt their mastication.

There is a short street of these stalls which I have mentioned between the main entrance of the chapel and the miraculous fountain, whereat St. Anne is accredited to have appeared on more

INTERIOR OF THE CHURCH OF ST. ANNE D'AURAY.

than one occasion. The waters of this are kept in three large basins, each accessible by steps. On approaching it to take a drink, no less than seven poor women, nearly all of whom were in a state of rags and each having a cupful of the water in her hand, came up to me simultaneously. Seven cups of water implied seven sous. So I sloped away without tasting; as my stomach could not endure to take the whole of the former, nor my pockets afford to expend the latter.

Beyond this, and at the corner of the Rue des Merciers is the *Scala Sancta*, or Sacred Ladder. This is a building of a square tower shape, and with a cupola top, steps being arched over on either side. It is where the mass is celebrated for such large congregations as sometimes come here on festival days—namely 20,000. Its orthodox use is for pilgrims to mount on their knees up to the top, just as is done with the *Scala Sancta* at Rome. The marble steps of the latter were taken by the Emperor Constantine from Pilate's house.

The church of St. Anne suffered in the Revolution of 1793. For at that period was destroyed, in its arcade, an exquisite group of statuary representing the "*Ecce Homo.*" The Père Martin tells us that this *morçeau* of art was the work of the grandson of Francis de la Barre, born in the town of Le Mans. He was an artist of superior talents, and flourished in the sixteenth century. These figures were replaced in 1815 by those of the Holy Family, taken out of an establishment of Brothers of the third order of St. Francis, styled "Cordeliers." It may be needful to explain that this title is derived from a badge of cord worn round the waist. All the square of St. Anne, except the spot on which the *Scala Sancta* is situated, is now occupied by secular buildings, although it is valued by the Carmelite friars (who are the custodians of the shrine) on account of sacred memories.

In this chapel we see three shelves at the upper end, which are valuable relics of the Renaissance period. The scroll work of the frieze has a remarkable grace and artistic relief. But the most wonderful thing to be seen here is the enormous quantity of *ex voto* offerings—silver, gold, jewels, pictures, marble, and wood, placed upon the walls as thanksgivings to St. Anne.

The sacristy behind the great altar is surmounted with an arch, sustained by four marble pillars. This arch supports the pulpit, which opens on the nave by a large gallery. At the extremity of the cloister begins the body of the

BRETON PEASANTRY (MORBIHAN) PASSING A CROSS ON THE ROAD SIDE.

Friars' building, of which the front gives on to a spacious garden. Towards the north the convent ground of the brothers is extended to an inclosure of fifty-one acres of land, shut in by a wall nearly five thousand feet in extent. Large meadows, prolific orchards, avenues of chestnut trees, rows of poplars, a canal, a good-sized lake abounding in fish; all contribute to make the monastic property at St. Anne a valuable one to the incumbents.

The Carmelite Nuns have a house behind the chapel to the right-hand side—that of the Friars being on the left—the sacred edifice standing between. At the opposite side of the village, and with spacious recreation grounds attached, is a large convent of Sisters of the Faithful Company of Jesus. In the latter establishment we find a considerable number of boarders, not a few of whom are from England and the United States.

Let the Puritan growl, and grumble as he may, there is something of a very exalted sublimity in the devotion of the people of Brittany to their patron Saint—St. Anne. The solitary Breton,—soldier, sailor, farmer, or peasant—often walks a distance of fifty, sixty, or even eighty miles, to make his devotions here. Even now-a-days this is done, when the pilgrim cannot afford the railway fare. Should he arrive, as sometimes happens in the middle of the night he lays himself down to sleep on the flag-stone outside the chapel door—happy in believing that he is under the protection of his holy patroness. This, for him, is far more agreeable than the comfort or luxury of the best bed at hotel or lodging-house.

When you enter the holy building, you can see that all around the small altar of the chapel on the right side of the transept, the wall is completely covered with *ex voto* offerings left or sent by pilgrims—the greater number of them for favours received. The crown of emeralds on the head of the statue of St. Anne is a present from Anne of Austria, as thanksgiving for the birth of Louis XIV. So far back as A.D. 1638, by the solicitation of Anne and her husband, through Marshal d'Estrées, Ambassador Extraordinary in Rome of Louis at that period, a Bull was granted by Pope Urban VIII. to establish a Royal brotherhood of St. Anne. Every one, familiar with French history, may probably know that Anne of Austria had been married to Louis XIII. for twenty-two years before their son was born. His birth took place on the 5th September, 1638. He was entitled "Louis Dieu-donné," or, "Louis given by

God;" and his reign extended over a period of sixty years. It was in gratitude for his birth, that the royal offerings were made at St. Anne's shrine in the period of which I am writing. I cannot ascertain whether Anne of Austria ever came in person to this part of the world. But I find it recorded, that a visit hither was made by the unfortunate Queen of England, Henrietta Maria, daughter of Henry IV. and sister of Louis XIII. (Anne of Austria's husband). She was also wife of Charles I. of England. One of the stained glass windows commemorates the presence of this Queen in company with her daughter, Henrietta Ann, Duchess of Orleans. The late Emperor of France Napoleon III. visited this chapel along with the Empress Eugenie, on the 15th of August, 1856. Another of the stained glass windows is put up at his expense. The chief tableau in that represents the Bishop of Vannes in 1826, giving directions to the priests of his diocese about the pilgrimage to this shrine.

From the top of the nave are suspended by long cords three models of ships, offered by some Bretons in the seafaring line. Facing the small altar, which I have already mentioned as surrounded by gold, silver, printed inscriptions, and marble tablets, is a rude painting, on which are sketched two sailors, with their hats off, supporting a shield between them, surrounded by cannons, flags, a vessel in the back-ground, gun-carriages, ammunition, and other contingencies of war. In the centre of the shield the story of it is told. One day in the month of July, 1870, there marched into the little village of St. Anne, seven hundred sailors of the conscription, who had come from Vannes to put themselves under the protection of their patron Saint. After their devotions were completed, they went away to the war with Prussia. Everywhere foremost in the fight, and frequently under fire for many hours, yet in March of the following year, as soon as they could do it, after the armistice was signed in Paris, they returned to Vannes without the loss of a single man's life, and having only two of their company wounded. So, once more the same seven hundred sailors marched into the little village,—returned thanks with religious devotions,—made offerings in contributions to the completion of the chapel,—and put up the little picture as a memento of their gratitude.

Besides these we find many other acknowledgments. In A.D. 1651, a tribute was given by Marguerite de Lorraine, Duchess of Orleans, in gratitude for the birth of the Duke of Valois.

This is a bas-relief in silver. Another offering is a rich silver lamp, from the wife of the Grand Dauphin in A.D. 1628, on account of the birth of the Duke of Burgundy (subsequently the pupil of Fénélon), and who died of small-pox. Again in A.D. 1729, the Queen, Maria Leczinca, wife of Louis XV., made a like donation for a similar reason. Her son, unfortunately, departed this life before he could ascend the throne.

The register books of the confraternity are full of Royal and noble names of those, who have acknowledged their gratitude for favours received, and who have thus helped to swell the coffers of the voluntary offerings towards keeping a permanent chapel here. The new building, when completely finished, will have cost a million and a half of francs. It is a very handsome piece of ecclesiastical architecture.

From the period of the first discovery of the statue of St. Anne in March, 1625, by a humble peasant, named Yves Nicolazic, of the parish of Plumeret, the pilgrimages have been carried on with a steady Christian self-denial, and an abnegation of everything outside the aim of arriving at the shrine. The chapel in which the statue had been originally placed, tradition says about the fourth century, was somehow or another destroyed in A.D. 699. So that the sacred figure was out of sight for nearly a thousand years.

Next to Normandy I believe Brittany was one of the parts on the Continent in which the Christian religion took earliest root. Even so far back as the third century, it is recorded, that the Gospel was preached to the Venetians by St. Clear, the first Bishop of Nantes. A century afterwards St. Patern had founded the Bishopric of Vannes, in which St. Anne, where we are now, is part of the diocese.

There is a full account in a little book (which has reached the seventh edition) by a Jesuit Priest, the Père Martin, of the various incidents that led Nicolazic to the discovery of the statue. Another work of about the same size, by the Abbé E. Bernard, gives equally ample details, together with particulars of many miracles, that have been wrought. In both we are told of the original revelations, conveyed by what he considered a holy flame over the spot from which the sacred figure was taken; of the bullocks that had been used to plough in the field, always refusing to go over that particular place; of spades and hoes being invariably broken when attempted to be worked with on the same bit of field; of the Curé at Plumeret remaining obstinate in disbelieving it, until the Bishop of Vannes ordered a judicial examination into the facts and circumstances. When these were fully proven, Nicolazic triumphed not only for his own credit, but "for the glory of God, and the benefit of humanity," as it is summarized by one of the narratives. Even the shortest possible abstract of the dozens and scores of miracles that are recorded, would fill half a volume. I must therefore refer those, who are interested about the *minutiæ*, to the small treatises I have mentioned. They are published at Vannes, and doubtless could be obtained through any Paris bookseller.

Meantime the people of Brittany, without waiting for the decision of the court of inquiry, expressed their faith by coming in large crowds to offer up prayers at the shrine. Their belief was quite settled in the conviction that St. Anne, the mother of the blessed Virgin, had miraculously brought to light the Cross, ever the symbol of Christian belief;—that she constituted herself their friend and patron;—that this revival was to stir up in their hearts the holy zeal of their forefathers;—that her spirit was to be with them, and amongst them, henceforth and for evermore. Then began the building of a chapel over the site where the statue was found, and simultaneously commenced the organized pilgrimages. With great pomp, the first holy edifice of the renovation was consecrated in A.D. 1628, when the Carmelite friars had come to replace the Capuchins, who were custodians for two years after the discovery. During the brief period, last mentioned, many pilgrimages had been made ; the largest of them being on the feast day of St. Anne, the 26th of July,—the date which finds us spending part of our holidays here.

Some of these counted in numbers from forty to fifty thousand people attendant. Several miracles had also been registered. The chaplain of the community informs me that more than forty thousand people had received communion on one festival day, since his coming to take charge. I have already mentioned that for such a large congregation mass is celebrated in the open space in front of the Scala Sancta. But this would not hold one fourth of such a number. They are divided between that and the chapel,—masses being said every half-hour from 5 a.m. to midday. During the last year the chaplain says nearly 200,000 people visited the shrine of St. Anne d'Auray.

A short notice of some of the pilgrim-bands

in the olden time may not be uninteresting. In
A.D. 1629 (it may be remembered, one year after
the chapel was consecrated, and three years subsequent to discovery of the statue), a large body
of pilgrims came from Guelon, near Granville,
in Normandy, to implore the intercession of
St. Anne, after a long drought, which had destroyed their crops. To judge of the distance
in these days of trudging it on foot, I must ask
my readers to look at the map, where they will
see Granville considerably to the north of St.
Malo. Of the result in this case we are not informed. But in A.D. 1634, nearly the whole
town of Pont l'Abbé walked hither in solemn
procession, the distance being twenty-five
leagues, or nearly eighty miles, by French
measurement. This was done for a like object
as the previous, on account of an epidemic at
the time desolating the locality in question.
Ere the organization had been completed, the
epidemic ceased. Yet such was the pious spirit
pervading the people, that, now joining to it the
sentiments of gratitude, they made the journey
as the Guelon one was done, on foot. Rich and
poor, clergy, nobles, tradesmen, professionals,
farmers and peasants, all joined in the march.
Amongst them was an old man, exceeding

seventy years of age, who insisted on walking the whole distance, although he had been offered a horse at more than one stopping-place. Setting out in perfect discipline as regarded order of march, they only rested for a short time at such places as contiguous to the chapels of St. Roch and Quimper, both of which were *en route.* These were selected, no doubt, that after taking necessary repose and sustenance of food, they might have their spiritual recreation. The procession was headed by over thirty priests, walking four abreast, carrying crosses and banners. From time to time, and at certain positions, arranged in the programme, they gave out sacred hymns or canticles, in which the whole company joined. This is not the least of the impressive features connected with these pilgrimages. Following the clerical *avant-garde*, walked the laity in threes, and after them came the women. The whole assembly extended for several miles. When they arrived at St. Anne, their joy was indescribable. Late though it was in the evening, no fatigue or weariness was felt, and they slept soundly as contentedly, many of them in the fields, or on the pavements.

Subsequent to this, another band of pilgrims arrived here, from the Ile de Dieu, after a walk of sixty leagues, or beyond 180 miles. But such journeys as these could be multiplied in their narration, were I not afraid of tiring my readers.

To-day the devotion of the Bretons is as strong as it was three centuries ago. The religious enthusiasm in these *pardôns* or pilgrimages, evidenced by the thousands of bare heads, the dozens of gorgeous banners, and the singing of hymns at these pilgrimages is a picture that cannot be conveyed to paper. Joined to those is the energetic expression, which conveys the idea of a faith-proclamation to the whole world, when they chant with hundreds of singing voices the following chorus, which must be heard to be appreciated :—

> O Marie, ô Mère chérie,
> Garde au cœur des Bretons la foi des anciens jours :
> Entends du haut du ciel le cri de la patrie :
> *Catholique et Breton toujours!*

In the Revolution of 1791-93, the chapel of St. Anne and its treasures were not overlooked by the followers of Robespierre, Mirabeau, Danton, and their *confrères*. All of the diamonds, precious stones, gold, and silver offerings that could be laid hands upon by the marauders disappeared. Even the venerable statue was rescued by some pious inhabitant of Auray, and for more than a year it had to run the gauntlet from house to house to insure its safety. At length it was brought to some depôt where other articles of church property were deposited, and with them it was consigned to the flames. The body of it was burned, but the head was saved; whilst through the courage and piety of an inhabitant of Vannes this was restored to the chapel. It is now contained in a small box with a glass front, and is under the pedestal of the new statue of St. Anne. The last-named is is on the small altar previously alluded to, as at the right-hand side of the transept. It was crowned, in the name of Pope Pius IX., by Monsignor Bézel, the Bishop of Vannes, on the 30th of September, 1868.

CHAPTER V.

Round and about Auray—Curious rocking-stone—Horse named Bismarck—How it was made by the coachman to travel—Valley of Tre-Auray—La Chartreuse—Battle of Auray in 1364—College of St. Michael—Erected on account of a vow—St. Bruno, founder of La Chartreuse—The precious liqueur—Damage done by Revolution in 1793—Austere lives of Carthusian monks—Dispersion of goods and chattels—The order in England—"*Les Sœurs de la Sagesse*,—Deaf and dumb porter—Invention of substitute for bell—Monument of Quiberon—952 martyrs—"*Droits de la couronne*"—History of St. Bruno—Carved oak in Chapel—Umbrageous tree—"*Champ des Martyrs*"—*Hic ceciderunt*—Valley of Kerso—Poor Bismarck.

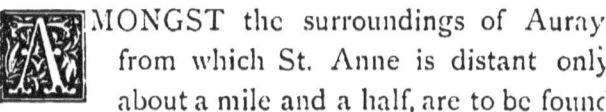MONGST the surroundings of Auray, from which St. Anne is distant only about a mile and a half, are to be found some of the most interesting historical and antiquarian relics that can be met with in France. We hired an open carriage at Theuff's Hotel,—fifteen francs or twelve shillings for the whole day,—to take us round by the celebrated convent of La Chartreuse, and crossing past the pillar on the old battle-field, to visit the Champ des

Martyrs. Thence, after resting the horse for a short time at Auray, whilst we dawdled about its streets and into its old churches, our further programme was to go by Plouharnel to the Druidical monuments at Carnac,—returning to the hotel for night time.

Starting as soon as we could after breakfast at nine o'clock, our route was to the west and south, from the village of St. Anne to where meet the high roads to Lorient and Pluvigner. A very curious rocking-stone is soon passed as we descend the declivity near Brech. The road was very rough from being newly laid down, and the driver whipped the horse now and then most unmercifully. The animal did not seem as if he could bear much of the castigation he was getting, used to it though he appeared to be, from a peculiar shuffling pace that he had in his hind legs, and a helpless manner of twisting his head around as if trying to turn back. "What is the name of your horse?" said I. It would be difficult to convey an expression of the fearful thump he gave the poor beast with the whip, as he answered emphatically, "Bismarck, Monsieur." "But," I replied, "if you punish the animal in that manner, you will fatigue him more than if he were drawing us in a carriage

THE VALLEY OF TRI-AULAY.

for several days." "No, Monsieur, he always needs to be well flogged before he goes on a long journey." And here suiting the action to the word, down comes another awful whack on the back of poor Bismarck.

To this logic I could make no reply. But I must, in justice to the horse, record that he did his day's work well; whereas his driver got muddled at Carnac, in fraternizing with some brother Bretons at an auberge there, whilst I was visiting the ruins of Mr. Milne's excavated Roman villa.

From the bottom of the hill at Brech, and close to the waterworks of the Railway company, we pass across the pretty valley of Tre-Auray, and advancing along a completely shaded avenue of oak-trees, pull up at the outer gate of La Chartreuse.

This is a very spacious building, which has had a most interesting bearing on the fortunes of the vicinity since the time in which it was erected. Originally a collegiate institution, the staff of which consisted of a dean and ten chaplains, it was founded by Jean de Montfort after the battle of Auray in September A.D. 1364.

Here was the last great fight of the wars of succession, when Charles de Blois was not only conquered, but as M. Rosenzweig, the

Archivist of Morbihan, tells us,—"*Charles prisonnier est tué lâchement par un soldat Anglais.*" The reason of erecting the College is thus explained. Jean de Montfort, uneasy about the results of the battle, made a vow, whilst it was still going on, as was the custom in those days to do, that he would build a sacred edifice if the victory proved on his side. His soldiers gained in the fight, and the result was a college dedicated to St. Michael, which soon received large endowments from its founder, then become John, fourth duke of Brittany.

In subsequent periods of the Church militant it went through many changes and vicissitudes; through the reigns of John V., Francis I., Peter II., and Arthur III.; till by a bull of Pope Sextus IV., issued in October 1480, or a trifle over a century after its first foundation, it was rebuilt and converted into a convent for the Carthusian monks. The title of "La Chartreuse" is derived from the name of the place near Grenoble in the diocese of Rheims, where the order was first established by its founder, St. Bruno, in A.D. 1084. At the latter place was invented that precious liqueur, known to every continental traveller as "*La Grande Chartreuse.*" About which, it may be remembered, there was a law-suit some few years ago, in reference to one of the monks who had left the convent, not only betraying the secret of its composition to an outsider, but having assisted in selling the illicit article to the detriment of the Chartreuse Treasury. My readers may recollect, likewise, that the community gained the restoration of their privileges for the exclusive manufacture of the liqueur. Their first house in Brittany was at Nantes, whence they came to the neighbourhood of Auray, through the papal bull to which I have referred. This was obtained by the influence of François I. and François II. during their successive reigns as Dukes of Brittany.

From A.D. 1482, when the Carthusian brotherhood took possession of this place, which they occupied till they were turned out by the Revolutionists of 1791, they led the most austere of lives. They did all their own mechanical work of masonry, carpentry, ploughing, and reaping: building up chapels, cloisters, and cells, planting trees, and cultivating gardens. During these three hundred years, their community was much increased in numbers, and their property considerably augmented. Their chief vexations were of quarrels with the officers of woods and forests, in regard to their privileges and immunities. But the thunderbolt of the great Revolution came down on them, in common with all other religious communities in France.

Their goods, chattels, and furniture were confiscated and sold. Their library of rare books was sent over to Auray, where it is still to be seen at the Hôtel de Ville, though much curtailed of its contents. The archives of their three hundred years' ministry were packed away to Vannes. If the disciples of Mirabeau and Robespierre had got up to the ferocity which they manifested four years afterwards in the slaughter on the Champ des Martyrs—only a few hundred yards off—possibly the monks would have been shot, and the library contents as well as the archives burned. They were satisfied, however, to let the poor monks go whither they pleased, as the world was supposed to be wide enough for them. Then the marauders sold the whole of the buildings and estate to a Sieur Leconte of Lorient for £94,000. It was rebought in 1810 by Monsieur Le Gal, the Vicar-General of the diocese of Vannes, and Monsieur Deshayes, a very celebrated man, who in his time was the Curé of Auray. From them it passed into the hands of "Les Sœurs de la Sagesse," whose care is employed in instructing the deaf and dumb.

They were the occupants of it when I visited in last July. Of the order, the sister who accompanied us through the building tells me there are fifty houses in France, with an aggregate community of 3500 sisters. In this there are 150.

The deaf and dumb porter here, named Henri Cohanne, is quite an original in his way. He corresponds with visitors by means of a pencil, and a small piece of slate. With a most courteous smile he wrote on the slate a request for me to come into his little lodge to look at the bell, by which I summoned him to the gate. Because having pulled a brass handle at the outside, and seeing it answered by this man, whom our driver told me was deaf and dumb, I was anxious to know how he heard the sound of our summons. On going to the small room it was explained. His eyes gleamed with delight, as he wrote down his name on the slate for me to read, then tapped his breast several times, pointing with the other hand to the machinery. This was a large mass of iron, from seven to eight pounds in weight, so arranged with a small hook, that when the latter was detached by the traction of the wire from the bell-handle outside, the iron fell against a wooden partition. The house being all of wood, the striking of the partition made a reverberation sensible to his feelings, whereupon he looked up, and seeing the piece of iron had fallen, proceeded to the outer gate. He is a shoemaker, and works at his trade. Another porter to relieve guard, and a brother craftsman in the St. Crispin profession, dwells and works in the same house.

The principal attraction of visitors to La Chartreuse in the present day is to see the monument of Quiberon, which is in an apartment built up against the side wall of the convent, and facing the front gate. At the base of the architrave we see over the door in large Roman letters :— " GALLIA MŒRENS POSUIT." The inside is elaborately done up in marble slabs on the walls. The chief of these represents the Duchess of Angoulême, laying the foundation stone of this mausoleum on the 20th of September, 1823.

On a square block in the centre, surmounted by a cenotaph, are engraved in black letters, the names of 952 martyrs, of whom 743 were shot in the meadow near at hand, whilst the rest comprise a party of the Royalists who were executed somewhere else. Should the visitor desire it, the deaf and dumb porter will open a small barred gate, which is at the end of the mausoleum, and lowering a candle down into a vault, show you a few skulls, and a large number of human bones. On entering you see in front a square piece of black board on which are printed in white letters: "Tombeau des Royalistes —courageux Défenseurs de l'autel et du trône. Ils tombèrent martyrs de leurs nobles efforts. Quel Français, pénétré des droits de la couronne, ignore ce qu'il doit à ces illustres morts?"

I am afraid the mausoleum has many visitors in the present day who do not sympathize with the *droits de la couronne*. The roofed arch of ceiling is fretted with *fleur-de-lis*, and has painted on it the Imperial crown. The top of the monument is ovoid with a small marble cross at its front. The Duchess of Berry is said to have made a visit to this place in 1828. And we are further informed by the good sister, who is here with us, that the larger number of skulls and bones pertaining to those who perished in the slaughter of 21st July, 1795, are not in this, but in the vault of the chapel of St. Louis beneath the cathedral of Vannes.

The sister conducted us round the cloisters, which are very extensive. In one square of corridors, the history of St. Bruno, the founder, is painted on large canvas, about the size of the frescoes in the lobby of the House of Commons.

There are twenty-one different scenes, and they were done by the celebrated Breton artist L'Hernutais, who died at the early age of forty-one. We went into the chapel likewise, where the carved oak pulpit and panellings, worked by the Carthusian brothers, are wonderful realities of art, to look at, and bear memory of. Thence into the refectory, with its arched wooden roof, painted in the year 1750. It bears also symbolical records of the union of Brittany and La Vendée. Out into the garden also, where there is a large tree called " La Charme," beneath the perfectly umbrageous shade of which, spreading over a large extent, are seats and *pric-Dicus*—most grateful resorts in such scorching weather as we have now. Driving again down the avenue of oak-trees, through which we came up, and out upon the highway, we leave the railroad station of Auray to the right, and come to a spot where three roads meet. In the centre of this is a cross about twelve feet high, with an inscription on its base to the effect that it is in memory of the battle of Jean de Montfort and Charles de Blois, in 1364, —the battle-field was around here—and that it (the cross) was renewed by Jean le Boulch, Mayor of Brech in 1842.

A few hundred yards farther on, is an inclosure

of about a square acre, an iron gate in front, and a row of lofty pines on each side. Within this— the veritable "Champ des Martyrs," on which the 743 Royalists were shot, we see a square chapel with four large pillars supporting a triangular top, on which are painted the simple words—"*Hic cecidcrunt*" (i. e. Here they fell). The whistling of the wind through the pine-trees —the incidents which the Expiatory chapel is built to commemorate—and a *je ne sais quoi* of sombreishness hang about it. So that we concluded once in a lifetime is enough to pay a visit to the Field of the Martyrs.

Coming out, and directing the driver to go on to Auray, we cannot avoid a trifling meditation. This valley of Kerso, through part of which we are driving now, has had blood enough shed in it, God knows. For besides the battle of Jean de Montfort in 1364, and the massacre of the Royalists in 1795, it witnessed in June 1815 another fight between the Bretons and the Federals. But having come to these facts, I am inclined, on second thoughts, to doubt whether I, as a holiday-roamer, or traveller for my pleasure in France, have any right to deduce inference from my meditations, however trifling they may be. I therefore tell our coachman to drive to whatever hotel he thinks the best, and let Bismarck have an hour's rest. Whereupon with a "*Oui, Monsieur*," down comes the whip on the poor animal's flanks, and in about ten minutes we get out at the door of the Hôtel des Postes.

CHAPTER VI.

The city of Auray—Likeness to Chester and to Dol—Sleepy town—Antiquity of cathedral and of château—Hôtel de Ville—Chapel of Cordeliers—Gloomy castle of Treulan—Inhabited by bats or toads—Bismarck *en route* for Carnac—Barren and savage country—Village of Carnac, with nothing to speak of like a street—Church of St. Corneille—Church of St. Michael—Built on Druidical tumulus—Explorations in 1862—Dolmens found—Mr. Milne's diggings in the Roman Villa—What he has turned out—Avenues of large stones—Stretching to Kerlescan and Plouharnel—Sonorous stone masses—15,000 in sixteenth century—Modern Vandalism—Guesses about the monuments—Dolmen at Corcoro—Oyster parks—The Baron de Wolbock—Enormous profit—Curious grottoes—Old town of Locmariaker—Visit of London Anthropologists—Analogies of Archaic Anthropology between Bombay and Carnac—*Embarras des richesses* about Auray.

THE city of Auray has the same style of quaint old houses in it, that I have described at Dol, as bearing so much resemblance to those of Chester, as to some that can be seen a little further on at Quimper. The narrowness of passages, the balconies, the gable-ends of dwellings turned street-wards, the painted beams and joists, that mark the mechanical style in which they are put together, the small panes of glass in the windows, and the general hoariness of the architecture plainly proclaim the middle ages. A new house here and there seems like a fish out of water. On this hot summer's day it is the sleepiest of sleepy towns, bringing back memories of those locations on the Pampas of South America where the inhabitants are hereditarily predisposed to a siesta from ten in the morning till four in the afternoon, and where, in such a scorching sun as we have here, no living thing is outside the doors except lizards, mad dogs, and Englishmen. Very old is the Cathedral—I can scarcely help wondering how nearly every small town in France has a cathedral—but older still is the Château, from which stones were taken in the sixteenth century for the fortifications of Belle Isle. One of the chapels here, that of the Holy Ghost, dates from the thirteenth century. This is not used for worship, being in rapid progress to ruin. At the confluence of two streets, the first leading from the railway station, the other from the parish church of St. Gildas, is the Hôtel de Ville, now used as the Mayor's official residence. Being flanked by the ends of the streets, it can be passed from one to the other, through the market, which is underneath, and posterior to the hotel. Cooler though it be here than outside doors, the woodwork appears all decayed, whilst the fish, potatoes, and meat that are for sale, communicate a musty ambient to the place. In one of the chapels at Auray—that of the Cordeliers—is a number of richly-carved oak stalls taken from La Chartreuse. The town is about three quarters of a mile from the railway station, but omnibuses from two or three different hotels ply to and fro, every train that arrives. The whole of Auray has such an air of antiquity about it, that it seems no wonder the railway did not approach nearer.

Yet venerable as are its churches,—older still its château,—still many centuries more antique than these is that ruined windmill near the station. A hoary companion to the latter is the gloomy castle of Treulan, in which one can scarcely imagine anything livelier than bats or toads to be dwelling. But these things are all of modern date when contrasted with the Dolmens, and Menhirs, the relics of Celtic and Druidical architecture at Carnac and Plouharnel. To which, after a good luncheon at the Hôtel des Postes, and with Bismarck no doubt refreshed by his feed, we set out for a visit.

For several miles outside of Auray we had evidences of comfortable farming on each side. The farther we penetrated the more desolate and barren the country became, and the odd spots of cultivation were not set off to much advantage side by side with extensive tracts of gorse. I therefore began to cogitate, that the road across Salisbury Plain to Stonehenge must be very dreary indeed if it be more desolate than the scenery as you approach Carnac on the way from Auray. Its wildness increases as you find yourself skirting the rows of tall stones on the right-hand side on approaching the town. Hence starts up the question why were such dismal *locales* selected for Druid worship?

The little village of Carnac has nothing in it that one can call a street. It is a continuous turning round corners, as of going up and down declivities. There is one small slice of a *rue* in which the Hôtel de la Marine is situated, and something like an attempt at half a square, wherein you find the Hôtel des Voyageurs and the chapel. This latter, grand enough to be a cathedral, and dedicated to St. Corneille, was erected in A.D. 1639. It is so full of ornamentation of the Renaissance period as to be quite a studio for artists, though doubtless very few

Academy men go so far out of the world as Carnac. At the part of Quiberon Bay which is in front of this the emigrants landed in 1795,—the victims of the Champ des Martyrs. On a hill about a quarter of a mile from the village is the old church of St. Michael. Here again is the same kind of mistake as I committed at Auray— to style this an *old* building, although it is semi-ruinous and disused, for I am told the hill on which it is erected is a tumulus supposed to have been constructed by Celts or Druids. In 1862 some explorations were made in this mound, beneath the church, and a subterranean Dolmen was discovered, which measured eight feet in length, two feet in width, and one foot in height. Within the latter were contained calcined bones— no doubt human—Celtic tools, I believe of flint, heads, and other matters. A report on the subject has been written and read before some Archæological society.

A quarter of a mile farther on Mr. Milne, a Scotch gentleman of antiquarian tastes, is having excavations made on a Roman villa, from which he has got a large number of items of very great interest. At the Hôtel des Voyageurs where he is staying, and at which we visited him, he showed me deers' horns, fragments of glass and pottery— bones, iron, statuettes in bronze. On the day of my being here they had turned out two fragments of Samian ware, bearing the maker's names stamped on the feet of the vases. I went down to see the workings, but cannot say much about them—as they are yet incomplete—except that they reflect the greatest credit on the assiduity and perseverance of Mr. Milne.

Nearly a mile from the village and on the farm of Menée, we can see eight avenues of these large stones—nearly all of them having the bigger end upwards. There are ten rows stretching hence to a distance of not far from three miles—to the hamlet of Kermaux. Behind some houses at that spot, they again reappear in a large field containing forty tall stones, and the ruins of a covered alley. In fact all around the country by Kerlescan and Plouharnel—to a stretch of many miles (Mr. Milne tells me)—the plain is thick with these monuments, as with several of the altar stones, such as we see in Stonehenge. Some of the former are nearly ten feet in height, but the average are not above five. A bevy of half a dozen little boys accompanied us as we strolled amongst them, and showed us three or four large masses, each of about five ton cube, that, on being struck with a piece of rock, sounded as

DRUIDICAL MENHIRS AT CARNAC.

if they were hollow. I believe this sonorous result to be from the innate nature of the stone, not from any cavity. In the sixteenth century Deacon Moreau counted from twelve to fifteen thousand of these. Yet now in consequence of having been broken up by modern Vandalism, to make roads, build walls, and erect dwelling-houses, they do not exceed five to six hundred.

Curious it is to speculate,— not only for what object these enormous stones were thus placed, but by what mechanical agency they were arranged *in situ*. It appears that some writers only go as far back as Cæsar's time in guessing they formed part of his camp. Strong as Cæsar's men might have been, they were scarcely likely to have spent their energies in erecting these pillars, with the additional labour of bringing them from whatever position they were taken elsewhere. For I understand they are not of the same geological nature as the rock-stratum of Carnac's neighbourhood. Others say they constituted part of a temple for serpent worship. The idea of a single temple of the extent of ground, covered by these Menhirs, is simply preposterous. Several authors conjecture that they mark the burial ground of great men. Whilst the natives of Carnac adhere to the belief, that they were Pagan soldiers metamorphosed into columns of stone by St. Corneille, when they followed to persecute him. Monsieur Adolphe Joanne, in his " Itinerary of Brittany" tells us that they are called "soldiers of Saint Corneille," though why we can scarcely guess.

On our return by the road coming from Plouharnel I got out of the carriage to look at two of the Dolmens. These had a deep cavity under each—although supported on the sides by massive uprights. Near the hamlet of Corcoro, about three miles from Plouharnel, is to be found the largest in the valley of Morbihan. It is called "*La Rocher des Fées*," or Fairy's Rock, and is used to day as a farmer's barn. The total length of this was originally fifteen yards, though it is now no more than eight yards in length, four and a half wide, and two in height. The top, or table-part is composed of two flag-stones, one of which measures thirty-eight to thirty-nine cubic yards in superficies. In fact, the whole country to Erdeven, twenty-two miles from Auray on one side, and Etel, twenty-six miles on another, is full of such relics.

I had intended to have called at the Hôtel du Commerce in Plouharnel, where I am told the proprietor M. Bail has a goodly collection of

Celtic relics, excavated in the neighbourhood. But our coachman having already paid his devotions to the auberge near Mr. Milne's workings, and showing symptoms, as well as smelling strongly, of Absinthe when he came up, I was afraid, in pity to Bismarck as well as on account of my companion's safety, to run the risk of going within the temptations of a hotel.

The neighbourhood of Auray has many charms for the idler in Brittany. Besides those I have mentioned—although it may seem but the step from the sublime to the ridiculous—at Etel there is an important establishment for the preservation of sardines, where they can be had at any time quite fresh from their native element. Whilst not far from Carnac, at La Trinité, one can feed himself to repletion on excellent oysters, if he be there during the season months.

In this vicinity may be seen at the small bay of Keriolet one of the finest, best arranged, and most productive of oyster *parcs*.

This was first begun in 1867, but in 1869 and 1870 the Baron de Wolbock took the entire charge of it. Some of the results of the excellent management of oyster culture here may be imagined from the fact that now "the value of the works carried out, of the plant erected, including collectors' boats, and other contingencies, is estimated at £20,000. The worth of the stock of oysters, adult and at present preparing for the market, is calculated at between £20,000 and £30,000 a year."[1]

In the harbour of Pontivy, which is on the western side on the Presqu'Ile de Quiberon, there are some very curious grottoes near the sea. This "almost island," as its name indicates, is barely joined to the mainland by a spit on which the Fort Penthievre is situated. Close to the Bay of Morbihan, which is to the eastward of Quiberon, stands the old Breton town of Locmariaker, in front of which are the two islets of Long Island, and Gavr'Innis. Besides a curious Celtic grotto, as it is styled, with hieroglyphic characters on it, at Locmariaker, there are several Dolmens and Menhirs about.

One of these is described by Dr. Charnock[2] as "a colossal Menhir near the ground, broken into four pieces." The four blocks lay as shown in the rough plan drawn by the author of the

[1] Vide *The Colonies*, S. H Silver and Co., 66 and 67, Cornhill, Oct. 30, 1875. p 346.
[2] *The Anthropological Review*, No. 26, July, 1869, p. cxxii. Asher and Co., 13, Bedford Street, Covent Garden, London.

paper, but, unfortunately, this plan was not preserved. Dr. Fouquet thinks the Menhir, when whole, may have cubed 250,000 kilogrammes. Measure of each of the four blocks was taken by Dr. Charnock. The largest of these was thirty-two feet and a half, by thirteen and a half; the smallest ten feet by six and a half. When upright this Menhir must have been *seventy-two and a half* feet in height.

In or about the period of Dr. Charnock's visit hither, came also Dr. James Hunt, President and founder of the Anthropological Society. There is only an abstract of his paper published;[3] and I regret to add none of the illustrations that accompanied the Memoir, which was only read a short time before his premature death.

One of the most striking analogies of what Dr. Hunt styled Archaic Anthropology may be seen by comparison of the Dolmen at Corcoro with the Cinerary at Shillong, Khasi Hills, in the territory of Bombay.[4] A similar resemblance may be said to exist between the Megalithic

---

[3] "On Carnac in Brittany," last work cited, *Anth. Review*, p. cxxiii.

[4] *Vide* "Monuments of the Khasi Hill Tribes," by Major H. H. Goodwin Austen, F.R.G.S., &c., in *Journal of Anthropological Institute of Great Britain and Ireland*, vol. v., No. 1, July, 1875, p. 40.

Monuments of Nongshai in the same part of the world (vide same Journal) and those at Carnac. They all seem as if they were designed by the same architect and erected for a like purpose.

In fact, the summer tourist who may be disposed to pass a few weeks in the neighbourhood of Auray will have nothing to complain of—except perhaps *un embarras des richesses*—in the way of enjoyment.

CHAPTER VII.

A trip to Basse Bretagne—Red petticoats in the fields—From Auray to Landernau—Junction to Pontivy and St. Brieuc—Pretty view of Hennebont—Ships amongst the houses—Lorient and the river Scorff—Large water basins—Old East Indian company—Gestel and Guidel—Limits of Morbihan and Finisterre—Dolmens and Menhirs—Quimperle—*L'Arcadie* de Basse Bretagne—Mail phaeton—Where are the letter-bags—Abbey of St. Croix—St. Gurloës—Cure of the gout—Galloping madly—Charming country—Vile huts of peasants—Fancy ploughing by pigs—Church of St. Fiacre—Dirty town of Faouet—Church of St. Barbe and the "Pardon"—Apparition round the corner—The *gendarme* again—Spurs and white gloves—Fibrous apples and old men of same class—Capot and coif—Gourin—The Black Mountains—Château de Kerbiguet—More Dolmens and Menhirs—To Scaer and through the Landes.

DESIROUS to see some part of Lower Brittany outside the beaten track of tourists, we started the morning after our visit to Carnac by the train passing St. Anne, which leaves Redon at 10.45 a.m.

We took tickets for Quimperle, where we arrived at ten minutes to one o'clock. Between St. Anne and our stopping-place I observed the women working in the fields, and wearing red petticoats—the same as they do in Galway.

The chief stations passed in the first stage of our day's trip, are Auray, Landernau, Hennebont, Lorient, and Gestel. After which comes Quimperle.

Landernau is about four leagues beyond Auray. Not very far from the latter, we go by the junction from which trains proceed to Pontivy and St. Brieuc. There cannot be much of the ancient about Landernau, as its church was erected between 1834 and 1837. It does not present a considerable appearance of a town, and seems about 500 yards from the station. Hennebont shows a very picturesque spot at both banks of the river Blavet. On the inland side of the railway bridge which crosses here, we see up amongst the houses a few large vessels with sails furled, that give quite a maritime look to the place. Ships of 300 tons burden can go to the quays at Hennebont on high water. Of its Château there exists only a fragment of wall. Beneath one of the houses in the main street of what is called *La Vieille Ville* is found a rectangular cave, four yards by six, which was said to communicate from the castle to the fortified part of the town, styled *La Ville Close*. Like Dol and Auray, it has several twelfth-century houses, with their gable-ends to the street. Some made jointly of planking and stone, with the beam portions painted black on white grounds. Ruins of convents,—of a large gate with towers on the quay side,—of chapels, and of a prison, show that it must have been a place of importance in the middle ages. Amongst these are the relics of the Abbey of Joy, about a mile above the town on the right bank of the river. This was founded in the thirteenth century by Blanche de Champagne, wife of the Duke of Brittany of the period, named Jean de Roux.

Six to seven miles further on, we halt at Lorient station, after passing over the river Scorff, which has a large basin on either side of the railway bridge. That to the right is more of mud than water, unless at high tide. It is flanked on the north by a long and graceful-looking suspension bridge, which communicates one of the country roads with the town. The water space to the left is of great extent, dotted with ships and steamers, as well as surrounded by military stores, and all the appurtenances of an arsenal.

Lorient first became a port of consequence at the beginning of the seventeenth century, through some Breton merchants establishing goods-sheds here on the river Blavet, at the side of Lorient Roads. In A. D. 1628, these sheds were found insufficient for the increasing trade with the East Indies, and more were added on the opposite side of the bay. From the traffic still increasing, it resulted that a new Indian company was formed in 1664, and furnished with letters patent from Louis XIV. Its success as a basis for commercial operations with India, was shaken by the English on their capture of Bengal in 1745. Now-a-days it is a maritime prefecture; a military port and place of war of the third class; and has 34,600 inhabitants.

As we emerge from the station, on our right appears the tower of St. Cristopher's church, with one of the prettiest spires I have seen for a long time.

Nine kilometres farther on bring us to Gestel; of which I have only to record, that between it and Pontscorff—a small *bourg* of under two thousand inhabitants—is a chapel of the fifteenth century, which was once a famous pilgrimage. Then at Pontscorff there are houses still standing and inhabited with inscriptions on them of A.D. 1565. One of these is accredited to have belonged to the Templars. At Guidel, a few miles more distant, is a modern church, adorned with pretty wainscoting. But this town, with its 5970 inhabitants, comprises a very extensive parish, bounded by the Laita, as well as the Elle rivers, which divide and limit the departments of Morbihan and Finisterre. In this district of Guidel, an immense number of Druidical Dolmens and Menhirs is spread over the country. Yet nobody here seems to take any interest in them. As we have already had *satis-superque* of these for our holiday trip—to which they may be considered somewhat of a damper—we may let them alone!

Out of the train at Quimperle we proceed in an omnibus to the courier office, to take our seats for the ride to Gourin. The town is beautifully situated in an amphitheatrical sort of a valley, a little below the confluence of the rivers Ellé and Isole; the junction of these two streams at Quimperle taking the new name of Laita. This place has been entitled *L'Arcadie de la Basse Bretagne.*

It is just the kind of spot that a lover of the antique would respect and reverence. For there are no new buildings to grate on the sensibilities of the old, except one nearly in front of our starting-place with the mail carriage. This was a chemist's shop, having glaring red bottles. We have but a quarter of an hour to look round us, and buy a few buns for our journey. It gave quite a *dolce far niente* aspect to the surroundings, to see a few men fishing with rods on the right bank of the river, and in a street. But here comes the trap. And after a good deal of talk, without which it seems nothing can be done in Brittany, we are packed into the most limited space of a covered phaeton, that could possibly be devised to hold five. My wife and self, two other passengers, and the driver,—the latter seated on a perch in front. But the mail-bags: where were they? Probably in the coachman's cap, or his pocket? For I should imagine the correspondence hereabouts rarely exceeds half a dozen letters.

So away we start;—the horse put into a gallop at once;—over the bridge of the Jacobins;—across the Laita;—through a square, with some seats and trees in it, and the Abbey of St. Croix to the right. The steed, no doubt, is acccustomed to the pace, for though he is not whipped by the coachman, he gallops along,—(I cannot help thinking if he be any relation of Bismarck's) up through the Rue du Château, which is the aristocratic quarter,—rattling on the rough blocks of pavement, as if the town of Quimperle were about to be bombarded, and it was a matter of life and death to get out of it at express speed. We have twenty-one leagues to Gourin, but this horse is to be changed for another at Le Faouet, which is nearly half way.

The upper part of Quimperle is covered with convents, houses, gardens, and sloping orchards. The Basilique of St. Croix, founded in A.D. 1029, was knocked down in 1862. It has been since rebuilt on the circular plan, in imitation of the Church of the Holy Sepulchre at Jerusalem. Within it is preserved a crypt of the eleventh century, which contains the tomb—erected in the thirteenth—of St. Gurloës, first Abbé of Quimperle, who died A.D. 1057. The Bretons style him St. Urlou, and invoke his aid to cure the gout. Here also is a church of St. Michael, the spire of which, made of lead, was taken down to be melted into bullets by the Revolutionists of 1791. The church of Saint Columban is in ruins. It was the parish of the Château, which has wholly disappeared. The convent of the Dominicans, afterwards styled that of the Jacobins, was founded in A.D. 1255. Of this the church is likewise a wreck.

Some little distance,—five hundred yards or thereabouts,—to the south-east of Quimperle, is the chapel of St. David, dating from the sixteenth century. In this is to be seen a sculptured group of life-size figures,—eight of whom are in the costume of the period when the church was built,—representing Christ in the tomb.

Away we go, galloping up hill and down dale. To me there is always a pleasure in travelling on French roads: even after the heaviest rain they are dry, and invariably void of ruts. On the sideways are reserved heaps of broken stones, done up in such tidy squares by the large wooden measure, resembling a Brobdignagian barrow, without a wheel or a bottom.

Then you have your progress indicated by the "*bornes,*" that you may call mile-stones, and on which are painted the number of Kilometres[1] *from* the place which you have left, or *to* that whither you are bound.

Through a country in many of its features reminding us of a park in England. Now and then its beauty was sadly marred by coming in view of a peasant's hut, that seemed to be constructed only for filth, and discomfort. Generally a few feet below the roadway—possibly

---

[1] A Kilometre = 1093.633 metres, or nearly five furlongs. It may be better defined by counting 4 kilometres = 3 English miles, or one league. One metre = 3 feet $3\frac{3}{8}$ inches.

INTERIOR OF A BRETON PEASANT'S HOUSE (MORBIHAN).

that the rain-water might flow in without further trouble. No chimneys, and no windows;—unless the latter were at the backs of the houses. The straw or rush roof saturated with smoke, and brown as the dungheap, that is invariably at one side or the other of the door. Some pigs doing fancy ploughing in the ditches hard by, and a small orchard, with apples, shrunk and dried up. In many cases a field of *blé noir* was near the house. The tall men, with long flowing hair, broad-brimmed, low-crowned hats, and coats with stand-up collars, who now and then appeared at the doors, had an aspect as if they had never eaten anything more wholesome than that black corn, or those shrivelled, juiceless apples. This was not exceptional. The dirtiest house we saw, with a great cloud of smoke coming through the roof—for it had rained a shower or two the night before—was on the right side before we mounted the hill near the little chapel of St. John, and within sight of the lofty towers of St. Fiacre church.

This latter is a building of the eleventh century, and stands about half a mile from our temporary stopping-place to change the horse, namely Faouet. From what I learn of it, I believe it to be a fine specimen of ancient architecture.

We had not time to stop and see it—I suppose on account of the mails. Our coachman told us the statues which adorned the cloister are to-day,—with the exception of the colossal figure of St. Christopher,—scattered about the church-yard. On some of the stained glass windows, still preserved, are depicted the Resurrection, the Crucifixion, the legend of St. Fiacre, and a few others.

The driver pointed out the church of St. Barbe in a curious position, about a mile and a half to the north of Faouet. At this place there is a religious function every year,—a sort of pilgrimage or penance, which is entitled the "*Pardón.*" The church is built on the top of a sharp rock, 178 yards high, and commanding a view of the river Ellé. It was founded in A.D. 1489, and like its neighbour St. Fiacre, the greater portion of its statues have been broken. Only a few remain, including those of the Virgin, St. Corentin, St. Ursula, and St. Barbe. In going through the penance for the Pardón, the pilgrims have to make a tour round some steep and dangerous part of the rock, which they effect by holding on to stout iron rings morticed in the stone. All through Basse Bretagne they have somewhat similar formalities of pilgrimages,

CHAPEL OF ST. FIACRE (MORBIHAN), NEAR LE FAOUET.

which are entitled Pardons. Of these I shall give more details in a subsequent chapter.

At Faouet, as dirty in its streets and dilapidated in its houses as you could see a village anywhere, our horse is changed at the Hotel of the Golden Lion. Being now past four o'clock, and having eaten nothing but buns since morning, we regaled ourselves on a basin of *bouilli* and a glass of beer. Such beer too! It must have been made out of the apples, or possibly the *blé noir*. Amongst the black mud and the ruined walls of habitations which I was contemplating from the hotel door, whilst lighting a cigar, and after finishing our soup, an apparition glides round the corner. As I live, it is the ubiquitous *gendarme*—the *alter et ego*, if not the self-same that I saw at St. Malo, and at every railway station or *diligence* office that I have visited since. Surely in these sloppy streets his spurs are not wanted? But he has them on nevertheless; as he saunters by the hotel door with his white gloves, sword, cocked-hat, and not a single button, or piece of silver cord out of place.

Faouet does not seem to me an attractive settlement to live in. Its hotel is too much of an auberge, or a carrier's place of stopping; and on inquiry I find the prices for bed and fare are equal to those of good hotels in Nantes or Angers. The chapel at the corner is so musty and frowsy-looking outside, that I did not care to look in. One part of it was erected in the thirteenth century, and another portion in the sixteenth. The old men, whom I see here, appear more stringy and fibrous than any I have met before. The majority of the women in the streets of Faouet, like many we have met on the road, wear for head-dress the black *capot*, which resembles in shape one of our own men's chimney-pot hats, but much shorter, and without the brim. Others wore the white cap or *coif*. And though we have the quasi-military evergreen of the cocked-hat, spurs, and white gloves, he is becoming a little *de trop* of a *toujours perdrix* to be wholesome!

With a fresh horse we proceed in the same tear-a-way style as before, and arrive at Gourin about six o'clock. I had ascertained, before starting from Quimperle, that the return mail-carriage, the only communication between these two places, except a hired or a private vehicle, was to leave every morning at 1 a.m. Still on account of having come to see something I did not like to turn back, without attempting part of our design. So we put up for the night at

INSIDE OF A BRETON CABIN NEAR FAOUET.

the Cheval Blanc, after having engaged a horse and *cariole* to bring us in the morning to Bannalec,—the next station to Quimperle, and four leagues beyond. By this journey we should see a little more of the country than in returning the same route as we came.

Gourin, with a little over 4000 inhabitants, is situated on the side of a hill, from which there is a very pretty view of the Black Mountains. It is within reachable distance of the Ster-Lacrinam, the Isole, and the Ellé rivers, as well as some of their affluents; in all of which is to be found an abundance of trout. One of its chapels, that of St. Nicholas, dates from the fifteenth century. An old castle contiguous, the Château de Kerbiguet, has been despoiled many years ago, and is now converted into a farm-house. On some of its rooms there are frescoes and inscriptions, which are probably unintelligible to the modern Breton, or we might be told what they are. In the neighbourhood of Gourin are three Dolmens, some Menhirs, and traces of a few Roman camps. The only other thing that I learned of the place is that the hotel charges are as high as those in Faouet. Amongst the items of my bill for breakfast was charged " café et un œuf, 1 franc." But I deducted ten sous from this particular figure, and gave the landlord a bit of my mind about it.

Setting out early, so as to catch the train from Brest, on by the line we came yesterday to Redon—thence to Savenay and *viâ* Donges across the Loire to Préfailles, our drive was a most enchanting one. The first part from Gourin to Scaer was by thick oak forests on each side of the road as we went along. Sunshine glimmering through the leaves, and falling in a golden shower of sparkling light upon the fern, gorse, and heather-carpeted ground! Mounting a hill on the road, and looking down on the silver stream of the river Isole—that glides through the valleys in such a serpentine course—as if regretting to leave so much beauty!

In many other parts of France, through which I have travelled, the high roads present a long straight line, with a row of ghostly poplars on either side, and nothing visible at the end but sky. Such a prospect has been to me always wearisome from its monotony. But all through the *route* we are going to-day, no reach of it is more than a few hundred yards in length. And at every bend new beauties open before us. Twisting and turning like the river.

Thus it was as far as Scaer—a quaint, clean,

ANCIENT BRETON HOUSE AT QUIMPER.

Page 84.

compact old town of 4394 inhabitants, and chief place of the largest parish in Finisterre.

There was a number of people at one of the houses near the chapel, all dressed in their holiday garb, waiting we were told for a wedding, I should like to have remained to witness the ceremony, as well as to hear the peculiar music of this part of the world. But we had limited our stay to the 5 p.m. arrival at Redon, and were therefore obliged to be content with seeing a man walk up the streets—having a large bagpipes under his arm. Some people may think it was almost as good as hearing the music. But I am disposed to believe it was a great deal better.

Here the church is dedicated to St. Candide, who, according to tradition, made a miraculous fountain spring up in the neighbourhood with a stroke of her cross. The old church, and a new one are alongside of each other, like mother and daughter. A pretty stone crucifix of the sixteenth century is preserved at the rear of the cemetery. Indeed along the road at many parts of our journey to-day, we passed several of these on stone pillars ten to twelve feet high. Some of them bore large tufts of moss—so ancient were they. Occasionally at the corners of cross-roads we saw pillar boxes—

in shape like those at home for receiving letters, though not more than half the height. On stopping to look at one, in memory of the mail-bags from Quimperle, I found it with a very post-office mouth, but the words, "*Tronc pour l'Église*," printed in black letters. At this point, glancing round, we invariably recognized the spire of a church looming amongst the trees.

After passing Scaer we come upon some tracts of soil, on which little or nothing but heather, fern, and some gorse was growing.

The bright purple blossom of the heather, obviates the dulness of this herbage. These are part of the *Landes* of Brittany, on which a French friend once spoke to me of *La Sauvagerie des Landes de Bretagne*. Looking at it in this bright sunshine, and balmy air, it seems a very mild kind of savagery indeed. As if nature, in designing it, had held back the stern rigour of her pencil, such as we are apt to associate with savagery, and thus painted as little as possible of roughness on the fair face of *La belle France*. Here too we see the small Brittany cows feeding in the *Landes*.

All through the part of Basse Bretagne, in which we now are travelling, the chief agricultural produce is the *blé noir*. Maize is coming into use, but not so much in Low Brittany as in the high parts. Square heaps of about three feet high in the fields point out where the dung is put into practical use of hot-beds, upon which to raise pumpkins. But orchards of small withered-looking apples are everywhere. These are to make cider of, as well as probably to feed the old men: with what results as to appearance of physique in the latter case I have already described. But I say, God help the man who on a hot summer's day in the Landes has nothing to assuage his thirst or refresh him, but the cider which is made from the demoralized crab fruit that we see around!

CHAPTER VIII.

One of the conscripts—Talk about past and future German wars—Bannalec to Redon—St. Gildas des Bois—Pont-Château—Savenay Junction—"Sillon de Bretagne"—"La Grande Briere"—Salt making at Guerande—Isolation still existing—*Égalité et Fraternité*—Stand-offishness in the church—Varieties of dialect—To Donges, and across the Loire—Druidical remnants at Donges—Old priory—Paimbœuf—Relation to the Sea—Derivation of name—Formation of sand-banks blocking up the Loire—Change of scene—The *Quenouille* and *fuseau*—Ugly Duc de Guesclin—From Paimbœuf—Architecture of churches—Through St. Brenin, St. Père Retz, and La Plaine to Préfailles—Pornic and Kirouard.

SOON after starting from Bannalec, we got into conversation with some of our fellow-passengers, one of whom was a young man, not much beyond the period of boyhood, now *en route* from Brest to Bordeaux to join a regiment of artillery. He was of those who had been recently drawn in the conscription. In him we soon recognized the type of several that we have met during our rambles, and whose talk, on whatever subject it may have commenced, invariably glides off, not only into the late German war, but into that which is to come. His father had been killed in the last campaign, I forget where—but in the next —*parbleu!*—the Prussians would have a different story to tell. They would be forced to spit out (*cracher*) the indemnity money;—they would be trampled on, and made dung of under the feet of Frenchmen! And when the latter went to Germany, they would spare neither age nor sex! I regret being obliged to confess that I have heard too much of this morbid gasconade, and senseless braggadocio in my tour of last Summer.

After Redon, to which we now go on direct, our first stopping-place is St. Gildas des Bois, where there is a convent of the Sœurs d'Instruction Chrétienne for the teaching of young women. This is constructed out of the houses and cloisters of the old abbey of Benedictine monks, founded in A.D. 1026 by Simon de La Roche. The existing institution was established here in 1829 by the venerable Abbé Deshayes, who organized the order of nuns by whom it is now occupied in the previous year, 1828, at Beignon. We can see, as we pass by, the tower of the chapel, and an extensive appanage of buildings mixed up with large trees. Indeed, St. Gildas of the Woods does not belie its name, having a very arborescent surrounding, chiefly consisting of pine-trees, planted by order of the government during the reign of Louis-Philippe. Outside of these, on every point of eminence, is a windmill.

By the station of Dreffeac, and then on to that of Pont-Château. The latter derives its name from an old castle that is accessible only by a bridge across a lake which encircles the building. It was erected in A.D. 1478 by the Baron de Roche Bernard. In the neighbourhood are to be found ecclesiastical relics of architecture more ancient than the castle, amongst which are ruins of an abbey built in A.D. 1046.

Hence we go on to Savenay, at which there is a junction of the lines between St. Nazaire and Nantes, as well as the last named city and that by which we are travelling—the line to Brest. By the same come all the trains from Rennes *via* Redon. Savenay is chiefly interesting from having in its neighbourhood a field, where the Vendeans were routed in battle with Generals La Hoche, Kleber, and Marceau, on the 23rd of December 1793. After this began the guerilla warfare of the Chouannerie, which continued till the death of Charles X.

The height on which this village is built forms

part of a chain of small hills, styled the "Sillon de Bretagne." That extends along the right bank of the Loire, though separated from the river by meadows as well as by low and marshy lands. Of these there is a large tract called *La Grande Brière*,—a turfy marsh of twelve miles in length, and ten in breadth. We are leaving it to the right in our journey of to-day, as it extends nearly from the Villaine river to the back of St. Nazaire. Alternately lake, meadow, turf-field, the district is inhabited by the Briérons, relics of an ancient tribe, whose wretched huts are erected on slight eminences over the turf-holes. They cut thousands of tons of this turf every year, which is sent to Nantes, to Vannes, and to La Rochelle. The Briére district is separated from the Atlantic Ocean by the wooded hills of Guerande, not far from which are the several bathing-places of the Bourg de Batz, Poliguen, and Croisic. The chief commercial operations hereabouts are making salt and curing sardines. Of these two trades, the largest operations are carried on at Guerande, in which alone there are 35,600 of pools (called *œillets*) for evaporation, occupying a superficies of about 7000 acres, and producing an average annual amount of eighty million kilogrammes of common salt, without reckoning the white. The Custom House duties on this realize a yearly revenue of thirteen to fourteen millions of francs. Here as at Noirmoutier the coarse salt has the odour of violets.

In the neighbourhood of the Loire mouth—of which I am now writing—we find the relics of the old tribes still adhering to their ancient system of isolation and exclusiveness. It is the more remarkable in a country where we so often hear the bluster of "*Égalité et Fraternité.*" On the left bank of the Loire the peasant speaks the idiom of the Poitevins; near Ancenis and Varades the provincialisms of Anjou prevail; whilst about the Bourg de Batz they talk a corruption of the Breton tongue. At Guerande not only are the farmers, salt-gatherers, and fishermen assembled in different parts of their churches; but they never associate outside of doors, nor do they ever intermarry with one another.

From Savenay, instead of going on to Nantes, we wait for the train from the latter place bound to St. Nazaire, and proceed in it to the first station at Donges. This is another of the towns in which we can find not only ecclesiastical relics dating from the Roman period, but Druidical remnants likewise. Near the station are the ruins of church and priory of Notre-Dame, erected in the eleventh century. Steamboat communication twice a day between this and Paimbœuf at the opposite side of the river Loire. As we are only able to catch the 7 p.m. steamer, we must sleep for the night at the hotel of Monsieur Tremblet, to go on next day at one o'clock with Serene—the *Vermouth*-iest of men, but the best of drivers!—in the diligence to Préfailles.

Paimbœuf is a very frowsy-looking old town, as it appeared to me next morning when I went to ramble through its streets. It is on the left bank of the Loire, and bears about the same relation to the sea that Runcorn on the Mersey does to the Irish Channel. The population is stated to be nearly 3000. Some old legend tells of the original foundation having been here in the second or third century, when the Picts and Visigoths flourished on opposite sides of the river. But on which side respectively I cannot tell. In part of the suburbs are still visible remains of walls that sometime or another, in prehistoric ages, guarded the town. The name of the place is derived from *Paim* (Breton for *head*) and *bœuf* (French for *ox*);—from the resemblance to a bullock's or cow's head of a piece of rock, in the neighbourhood, on the river's side. I strolled up to the chapel, which has in it a very fine painting of the Miraculous Draught of Fishes. Its grand altar is of the seventeenth century period. Quite close to it I see a spacious hospital, to which is attached another chapel, marked as erected in A.D. 1696.

Up to fifty years ago, Paimbœuf was an important place. But the silting up of mud, and the formation of sand-banks in the river, have obliged the navigation—especially in regard of ocean ships and steamers—to be limited to St. Nazaire,—ten miles nearer to the embouchure, and on the opposite side.

Like the change in a pantomime comes the transition, from docks and steamers, to a scene that passes me by just now. When turning into the hotel, I saw coming up the street, a woman, preceded by three sheep and a dog. Her white *coif* and *sabots* would proclaim her a *Bretonne* all the world over. Yet with these she has another special mark and token. As she walks along after her small flock and canine lieutenant, her hands are occupied with the industry of spinning flax from a *quenouille*. This is a small, straight staff round the top of which a bundle of flax fibre is attached. The staff, at its other end, is fastened to the dress at the waist; whilst the thread is spun on to a piece of stick, that is uninterruptedly twisted round, and to which the left hand acts as a mechanical revolving power, that on which the thread is rolled being styled a *fuseau*. All through Brittany, the women, when outside of doors, engage themselves in this work or in knitting. The incident before me brings to mind a story about the Duc de Guesclin, who was put under arrest some time before the battle of Auray in A.D. 1364. Although knowing that he was considered the ugliest man in the country, he is said to have boasted that so loyal were the women of Brittany, they would sell their *quenouilles* to get him out of prison.

From Paimbœuf to Préfailles, whither we are bound for the sea-bathing season, there are two different roads. One to the right passes by a large rope-factory, and through the little village of Corsept. With its single street it has a chapel that appears nearly as large as all the other houses would seem if put together. The churches from Paimbœuf inwards on this side of the river are built on the same models of architecture; namely, a long nave surmounted by a massive tower in the shape of a huge extinguisher, which is slated from base to summit. There is a large Druidical Dolmen somewhere in this neighbourhood. Thence on to lofty eminences of roads in the vicinities of St. Père Retz and St. Brenin; from both of which, if outside with the driver, or even in the *coupé*, you have charming views of a large stretch of landscape, whilst the sea bounds the horizon before, and on the right-hand side. Another small village called St. Michael is passed; and in half an hour afterwards your horses are whipped round the sharpest of corners, and narrowest of streets, through the little bourg of La Plaine.

This, though the chief town of a parish, holding about 1500 inhabitants of native population, is a very diminutive place. There is in it a pretty chapel, erected in an old church-yard—guessed as antique at first sight, from its tombstones, its crumbling walls, and its overgrowth of rank weeds. On inquiry, you find this suspicion to be correct, as the ancient chapel of Notre Dame, which was built on the same site, is reputed to have been standing for a thousand years. The present one is dedicated to St. Louis.

The district of La Plaine has not much of the picturesque about it. Yet there are some peculiarities in which it differs materially from English scenery. To Paimbœuf on the northern or river flank, from Pornic on the southern or seaside, may be considered the base of a promontory, which comprises the land on the left of the Loire near its mouth, and which is washed on its opposite side by the Atlantic Ocean. From the village of La Plaine to the Semaphore, where the telegraph-office stands, at the Loire's embouchure, is a distance of about four miles in a straight line, and an average of three miles across from sea to river. All through this, whether walking in wheat-fields, amongst vineyards, along roads or pathways, the only landmarks to be seen are windmills, stone and wooden crosses amongst the crops, or at the corners of the high roads, together with telegraph posts.

I am afraid I have delayed too long to relate all this about La Plaine. For Serene is cracking his whip with vigour, and talking strongly to the horses, whilst they are careering through the little hamlet of Kirouard, round the corner by M. Peigné's new and big house, down the slope past the Hôtel Sainte Marie. Till with a twist of the *Diligence* they are pulled up in front of the Hôtel Simoneaux at Préfailles; where we see the worthy and obliging hostess, Madame Menard, standing outside the door, cheery and bright,—with her usual look of welcome, that promises comfortable quarters.

CHAPTER IX.

Nooks and corners of Brittany—Topographical position of Préfailles—Outside of Mrs. Grundy's territory—"Deportment," and "the proprieties"—Geographical divisions of France—Noirmoutier and the Pillar Rock—Away, over the Bay of Biscay, oh!—London to Préfailles in twenty-four hours—Ménage at Hôtel des Voyageurs—"La Source"—The Chalybeate well—Pleasant and homely scene at the spring—Varieties of company—Analysis of Source water—Gasifying it—Good only when drunk at the fountain—Other hotels—Lodgings of entire cottages or of chambers—Artistic grouping of houses—"Établissement Hydrothérapique"—Breton English—Ancient use of Préfailles chalybeate—No paradise for the Artist at Préfailles—Tranquil beauty everywhere.

AMONGST the nooks and corners of Brittany, which I have visited, there is not one of them that has for me such charms as the bathing-place of Préfailles. Yet I feel little doubt, that the majority of my readers know nothing of its name or whereabouts. Since my first visit here in 1873, I have felt it to be such a delightful spot, especially for those who like the purest of air,—who do not care to bring fashion and elegance to the seaside,—and who desire to be perfectly at their case, that I should like to have some gossip about its enjoyments.

The topographical position of Préfailles is likely to secure it for many years from the invasion of Mrs. Grundy, and her disciples. Unless indeed the line of railway, opened last year from Nantes to Pornic, only six miles distant, should assist such an incursion. To my taste, freedom from the trammels of society, which come under the definition of "deportment" and "the proprieties," is not the least important item in the *régime* whereby one hopes to derive advantages from sea-bathing. This freedom you have in its perfection at Préfailles. Of its other charms, and enjoyable features we shall chat as we stroll along the cliff.

I do not know a map of France on which Préfailles is marked down. Yet on the small chart of the country that accompanies this book, you can see it at that part of the south-west coast, where the river Loire flows into the sea, after passing St. Nazaire. It is situated about a mile and a half to the left of the embouchure, and facing the Atlantic. The bay in front, from the Loire corner down to the bight, in which stands the town of Bourgneuf-de-Retz, is called the Bay of Bourgneuf. Here we are—and have been ever since crossing the iron bridge at Redon, which shuts us out from Morbihan department,—in that of the Loire Inférieure. *En parenthèse*, it may be interesting to some of my readers to know that the geographical division of France into 32 provinces, which existed in 1790, has been changed into 89 departments, subdivided into 373 arrondissements (or counties), 2938 cantons (or districts), and 37,510 communes (or parishes).

Nearly six miles distant to the east is the larger and fashionable bathing-place of Pornic. Out in the sea before us are the island of Noirmoutier, and the Pillar Rock; on which latter there is a tower with a revolving light, apparently bounding the horizon. Beyond that horizon (visible from our hotel-garden) you can go across the Bay of Biscay,—out into the Atlantic Ocean,—amongst the Madeira, Canary, and Cape Verde Islands,—speeding away down south, between the continents of Africa and South America! Then you could turn round to the left, by the Cape of Good Hope, into the Indian Ocean, or by the right through the Straits of Magellan, or past the dreadful Cape Horn to the Pacific. Doubtless all my readers are acquainted with these facts. I only repeat them here for the purpose of adding, that in all the score of times I have made these voyages in much of the *routes* indicated, not one has given me such pleasure as I now enjoy of them, in memory and fancy every day, whilst lounging on the green sod of the sea-bank, overhanging part of the northern boundary of that same Bay of Biscay at Préfailles.

From London the holiday party—be it one or twenty—can come to Préfailles in less than twenty-four hours. Counting three to Southampton,—an average of fourteen across the Channel to St. Malo,—two from the latter to Rennes,—and three from Rennes, *viâ* Redon, to Savenay. Thence either on to Nantes, and by the opposite side of the Loire to Pornic by rail,—or from Donges across to Paimbœuf,—and by Diligence. as I came. Either of these lightning express, or Queen's messenger style of travelling, is not necessary, unless for those whose ambition is to try a style of Cook's excursion round the world in ninety days. Préfailles is a place to be enjoyed for its tranquil and healthful pleasures, of which I shall proceed to give details. It is in no way fitted for those who wish to rush over here in a few hours.

At the hotel of Madame Menard, my wife and I had a most comfortable and airy double-bedded room—linen being provided by the establishment.

Every morning at 6 a.m. tea was made for us, the congou brought from England by ourselves, —milk, sugar, bread and butter in abundance, candles for night, *table d'hôte* breakfast with lobster, soles, chops, and other contingencies of excellent *menu*. Dinner equally good—all of superior quality and first-rate cookery—the whole for five francs and a half per day = fifty-five pence = four shillings and seven pence sterling! I should add that extras to be paid for are such indispensabilities as soap, washing clothes, and so forth. For besides the condiments enumerated, you have included at breakfast, and dinner a bottle (or two if you desire) of *vin ordinaire*.

But who thinks of wine at Préfailles? When in any part of the village you are only a few minutes' walk from "La Source." This is the Chalybeate spring; and at it is the principal rendezvous for visitors; like the pump-rooms of Buxton, Harrogate and Cheltenham, but very unlike in the absence of all social starch, or stuck-up-ishness. Those, who are very constitutional, visit it in the morning before taking their sea-bath. The evening, however, is the most crowded time—after dinner—from half-past seven to eight p.m. It is not easy to imagine, and far more difficult to describe, the pleasant and homely scene of the few hundred people about;—everybody talking to anybody;—some drinking from the fountain,—others seated on the banks,—more dotted here and there amongst the rocks, especially if the tide be out,—and nearly all chatting with that graceful familiarity, *bonhommie*, and politeness, which is such a delightful characteristic of French society.

Amongst the company we have the Breton peasant, and farmers' wives and daughters, in their neat white caps, and always knitting. There are professionals, bourgeois, and shopkeepers, together with a sprinkling of priests and nuns. We have some few of the old Bourbon nobility from the valley of the Maine and Loire, all of whom are devoted adherents of the Comte de Chambord; and believing in the right divine of the *ancien régime*, they have a firm faith that the accession of Henry V. to the throne of France only requires a short time to make it *un fait accompli*. The water of "La Source" is a wonderfully curative, and strengthening chalybeate. A small pamphlet about its properties has been written by Monsieur Le Docteur Guepin. This is founded on the report and analysis of the Imperial Academy of Medicine, done in 1856 by order of His Excellency, the Minister of Agriculture, Commerce, and Public Works (of the period), M. Dubois. But I do not wish to bother my readers with chemical technicalities about chloride of sodium, magnesium, or protoxyde of iron. Who cares to know how many component parts of this, that, or the other ingredient are contained in any mineral water he drinks? Enough for us to see it pellucid and transparent as it flows out of the pipe, as to know it is delightfully cool and agreeable to the taste, and most invigorating in its effects.

On the high bank before going down, by a short winding road to the plateau of rock, in front of which the water runs out through a tube, there is a small wooden house, wherein an elderly man is gasifying the chalybeate liquid. This is bottled up, to be drunk either at the hotels of the village, or at any other part of the world to which it is desired to be exported. The operator before me is Monsieur Monier, Pharmacien de 1ere classe. I stepped in for a moment, and found myself in a laboratory of pipes, tubes, retorts, and taps.

"With what do you gasify the water?" I inquired.

"We do it with sulphuric acid and chalk," was the answer.

"At how much per bottle is it sold?"

"Fifty cents, Monsieur," that is, half a franc.

To which I replied, "Merci, Monsieur!" Then raising my hat with a "Bon jour," I went down to the well, where I had for nothing at all as much of the water as I desired to drink.

It may be a groundless prejudice, but to my unchemical mind the idea of chalk and vitriol having any concern with improving a liquid would prevent its doing me a benefit. Moreover I am not quite certain if the action of these ingredients does not, whilst gasifying, deteriorate the natural components of the water. As a general rule I do not possess faith in mineral waters that are taken when long removed from their natural sources. Under this idea I include those of Harrogate, Buxton, Cheltenham, and Préfailles. Drunk at their respective springs they are all good and useful, as they are prescribed by your medical adviser; but bottled, and taken away they must undergo some natural decomposition, which of necessity changes their thermal qualities. Dr. Guepin says of Préfailles:—"It is a great error to believe that this water has the same quality when taken at one's house, as it has when drunk at the Source."

Not only is this true, but I am afraid the iron water of Préfailles may do a deal of injury instead of good to those who imbibe it by the practice which now exists, that is, of drinking at the fashionable hours of rendezvous near the Source after dinner. I wish people would reflect, that the stomach, being employed in digesting the dinner food, cannot with impunity bear on it the additional load of iron water. Nor can I endorse the recommendation of Dr. Guepin, that the taking of the "Source" water be accompanied by "*une tranche très-mince de jambon entre deux lèches de pain*,"—which I need scarcely add is a very roundabout way they have in France of describing a sandwich. The best time for drinking the water is as early in the morning as you wish; then, after a short walk, have your bath in the sea, and another brief promenade succeeding will make the breakfast relishable. I do not think there is anything needed in the way of excuse for this long dissertation on the case in point. The majority of people who go to Préfailles visit it for the sake of the "Source," and I feel confident they will derive additional benefit if they pass seriously in their minds my observations on the subject. Nothing is farther from my intention than to deliver a lecture to people going to enjoy their holiday as every one does here. But wherever we go, these lines of the poet Thomson may be written in letters of gold, that

> "From the body's purity
> The mind receives a secret sympathetic aid."

There can be no purity where there is indigestion, so don't drink Préfailles Source water after dinner! *Verb. sap.*

Besides the Hôtel des Voyageurs (or Simoneaux, named from its original proprietor), there are two others here—the Hôtel Sainte Marie, and the Hôtel de l'Océan. I know nothing of their *ménage*. But they are both spacious; and I mention them to show that there is plenty of accommodation for visitors. Through the village, likewise, chambers are procurable—entire cottages and furnished houses as well. All cleanly and some luxuriously furnished, at rents varying from twenty francs a month to 360. I do not recommend any person coming here from England to undertake the management of a house, which is rented by the month. It will involve getting the alternative of French cook and servants, or of your own being fleeced in the shops and market. Whereas by going to a hotel, you can—not only leave on any day you wish, but will be able to live more economically. None of the hotels are farther than three minutes' walk from the bathing strand.

Along the bank, overhanging the sea, and wending eastward to La Source is a new macadamized road, constructed since my first visit. So either by that, or by the smooth grassy cliff on the opposite side towards St. Gildas is a most delightful promenade. At early morning in the month of July, the smell of wild camomile is wafted with the ozone from the ocean, and conveys to our senses a most agreeable combination. Whilst over the wheat-fields hard by, and still uncut, the larks are carolling above our heads. From the small chapel, quite close to our hotel we pass down between the Hôtel de l'Océan, and the bath establishment. All around here is a number of new houses—each one of different order of architecture from its neighbour; and no two in the same parallel of position. This gives them a most agreeable air of independence of each other, and helps to form an artistic grouping—so entirely different from the prim monotony of a terrace line of houses. What was a small bath-place—for douche and warm bathing—two years ago, is now raised up into a large red-tiled, and brown-painted building with a glaring sign-board of "*Établissement Hydro-*

thérapique."[1] At this you are provided with tickets for any kind of bath you desire, at so much per month. The proprietress, Madame Le Maire, is likewise the owner of the principal collection of boxes on the beach for dressing and undressing. As men and women go in the sea at the same place, here you can be furnished with pantaloons, blouses, shoes, and hats. I need scarcely say it will be found more agreeable as well as more economical, to take with you your own bathing-clothes, to any such place as Préfailles.

On my first evening's saunter in July last (1875) down to "La Source," I met a gentleman from Cueron (on the opposite side of the Loire, between Nantes and St. Nazaire), whose acquaintance I had made on my former visit two years before. This was brought about by his being the only English-speaking individual besides my wife and myself, who up to the period had penetrated into these parts. In the course of our conversation, I spoke of the British language having no hold on the country (Brittany) from which it derives its title; when he pulled out of his pocket a small bit of paper to prove the

---

[1] I may add this word should be Hydrothérapeutique, but the length of wall and size of letters perhaps necessitated the curtailment.

contrary. It had been pasted over a parcel of coffee, which he had recently purchased. I give it as the original—*litera scripta manet :—*

> This coffee, of succory and douce-acorn, prived ; is, in the Public delivered, with the system, which is preserving, the concentred perfume, delicious taste and alls goods nature of the most estimed plantations coffees ; doing of her composition party.
>
> His moderate price and in préparation great attentions very much given, his consummation will be sought for it more and more.
>
> The Boxes, you must hermitically to close, for conservation of perfume.
>
> That void Boxe, being in good order made, with note ; will be   pennys repayed ; because it his besides payed.

Is it not enough to make Lindley Murray and Dr. Johnson arise from their graves?

All my inquiries as to the first coming into use, or even the primal discovery, of the chalybeate Source have failed. In one of my rambles through a vineyard, I met an old woman who was minding a cow, and at the same time knitting. On getting into chat with her, she told me she was beyond eighty years of age; and in reply to my inquiry, she knew of the fame of the water as a curative since she can remember anything. Yet neither in Bradshaw's Handbook of Brittany, nor in Adolphe Joanne's Itinerary of the same, is there mention of even the name of Préfailles.

Here there is no paradise for the artist—no "sunset suffusing mountain heights in pink and gold "—no " bald wild peaks and ravines "— no "castled crags," or anything of that Rosa-Matildaish kind. But there is a tranquil beauty around you—joined with that most delightful of sensations, a feeling of health and vigour at every step you take—along the bye-ways—through the wheat-fields—and amongst the vineyards. Except twice a day, when the diligence arrives from Pornic and Paimbœuf, you are entirely freed from the vehicular clatter, that you want to escape, in order to enjoy the serenity of the sea-side. No one, I trust, will accuse me of affectation in the expression of my belief, that the most enjoyable of sounds in this place is that of "What are the wild waves saying?—sister, the whole day long " For the shriek of railway whistle, or the rattle of four wheels is incompatible with the peace and harmony which you desire to enjoy, and which make your sea-bath so appreciable.

CHAPTER X.

What about the sea-bath?—The season at Préfailles—On the strand and amongst the dressing-boxes—The Marquee—Traditional night-caps—Flopping up and down—*Le Baigneur*—On the bank to St. Gildas—Quadrupeds of Préfailles—Jerusalem pony?—*Comment s'appelle-t-il?*—Varieties of titles—Classical, historical, and mythological—Sexual difference not regarded—Chatty little market-place—"*Dam Oui*" or "*Dam Non*"—Derivation—*Émotion* at arrival of fish-boat—Breton coif—Increase of kid-glove-ology—Ozone and wild camomile—Agreeable recollections—General hybernation—Close of bathing season—Melancholy ocean—*Au revoir* to Préfailles.

"WELL! but what about the sea-bath?" some impatient reader may inquire. To which I reply "This is enjoyed at all hours of the day, from sunrise to sundown, and whether the tide is in or out.

During the season, which begins in the middle of June, and terminates about the 15th of September, the most usual period for the bath in the sea is from 2 to 4 p.m. Between these hours, more especially at the height of the bathing-period, in the month of August, the beach presents a very gay and lively appearance. The Hydrotherapeutic building, previously mentioned, stands on the bank, just over the bathing bay. At the back of this house, and on the slope is a spacious marquee, from which bannerets are floating all day long. Beneath it the non-bathers sit, shaded from the sun, and looking at the joyous medley all around. Men, women, boys, girls, priests, nuns, going in and out from their boxes, for dressing and undressing—as well as in and out of the sea. All garbed in the like costume of blouse, from neck to hips, and of drawers to below the knees. Many of these dresses are of stylish pattern, trimmed with red, yellow, or blue braidings. The caps are sometimes adorned with tassels, that bring to mind our grandfathers' traditional nightcaps of fifty years ago. The ladies going into the sea generally catch hold of a rope, which is extended out by poles. With this grasped in the hands, they flop down and rise up—often continuing this sousing for nearly half an hour. They invariably have their heads covered, with straw hats or oil-silk caps. These are used much more as a protection against the rays of the sun, generally so strong between 2 and 4 p.m., than to keep the hair from being wetted. But they serve both purposes.

Amongst the crowd of bathers is the *Baigneur*, the man who teaches swimming at half a franc the lesson. Occasionally his energies are called into action when any case of accident occurs. Indeed during our stay at Préfailles more than one person has been saved by him from drowning.

The duties of bath and the chalybeate being finished, what next is to be done?

After a capital breakfast, you can either go fishing for shrimps,—stroll amongst the vineyards, —walk along the bank to St. Gildas,—or join a party down to one of the small coves, to pick up agates and beautiful pebbles. If you be too lazy to walk you can have a ride upon a ——? I really cannot give to the quadruped at Préfailles the name by which he is known at Hampstead, New Brighton, or Blackheath. Shall I entitle him a Jerusalem pony?

"*Comment s'appelle-t-il?*" I inquired of the small boy who drove up to the hotel door with one of them, under a spring cart painted bright yellow, that I had hired to bring us over on a six-mile drive to Pornic. The answer of "*Framboisie! Monsieur!*" first suggested raspberry-jam to my mind. Till I found, on further investigation, that the name is derived from a comic song about some Duke of Framboisie, during the Crimean War. As we mount and take our seats, the young driver gives a chuck to the reins, and a crack to his whip, with the words, "*Allons, Mademoiselle,*" addressed to Framboisie. Need I say, that with the associations of a Duke, and the title of Mademoiselle, it would be perfectly outrageous to give either of the English appellations that are applied to the animal which my readers will no doubt have recognized? Our drive was an exceedingly delightful one, and on our return Framboisie seemed as fresh as when setting out.

There are many members of the Framboisie race at Préfailles. On several doors and gateways you see posted up on cards fastened to small square boards :—"*Ane à louer—avec selle, ou voiture.*" Amongst them I found the following names. One is called "Napoleon," another "Champagne," a third "Papillon" (the butterfly), and a fourth "Franqueur" (the free-hearted fellow). We have also "Voltigeur" (a flyer), "Bélisaire," "La Basilique," "La Violette," "La Bichette," and though last not least, our gallant little Framboisie. The names of Violette, Belisarius, Napoleon, and Framboisie are given indiscriminately to males and females—thus proving that no attention is paid to sexual difference in the nomenclature. Any of these can be hired from four to five hours—and saddled for a lady or gentleman—at the cost of a single franc.

The chatty little market-place in front of our hotel is a picture vividly impressed upon me. About twenty small tables of the most primitive style are left permanently at the corner turning round from the main road. As the sun rises you hear the cackling of ducks, fowls, and geese, with the gobbling of turkeys, and the chattering of the people, arranging their marketables on the little stalls. Cabbages, eggs, carrots, vegetables of all kinds;—fish, flesh, and garden stuff in abundance. At every bargaining you hear the *prononcé* peculiarity of the Loire Inférieure—"Dam Oui!" or "Dam No!" I cannot trace the derivation of this—unless it be, as a lady friend of mine guessed it, from the English; without the divine prefix which our sailors give to make it still more emphatic.

Then we often had a sort of *émotion* on the arrival of a fishing-boat from Pornic or Noirmoutier. The coming in of this craft is known before she is within a mile or two of the anchorage. So the hotel managers with the housekeepers flock down to the beach. Every one in the village who has nothing to do—of which there is generally a large number—join the crowd impulsively. As soon as the punt of the fish lugger brings its cargo on shore, there is quite a market established at the water's edge; and all the cargo is bought up in a few minutes. Ladies and gentlemen often carry crabs or lobsters home in their hands; and you may travel much further, I assure you, without meeting a tidier *bonne* than that cherry-faced girl with the white Breton *coif*, glistening in the sunshine, and a pair of soles, held with a morsel of sea-weed between her fingers.

Yet here although the summer holidays are drawing to an end I cannot help a regret at seeing them closing with such an increase of kid-glove-ology as the last fortnight has ushered in. Little removed from desecration, does it seem to me—along that bank, where I have so many times rambled, fanned by the ozone and odour of wild camomile, as well as soothed by the carolling of larks—to meet as I have met to-day (the 4th of September) half-a-dozen distressingly got up swells, with kid-gloves of bright gamboge colour. It is a holiday, and so they must come to do something *outré*. I turn back to walk to St. Gildas Point for a farewell to Préfailles for seven months—leaving it as nearly every one does with the impression of the most agreeable recollections. The universal exodus is approaching—for this is a deserted village in the winter time—its inhabitants being like,

> " Those birds that bring Summer,
> And fly when 'tis o'er."

As soon as the 15th of September has gone by, a general hybernation comes over the hotels— the bath establishment—the groceries and other shops. The market is also dispersed; and its ricketty tables stowed away till next summer. The butcher, and the baker cease their daily visits from La Plaine. The postman brings no letters nor newspapers from Pornic. Except the two officials at the Semaphore—the coastguards who are always watching "the melancholy ocean" on the look-out for daring smugglers that never come—a few old women with small flocks of sheep—and perhaps some of our useful quadrupedal friends of the Papillon, Bichette, and Framboisie species, everything at Préfailles is suspended during the winter period. So having passed a delightful two months of bathing season let us hope to return next year with the larks and the swallows;—and to find the old hotel under the same obliging and courteous management of Madame Menard.

CHAPTER XI.

Picnic to Noirmoutier—Beautiful morning—"*Le paradis des ânes*"—Charming programme—General success of impromptu pleasure parties—Terrific whistling of steamer's pipe—Delay of getting passengers on board—Doubts of the propriety of such a trip before breakfast—"They *do not* manage these things better in France"—At the island—Tediousness of getting on shore—Clamour at the hotel—Hurrying to and fro—Is it a fire, or a revolution?—No breakfast for anybody—Frantic gabble—Improvised cookery—Foray on bread-basket—"*Poulet pour trois*"—Scrap of liver and shaving of leg—Asses and mules—Progress to capital of island—Aspirations for oysters—Château—Church and *Paludiers*—Dirty water in the streets—Bad smells—Double *morale*.

"THEY manage these things better in France," is an axiom as old as the hills. But I feel very confident it cannot be applied to such a picnic as that in which I was participator, on Tuesday, the 13th of July last, at the island of Noirmoutier.

The morning was charmingly mild, the sea deliciously smooth. At about 9 a.m. I was seated on one of the chairs outside the bathing box, after taking my sea-dip at Préfailles. Suddenly I hear a shrill whistle, that continued for a few minutes, and looking in the direction whence it proceeded I saw a small steamer coming round the corner from the direction of Pornic. At once I recognized it as the lugger-steamboat, which, in its ordinary voyages, plies during summer-time between Pornic and St. Nazaire. Now and then it is detached for such a special service as that of to-day; explained to me by a few of our companions at the Hotel coming up at the moment, and inviting me to accompany them.

In reply to my inquiry of " To where she was bound?" the programme was at once detailed. For what we in England call a picnic,—to the island of Noirmoutier in front of us, and only six miles' voyage,—breakfast at the moment of arrival, as it had been ordered by telegraph at mid-day yesterday;—then riding on donkeys (at Préfailles this island is styled "*le Paradis des Anes*")—exploring the labyrinth,—visiting the Château,—eating oysters! In fact, enjoying ourselves to "the top of our bent" in an improvised feast day, and a day that seemed specially made for such pleasure! Fare thither and back only two francs! How charming!

Who could resist this tempting bill of fare?

Not I at any rate. For I had a long time desired an opportunity to visit the island. Here it happens as if specially got up for the purpose. Moreover I was inclined to look upon gatherings of this kind that come to one *impromptu*, as this did, with more hopeful feelings of success as a pleasure excursion, than where elaborate preparations are made. My day at Noirmoutier has somewhat modified this opinion as far as France is concerned. But I shall not anticipate.

The little steamer dropped anchor in the cove, still continuing her shrill whistle as if there was not a moment to be lost, and that she wished the passengers to understand, in case they did not come on board directly, she would have her anchor up again, and steam away *tout-de-suite* The excursionists, however, seemed in no hurry as they came slowly down from the different hotels, about sixty all told, and the work of getting on board was begun. As there is no wharf or quay at Préfailles, all had to be taken off in a boat. This latter craft belonged to the steamer, and could accommodate only five or six persons with the two men pulling the oars. The absurdity of having merely a bit of a float like this on such an occasion, never struck me till I found myself on the steamer's deck, in company with two ladies whom my wife had commissioned me to chaperon for the day. Then I saw the folly of it. For the lots of five and six in the small tub seemed to be " never done coming." To be sure, I had not eaten my breakfast. But that could have nothing to do with my anxiety to be away, or with the distress caused by the eternal going to the shore, and returning of the small punt. That abominable whistle still shrieking! Every moment I felt myself more conscious of the unpleasant sensations, caused by my long walk in the morning, having taken my sea-bath, and yet eaten nothing!

At last and about ten o'clock, the screaming of the engine ceased, anchor is up, and the screw thumps away. Everything looked fair and beautiful, as if presaging a delightful day. The calm sea, the bright sky, the glowing sun—the laughing, chattering crowd on board—the pretty cliffs of Préfailles, Sainte Marie, and Pornic, dotted with white houses, that we were leaving behind. The island in front with its two towers, its pine, and oak trees coming every moment into more prominent relief. Here we are at last!

Anchor is down under the lighthouse in the little bay of San Carlos. Now commenced another operation, which I maintain against all comers they do not "manage better in France;" and that is, sending people on shore from a steamer when they are hungry. The same small tub of a boat that was used at Préfailles is lowered from the davits, and again, one, two, three, four, five, six, seven, eight, nine groups of passengers go ashore. One of my lady friends, being in delicate health, I did not like to ask her to try in the crush amongst several of the first lots of disembarkers. But at length we reach *terra firma*. Only about forty yards from the landing-place was the succursal of the hotel, at which we were to have our breakfast. As we approached the house we heard a fearful noise of clamour and dispute. We also recognized a dreadful "running to and fro" of *bonnes* and *garçons*, becoming at the same time conscious of a tumultuous uproar that is indescribable. We stopped. Was it a fire? a free fight? or a revolution? " No," one of our fellow-passengers who was coming out with a face of despair, told us. Yet something that I may be considered highly depraved for characterizing as ten times worse under the circumstances. No breakfast had been prepared! The telegraphic message sent on yesterday had not been delivered till just as the steamer appeared in sight! When at the moment, the *maître d'hôtel* tackled all his establishment to get up as good a breakfast as could be obtained at the moment. Eggs, bread, cheese, potatoes, fowls, wine, were all now being operated on in the cuisine department. This explained the reason of three *bonnes* and two waiters rushing, like mad people, in and out of the kitchen, which was to the left, from the large dining-room on the right of the entrance. I made three steps to get opposite to the kitchen-door, where several girls in a frantic state of gabble,—of rushing about,—of taking pots and pans off the fire, and putting them on again, seemed to make confusion worse confounded. I was about to exclaim,—

" The pillar'd firmament is rottenness,
And earth's base built on stubble,"

But on second thoughts, as a waiter rushed by me with a dish of omelette in his hand, I caught him by the arm. As he was impudent enough to try and disengage himself, he may be contented that I did not throttle him. Then slipping a franc into his hand, and pointing to the ladies who were with me, I asked for something to eat. With a cautious look around to see if he were watched, he put the omelette on our little table and returned back with a run to the kitchen,—to get a new supply, no doubt, for those who had engaged that, which fell to our lot. We had fortunately got to a small round table, supplied with knives and forks. In the next moment I had made a foray on a basket of bread that was on the side-board. The same *garçon* now brought us boiled eggs, potatoes, cheese, and wine. All of which had to be partaken of during, the never-ceasing talking,—rushing about,—screaming,—and indescribable clatter. One of the *bonnes*, who had probably had *clairvoyance* of the franc in the *garçon's* pocket, came up breathless, and asked me if we desired some fowl, I replied "Yes"—the very thing we did want.

"For how many," she inquired, "Bring fowl for three," I said sharply, meaning of course for the two ladies and myself.

In almost as short a time as I take to record it, she returned with a huge dish, overflowing with potatoes. This she put precipitately on the table, with a crash that made several of the *pommes de terre* to scamper about on the table-cloth. And with a scream of " *Poulet pour trois*," away she flitted again. But where was the poulet? Amongst the potatoes of course! If it had left the cook's department, it must have betaken wing and flown away. For in all that large heap of potatoes was no semblance of fowl, save one liver, and the shaving of a leg! As my appetite was still lively, I went in for the esculent, which with butter and salt was very good. In this I was joined by the ladies. The fowl affair being somewhat of the smart, I set that liver and leg-shaving aside on a small plate. It was removed by the same *bonne* in ten minutes after, to whose notice I specially introduced it.

Then I paid the bill, without having anything charged for poulet, but gave nothing to the *bonne* who had tried to deceive us.

At the door was a bevy of about forty asses, the most miserable, worn-out looking animals it is possible to conceive. I can scarcely bring myself to believe they belong to the same race as our Préfailles quadrupeds. Mules and ponies too, all of these with an aspect as if they had never got anything to eat but the salt which is the chief product of the island, – and not even enough of that. The saddles are made of pieces of worn-out canvas, or sail cloth, stuffed with straw, or seed-weed (*alga marina*), and tied round the body with a piece of cord. There are neither stirrups, bits, nor bridles; but a small piece of slight rope is put round the neck quite close to the shoulders. This is for the rider to hold on by, and thus maintain his or her balance. My lady friends are obliged to mount the donkey as I do. They call it in France *à l'ancre*, or *califourchon*. The steeds are guided by the owner, who accompanies them stick in hand. Nearly all our party went to explore on the same kind of four-leggers.

Before leaving the small wooden house—*Succursale* of the hotel—where we had our memorable meal of this morning, I may note, that quite close to this stands a tower for which nobody knows the use. It is not far from the lighthouse, and was erected some few years ago by Monsieur Plantier, mayor of Noirmoutier. The cost of the building was from 15,000 to 20,000 francs.

Our road to the capital, the same name as the island, is through a wood of oak and beech. Of humanity on the route, we see only a few old women. At the city, the principal objects of notice are a big château, and a bigger church. I am told there is a labyrinth in the woods through which we have passed; but after the *fiasco* of a breakfast I find it difficult to believe in anything, that is not palpably before me.

The day was very hot as we arrived at the church, and dismounted from our donkeys to go inside. It is a spacious building, dedicated to St. Philbert, and resembles the majority of those to be seen in country places near the coast of France. There is a model of a full-rigged ship, hanging from the vaulted roof. I went down into a crypt beneath the altar, and whilst the Sacristan was sounding the Angelus, copied literally the following from a tombstone:—" Çy est le cœur de très hault et puissant Seigneur, Messire François Tremoille, Marquis de Noirmoutier, qui décédé le 14 jour de Fevrier, 1608." From which it may be surmised the church is one of considerable antiquity.

Out of the chapel, and close by, is the château, with a moat round it. No one is visible about the ramparts except a sentinel at the chief gate. Then we turn down by a one-sided street, where we were lured to stop, again dismount, and enter a house in search of oysters, from having seen some shells on the pavement. But there were none to be had, although I know of the bivalves having been furtively procured that day by one of our fellow-excursionists. It was out of the season, and therefore—

"Caution mark'd the guarded way."

We came from this on the quay of a canal, where a number of small vessels were being loaded with salt. Whilst as far as the eye could reach were heaps of that article, resembling in their conical tops, the military tents of a warlike encampment. These hillocks are to be covered with earth in the winter time, to prevent the action of hail, rain, snow, or frost. I have already explained how the salt is made by the evaporation of salt water in the heat of the sun.

Outside the boatmen, the chief inhabitants of Noirmoutier are the salt-gatherers, and their wives. The former scrape up the crystals, and the latter carry these small heaps to put them into the large cocks. It is a curious fact that much, if not all of the salt made at Noirmoutier, as at Guerande, has a strong smell of violets;— how derived I cannot guess. The chief products of the island are salt and wheat.

Noirmoutier is twenty-four miles in circumference, and has 6000 inhabitants. Besides its capital—seat of the big château, and bigger church, it owns the small towns of La Bodier, La Vieille, La Garnier, L'Epin, and Barbot. As we turn round the corner of the canal quay, and over a bridge, we get into the heart of the place. Dirty green water is lying in small pools through the streets, and bad smells are everywhere as we go along; of the same ammoniacal and filthy nature as those I have mentioned at St. Malo. Such as these are experienced in every French town, though not to the same degree of intensity.

Noirmoutier is every day losing its physical character as an island. For at low water, carriages can cross its shoals from the mainland to the eastward, either from the village of Bouin, or Beauvoir-sur-Mer. The island of Noirmoutier belongs to the department of La Vendée.

At five o'clock we were all assembled at the Succursale, and after the usual prolonged style of getting on board, arrived at Préfailles in time for a good dinner.

Sitting in front of the Simoneaux Hotel with my after-dinner cigar, I noted the *morale* of our day's picnic as simply an advice to my readers on two points:—

FIRST. Whenever you go Noirmoutier, always make your voyage after breakfast.

SECOND. If you visit the capital of the island and walk through its streets, it will obviate no small amount of discomfort to have with you a pinch of snuff or a bottle of smelling salts.

CHAPTER XII.

Préfailles to Nantes—Three different routes—Beauty of the old city—Hide-and-go-seek style of architecture—The Château—The Cathedral—The railway' station—Early foundation of Nantes—At what epoch?—Primitive Christian teaching and martyrdom here—Anne de Bretagne—Famous prisoners in the Château—Visit to Cathedral—Begun in Fifteenth Century and not yet finished—Deficient in harmony of proportions—Reign of Terror in Nantes—The Noyades, or Republican marriages—Narrative by one of the *employés*—Knocking the victims on the head—*Le mariage civique*—Five girls sent for execution with their mother—Motherly feelings of fisherwoman—Reward for Carrier—Clisson and its Inquisition memories—*Tivoli de l'Occident*.

FROM Préfailles there are three different routes to Nantes:—first, by the new line of railway extending to Pornic;—second, *via* Paimbœuf to cross the Loire, and go with the St. Nazaire train from Donges;—third, up the river in one of the Pyroscaphe Company's steamboats, that touch twice a day at Paimbœuf.

A beautiful city is Nantes, with a hallowed air of antiquity about many of its buildings.

Yet having a bustle of streety and business life, almost equal to London or Liverpool;—at the railway station, in several of its streets, and on the shipping quays. Here I could never feel the incompatibility which one might expect from the contingencies of our busy age, jostling with centuries of historic associations. It is built on an archipelago of islets, formed by the confluence with the Loire of the rivers Sevre, Erdre, Chesine, and Sail. Crossing these we find more bridges than a lazy man would care to count on a hot summer's day. Adolphe Joanne tells us there are sixteen of them. The architectural arrangement of the town seems to have been originally of the hide-and-go-seek style. For to a stranger no labyrinth could be more puzzling than the way in which bridges, streets, quays, archways, hotel-yards, courts, stables, and passages are inextricably confused.

Above the bridges, and within a stone's throw of each other, we find the Château, begun to be erected in A.D. 1466 by the Duke Francois II., to replace fortifications of the tenth century;— the Cathedral dedicated to St. Peter, commenced in A.D. 1434, though not finished yet;—and the railway station dating from ?—well!—from some years—few or many!—since you and I, dear reader, were born! Yet what a series of vicissitudes has not the site gone through, ere a stone was laid in the oldest of these. For Nantes was founded—who can tell at what epoch?—by the Namnétes, or Nannétes, a tribe of Armorican Gauls, that flourished here, when the Picts occupied the left side of the Loire, and long previous to the first Roman invasion, 56 B.C. The primitive Nannétes had an extensive commerce. It is even said that so far back as 400 years B.C. there was a flourishing trade at Couëron (a few miles lower down on the Loire), and where there is now a railway station. In the middle of the third century, Christianity was preached at Nantes by St. Clair, and in A.D. 290, Saints Donatian and Rogation, natives of this city, suffered martyrdom here. Besides the Cathedral it has fourteen churches, one of which, that of the Holy Cross, was first erected on the site of a Pagan temple.

The Château has an air of gloomy grandeur about it, as well as an appearance of strength, that seems to render it impregnable to time. Of the three towers erected at the period of its construction by François II. all are in as good a state as the like number done in the time of Anne de Bretagne. The former are at the

back of the building, whereas the latter face the
quay. Some time about the end of the fifteenth
century, a solemn entry was made into this
Château by the illustrious lady last mentioned,
with all the pomp which accompanied such cere-
monials in the middle ages. In or about that
period she was married to Louis XII., styled le
Père du Peuple. Previous to the epoch of this
wedding she was the widow of Charles VIII.
Her alliance with Louis ratified the union of the
crowns of France and Brittany. Various writers
say the marriage was celebrated in this Château,
within a small chapel that was subsequently
destroyed by an explosion in 1800. Whereas
others deny it. Indeed Adolphe Joanne records
it as a fact in his "Guide de Bretagne." Amongst
the most famous of the prisoners who have been
confined in this castle were the Cardinal Retz,
Fouquet, and the Duchesse de Berri. The last
named was sent here after she had failed in
organizing a rebellion of the Vendeans in 1832.
It may not be generally known that the Duchesse
was discovered concealed in a chimney, and it
was only through lighting a fire by which she was
severely burned, and her clothes materially injured,
that she consented to come out and surrender.

Strangers are permitted to visit this old castle,

on presenting their cards to the gate-keeper in the conciergerie at the end of the courtyard.

Through a very narrow tortuous street, two minutes' walk will take us to the Cathedral, in the Place St. Pierre. I have already mentioned that this was begun in the middle of the fifteenth century. It is not finished yet. The latter fact is evident by a large mass of scaffolding overlooking the promenade. But the real truth is, that a Christian church was erected on this spot towards the end of the third century, and this was reconstructed by St. Felix, in A.D. 570. That was again replaced by a Roman church after A.D. 1150, which was in its turn demolished— except the transept and the choir—to give place to the large Gothic Cathedral, of which the foundation was laid in 1434, and where we find ourselves now.

The inside of this large building appears to me deficient in harmony of proportions. The pillars are enormously large, and the vaulted roofs very high in their bearing to the length and breadth. It contains a number of small altars, several statues, and paintings. But its chief work of art is the tomb of François II. Duke of Brittany, and of Margaret de Foix, his second wife. The Cathedral itself as well as the tomb suffered many mutilations during the Revolution of 1791-95.

To go through Nantes and describe all its attractions would require a couple of volumes. It has Préfecture, Hôtel de Ville, Palais de Justice, theatre, public libraries, museums, the passage Pommeraye, Bourse or Exchange, and many other institutions.

Few cities in France suffered so much as Nantes during the Reign of Terror; although at the commencement in 1789 it embraced the Revolutionary principles quite enthusiastically. During four months of 1793, Carrier was here—having been sent down from Paris by the self-styled Committee of Public Safety. Finding the guillotine and shooting people did not exterminate with sufficient rapidity, he invented the *Noyades*, or Republican marriages. It would be impossible to make a calculation, even by the wildest guesswork, of the numbers of thousands of victims to this cruelty. A recent account of it is given in a work, "*L'Histoire de la Ville de Nantes*," par Messieurs Lescadieu et Laurent. Although the story is related by a Monsieur George Thomas, one of the health officers, as having been told to him by a boatman, named Perdreau, whose credit is said to be impeached by his having been a little tipsy at the time of his narration, I am sorry at having to record that its truth has been assured to me by friends of undoubted veracity at Nantes.

"Towards the end of Brumaire," said M. Thomas, "I was in a café on the Place Buffay, when a boatman, a short, stout fellow, named Perdreau, entered, who asked me for a pinch of snuff, which I gave him. 'I have gained a lot of money,' he said, 'by knocking off (*expédier*) seven or eight hundred people.' Whilst he was talking I saw that he was a little drunk. And this was a reason for my pursuing the question, to discover the truth.

"'But,' I inquired, 'how did you manage to kill so many people in such a short time?'

"'Nothing more easy,' he replied, 'When I go to bathe them, I strip the men and women. I search their pockets, and then put their clothes in a big hamper. Man and woman I fasten arm to arm, and wrist to wrist. I bring them to the edge of the Loire. They mount in my boat—two men push them from behind—and they fall head-foremost into the river.'

"Not being yet satisfied, and wishing to tear from this fiend the truth about his detestable work, I asked him if these people did not sometimes escape by floating on their backs, or by the use of their arms.

"'No,' he replied, 'we always put them to the river in good order. We have large sticks, with which we knock them on the head before sending them into the Loire. This we call *le mariage civique.*'"

I have the pleasure of knowing a lady, residing in the Maine and Loire department, whose mother was one of five girls that had to go with that parent to the place of the *Noyades* execution, which was in-front of the *Salorges.* Near the gangway a youthful officer stopped the group, and asked one of the young ladies if she would marry him. To which she replied, "Can you save my mother and sisters?" He answered "No! but I can save you." Whereupon she declared she would suffer with her relations.

It so happened that one of the five was no more than a child. During the brief excitement caused by the scene I have related, a poor fisherwoman, who was hard by and whose motherly feelings were no doubt impressed by the dreadful event, that was about to take place, drew the little one away, and hid it under her cloak. The mother, soon missing her youngest, turned round in affright to inquire about its fate. But a quiet signal from the fisherwoman with upraised finger, and a trifling opening of her cloak revealed what had occurred. Then hands clasped! eyes turned to Heaven! and an exclamation of "God bless you!"—the doomed parent was sent out in the boats with her four daughters, and they were seen no more.

The young one whose life had been preserved was recognized soon after in the market-place at Nantes by a French nobleman, who was a friend of the family. But he left her in the care of the good fisherwoman till the troubles were over. She belonged to one of the first families in Brittany.

This work, as I have already mentioned continued for beyond four months, till Julien, the Secretary of Robespierre, recalled Carrier, who, as a reward for his zeal, and probably *pour encourager les autres*, was executed after the 9th Thermidor.

About ten miles from Nantes, on the Roche-sur-Yon, and Rochefort railroad, which goes on to Bordeaux, as to the South of France, is the celebrated castle of Clisson, famous, or more correctly *in*famous, for having been one of the most notorious prisons of the Inquisition. Indeed not the least creditable of things, done by the

Revolutionists of 1793, was the partial demolition of this building;—revealing its dykes, and subterranean prisons, its *oubliettes*—holes in the walls for burying people alive—and numerous kinds of tortures. The towers which remain are nearly all covered with ivy. Some of the walls are more than three yards in thickness, and very high. Since its battering down in the Reign of Terror it has been rebuilt and decorated in the Italian style. The place is now owned by the descendants of M. Lenot, who bought it at the end of last century.

But all its decorations of Art, in the shape of statues, fountains, grottoes, seem but a burlesque joined to its new-fangled title of *Tivoli de l'Occident*, when one comes to consider the abominations of its ancient history; although this may produce no more vivid description than what our imagination can supply, of the sufferings endured in torture within these walls.

CHAPTER XIII.

Departments in Brittany—Château Villegontier—Hospitality of Baron d'Arthuys—Candé—A considerable barony—The Feudal period—A mother-in-law in these days—Fête at Candé—The town in its normal state—Grand names of hotels—Dead-and-alive commerce—Squealing of young pigs—Melancholy-looking shops—Comfortable farm-houses—Elegant châteaux—Cattle Show and Agricultural Exhibition—Merry-go-rounds—Monsieur de Falloux—Philanthropic Frenchmen—Les Prix de Vertu—Dr. Letort's speech—Anne Tessier—Her history—"God's ladies and gentlemen"—The prize for filial piety well earned.

AMONGST the eighty-nine departments, of which I have written, as constituting the territorial divisions of France since 1790, there are eight of these—some of which have the whole, whilst others have only portions of the area—that in the middle ages belonged to the dukedom of Brittany. They are the following:—

Department—Ile et Villaine		Capital—Rennes.	
Do.	Côtes du Nord	Do.	Saint Brieux.
Do.	Finisterre	Do.	Quimper.
Do.	Morbihan	Do.	Vannes.

DEPARTMENT	—Loire Inférieure	.	CAPITAL	—Nantes.
Do.	Sarthe		Do.	Le Mans.
Do.	Mayenne . . .		Do.	Laval.
Do.	Maine et Loire	.	Do.	Angers.

The bathing season at Préfailles being concluded for this year, I am now in the neighbourhood of Candé, enjoying the cordial hospitality of the Baron d'Arthuys, at his pretty Château of Villegontier. Candé is inserted in Adolphe Joanne's "Guide to Brittany," as "Chief town of the canton, with, 2011 inhabitants, situated at the confluence of the Erdre and the Mundy, on the confines of Anjou and Brittany. In former times," he adds, "it was a considerable barony." Any traveller can reach it by *Diligence* of three hours' journey to the east of the Varades station on the Paris and Orleans line of railway to and from Nantes; or by similar conveyance of four hours' journey from Angers—capital of the Maine and Loire Department—to which Candé asserts its belonging.

It was not, however, a barony until after the eleventh century. Previous to that epoch, and during the feudal period, Nomenoë, Herispoë, and Salomon, three of the Breton Kings, tried to prove their claim to jurisdiction in this part of the Anjevin territory.

When the counts of Anjou, at the beginning of the twelfth century, pushed forward the limits of their domain to Ingrandes—situated on the Loire, about eighteen miles from Candé, and the next station to Varades—there broke out between the Breton and Anjevin lords—they had titles of Dukes and Counts—a series of bloody wars, which desolated their respective countries for many years. Before the feudal period—neither the Andes tribe (after whom Anjou is named) nor the Gauls, Romans, or Franks, are known to have territorial divisions. For with them sufficed—

> " The good old rule,—the simple plan,
> That they should take, who have the power—
> And they should keep who can."

A Priory, or an Abbey was erected in Candé, and dedicated to St. Nicholas, in the early days of Christianity. Of the period in which it was founded, no legend or chronicle remains. But the place must have been of importance as Monsieur La Bessière tells us "it sustained a siege in A.D. 1106." On that occasion Geoffry Martel II.—Duke of Anjou at the period when Philippe I. was King of France—was mortally wounded with an arrow, poisoned, it is said, by his mother-in-law. This cruelty was done at the instigation of some revolted barons, who were then refugees at Candé. Of the Abbey there is not a single stone remaining. But the Mayor, Dr. Letort, informs me it stood on the "Champ des Foires"—the Fair Green—where at or about two o'clock to-morrow (the 8th of September) a historic cavalcade is to be organized, and a procession through the town commenced. Besides we are to have a grand festival on this, the anniversary of the Blessed Virgin's nativity.

The fête is to comprise a cattle show, agricultural exhibition, the gift of a prize to the person most distinguished for filial piety, a breakfast and speeches in a pavilion on the Prairie de la Porte; then the grand cavalcade at the hour I have mentioned; to be followed by music, fireworks, and illuminations in the evening.

Candé, in its normal state, is about one of the most humdrum places it is possible to conceive. Even the starting, or arrival of the *Diligence*, every day, to and from Angers and Varades, creates no more show of interest in the people than would the passing by of a wheelbarrow. It has fine hotels with very grand names—Hotel of the Golden Lion—Hotel of the Market Hall—Hotel of the Golden Ball—Hotel of the Three Merchants—Hotel of the Posts. I cannot help wondering what legend there may be about that of the Three Merchants, as I glance at its shabby-looking outside walls, or steal a look up the archway into its stable precincts. Perhaps some commercial bagmen of the middle ages, who murdered one another on the spot, at their disappointed hopes about finding anything like merchandize in Candé. Or possibly that the first hotel or auberge here could only accommodate three merchants at a time.

On market and fair days there is no life amongst the buyers and sellers: unless what may be created as evening comes on by the squealing of young pigs—that, not having been disposed of during the day, are being lifted into carts to be conveyed to their own grunting-grounds. Its few melancholy-looking shops have quite the air of being pretentiously bakers, drapers, coffee-shops, or tobacconists—but really subterfuges for the business of an undertaker in every one. Yet I am told, there is a large traffic done at Candé. In the centre of the town is a little segment of open space, in which there are three coffee and billiard rooms, *Diligence* office, dress-makers, drapers, jewellers, with the chemist's shop at the corner. This might have aspired to the nomenclature of a *place* or square in its younger days, were there not, about twenty yards off, and on opposite sides of what appears the main street, another open space, which, though smaller, has an aristocratic air about it from very large pillars facing the Hotel of the Market Halls, and making a piazza underneath. Two chapels in the town—post and telegraph office—a couple of blacksmith's forges, and a machine shop, constituted what appear the larger portion of the village, thus making the legend of 2011 inhabitants a difficulty to the stranger. Around its neighbourhood are many elegant châteaux, as well as comfortable farm-houses.

The Cattle Show, with Agricultural Exhibition, was held on the ground at the left-hand side of Beaulieu Road, as you enter the street by the southern entrance. This field is styled the Prairie de la Porte. Besides the items of exhibition, witnessed by from two to three thousand people, there was a number of small theatres, merry-go-rounds of wooden horses, and stalls having various commodities for sale.

The agricultural show of Candé, was first got up by the Baron d'Arthuys in 1862, when he accepted the post of secretary, with Count Villemorges (since dead) as president. Amongst the gentlemen in the marquee from which the prizes are given to-day is one of great fame in France—whose Château of Bourg d'Iré is only a few miles off. This is Monsieur de Falloux—member of the French Academy—a celebrated orator, and Minister of Public Instruction in the Government of the late Emperor Napoleon III. As soon as M. Le Cadiré, who is President of the Agricultural Exhibition for this year, had delivered the prizes, the mayor, Dr. Letort, then rose, and called the name of Anne Tessier. Whereupon, a middle-aged woman, dressed as Breton servants usually are—with an irreproachably white cap—advanced to the table. After a speech, brief though practical, the mayor handed her a medal and a sum of money, of which I shall explain the *raison d'être*.

More than a century ago, a legacy of 80,000 francs was left to the administration of the French Academy in Paris, by a philanthropic gentleman named Monsieur de Montyon, to found a yearly gift of some hundreds of francs, together with silver medals, to be given as a recompense for domestic virtues—applicable to all parts of France—awarded, in preference, to the poorest, and as much as possible to those who had manifested striking evidences of filial piety. Since that time a Monsieur Saurian and Madame Marie Palmyre Lasne have willed sums—though smaller in degree—to the same administration, and with a like benevolent object. Every year one of the directors of the Academy delivers in Paris an oration on these legacies, with an account of the different acts of virtue that have earned the prizes. By the discourse of Monsieur Cuvillier-Fleury, on the 13th of August last year, I find there were of the Montyon rewards, three of two thousand francs, four of one thousand, and seventeen of five hundred francs each. Of the Saurian there was one of a thousand, whilst of the Marie Lasne, there were two of three hundred each. Every one of those specimens of " Nature's nobility," or as an esteemed friend of mine designates them, " God's ladies and gentlemen," to whom a prize was awarded, affords materials for a biography, the interest of which is most wonderful. The Breton white cap of the woman before me at Candé seemed as if it ought to have a radiant halo of filial piety about it when Dr. Letort gave her history.

Anne Tessier, aged thirty-four, and a spinster, is servant of all work, with a druggist in the town of Candé. For seventeen years she has been daily and nightly doing—what she does still—

namely, toiling from morning till evening at her vocation in her master's house, whilst at night she walks home to her father's—distant a little over a mile from Candé. This is done whether it hails, rains, or snows. There she plies her faculties of a ministering angel. For her father is blind,—step-mother paralyzed,—and sister to that adopted mother in the same helpless condition as the last. All Anne's wages, except what is essential for her plain and unpretentious clothing go to the support of these afflicted relatives; and a large portion of the time at night, which with other people is passed in refreshing sleep, serves only to this devoted creature in looking after the wants and necessities of those under the parental roof. But she never fails to be back at her post as soon as there is light in winter time; and never later than six o'clock in summer. Whilst she is always gay, cheerful, and contented. The prize for "filial piety" was therefore well bestowed on Anne Tessier.

CHAPTER XIV.

Disregard of punctuality—"*Tout de suite*" not always "right away!"—Waiting for historic cavalcade.—Champ des Foires—Site of Old Priory—Musty, mediæval-looking Candé—Three gendarmes—Splendid fellows—Horses well trained—Noble Crusader smoking a meerschaum—Pages and equerries sucking çigaritas—François I. and Jean IV. of Brittany—Mounted trumpeters—Gaulois chief and soldiers—"Char d'Agriculture"—Franks—"Char des Fleurs"—"Char de l'Industrie"—Perfect order and discipline of cavalcade—Doubtless due to presence of the Ubiquitous—Illuminations at night—Music and jollification at Prairie de la Porte—Source of expenses—Menhirs—Bourg d'Iré—Segré—Laval.

S two o'clock approached—the hour mentioned in the programme—I strolled down to the Field of the Fairs; but there was no sign of *even* preparation for the cavalcade.

So I began to ruminate on the fact, how I have always found it a rule in France—that time is rarely kept to the period for which it is indicated. Even at railway stations you seldom start to the minute indicated in the bills. This, however, may be excused from the record of railway accidents being so rare in that country, I have observed the same disregard of punctuality with Spaniards and Italians wherever I have met them. In France—be it at a hotel or elsewhere—the words *tout de suite*, which ought to be synonymous with the Yankee "right away," is no sooner uttered than it is forgotten. Thence, whenever a *garçon* or a *bonne* promises anything asked for that it shall be ready *tout de suite*, I always ask a definition of how many minutes are meant? Sometimes the answer is "Five minutes, Monsieur," or as frequently ten. Yet in no case have I had experience of the five being shorter than fifteen—or of the ten being less than half an hour.

Whilst recording these experiences in my notebook I am seated on an empty cart in the shade of a stone wall opposite the Post Office. Perhaps not far from where the monks of St. Nicholas Abbey used to chant their hymns more than a thousand years ago. The sun is pouring down its hottest rays, In such musty, mediæval-looking towns as Candé, the solar heat always feels to me intensified in its sensation—as if everything was too much dried up to take in any of the hot air that is about. Half-past two—quarter to three—and two quarters after go by! Odd horsemen dropping into the open space—which by the way is not a field, as its title of the "Champ des Foires" would indicate, but is a macadamized piece of ground. These are dressed in their several uniforms of Gauls, Franks, Crusaders—pages, equerries, and other state officials. Now coming on with the crowd—but in the proper place to use the spurs, namely, on horseback—are three gendarmes. Splendid-looking fellows they are too, in what is the correct sphere for cocked-hat, epaulettes, sword, spurs, white gloves, and the other contingencies of their authoritative presence such as I have described it in my first chapter. Mounted on magnificent steeds, and not dawdling on the platform of a railway station. How they manage their horses in clearing a passage with so much skill and dexterity as if the animals had been trained at Astley's!

Some thousands of spectators are gathered by this time—half-past three—prominent amongst them being the white caps of the women. Something of the grandeur looked for in the coming spectacle is damped to me by observing a noble-looking Crusader, decked out with a highly-polished brass crown,—quite as good as gold though—a long scarlet cloak, that swept behind him from under the back of the crown, down over the horse's tail ;—coat of mail, glistening in the sunshine, red cross on breast—steed caparisoned with red velvet bound by ermine ;— sword, saddle, and bridle appurtenances all in exquisite trim, and the truth must be told— smoking a dark-coloured and dirty-looking meerschaum—as vigorously as if he were doing it for a wager! I cannot help wondering if meerschaums were invented in the times of the Mission to the Holy Land? But whether or not, the use of the weed is very general here to-day. Running about to find their places I see a number of pages, and other courtiers, dressed in caps with plumes, velvet tights, and much spangled embroidery, yet sucking paper cigarettes. I confess the sight made me feel queer. Particularly as I afterwards recognized some of these to be the pages of François I., the great King of France who was called the Restorateur des Lettres (A.D. 1515), and who after the battle of Pavia wrote to his mother an epistle, in which was included the memorable sentence—" *Tout est perdu fors l'honneur.* Is there not something of an anachronism in putting these incidents together? the *honneur* and the *cigaritas?*

As half-past three had come and gone, a shout arises; the gendarmes bustle about with renewed fuss; and turning towards the side from whence the cheer came, I see approaching, one after another, three triumphal cars that are to take part in the procession. Only ten minutes are needed to put them in their proper places, when the cavalcade moves on, as nearly as it could do, to the order laid down in the programme.

At the head went half a dozen mounted trumpeters from the 10th regiment of Cuirassiers, now stationed at Angers. Vigorously they blew as they marched along. To them succeeded a Gaulois chief, with twelve to fifteen soldiers—all on horseback. These Gauls were dressed in brass helmets, having small wings at the sides of this head-covering as we see it in Mercury, white frocks, with tight crimson trowsers, and a skin of some animal round the loins—no doubt as representing the period "when wild in woods the noble savage ran." Each held in the left hand a shield on which was emblazoned that chubby round face, usually depicting Sun worship. Then came a large four-wheeled cart, "*Char de l'Agriculture*," drawn by four bullocks, each body of which was covered over with nets and tassels.

The car itself was decked out with agricultural indispensables in the shape of tree branches, sheaves of corn, rakes, scythes, reaping-hooks, wheelbarrows, and so forth. From the centre went up a mast, at the top of which were half a dozen tricolor flags nailed on to a curved stick. The car also held about a dozen boys and girls,—all dressed in the best style of rural *coquetterie*. To these succeeded the Franks—a chief and soldiers. The first named had a long sweeping white cloak and a white metal helmet; but the latter seemed more like acrobatists for a circus than soldiers, as they wore bright blue, skin-tight pantaloons, that had a glaring scarlet stripe round the leg, of the fashion wherein it is seen on a barber's pole. They had white frock coats, white metal helmets, and spears. Next came a most tastefully decorated car, the "Char des Fleurs," drawn by four horses, a driver walking at the head of each, and seeming on its four wheels like a moving garden. Another bevy of children here; all young girls, decked out in the gayest of garlands, and freshest of bouquets. After these succeeded the group of Crusaders, the chief of whom was a very fine-looking fellow, and indeed would have appeared to me the most chevalier-like of the processionists had it not been for the memory of the meerschaum. But he was at present *sans pipe*, and passed on with his red-cross knights. Another large car, drawn likewise by four horses, held musicians, the village band of Candé.

Now appears François I., followed by pages, equerries, nobles, guards,—the *suite* being, like the grand Crusader, *sans cigarettes*. The King was dressed in the traditional flat beaver hat of the monarchs of the middle ages, with velvet coat, short breeches, silk stockings; his horse's trappings resembling those of the Crusader chief, purple velvet fringed with ermine. After the royal group follows the "Char de l'Industrie," drawn by six horses, each horse having a plume of white feathers at his head, and being ridden by a postilion. In this vehicle blacksmiths were forging iron, whilst carpenters plied the saw and plane. The fifth and last corps comprised John IV., Duke of Brittany, followed by a number of nobles, pages, and guards on horseback. He looked every inch a king—a fact in which I hope to be pardoned for having a little vanity, when I remembered this was the Englishman Jean de Montfort, who won the battle of Auray in A.D. 1364,—who erected the College to St. Michael where now stands La Chartreuse in Auray,—and who afterwards came into power as John IV., Duke of Brittany.

The cavalcade went through every street in the town, round about, backwards and forwards, continuing the marching, the blowing of trumpets, and the music of the band till half-past five o'clock, in the most perfect order and discipline. Although this last was not observable in its minutiæ, still no one could doubt its being due to the four gendarmes who came out in their usual stately ubiquitousness wherever the procession wound its way. Were a collection of people too crowded at a corner?—there was a gendarme so politely but effectively dispersing them. Did a block occur in the procession itself?—the same magic influence at once set it right again. A car, carriage, or horse coming unwarily from a street crossing, was removed as nimbly as a scene-shifter would do his slides in a theatre? —for the cocked-hat was always hard by. About 5 p.m. the various sections of the cavalcade separated by divisions, going off at respective tangents.

At night the town was illuminated with lamps, candles, and Chinese lanterns, for gas has not yet penetrated to Candé. The trumpeters, after a few hours' rest, appeared on the grounds of the Agricultural Exhibition at the Prairie de la Porte. The village band likewise came out with energy. In some of the booths dancing was got up, whilst the merry-go-rounds and other spectacles did a roaring trade.

All the expenses of this festival are made up from two sources. That of the Cattle and Agricultural department is effected by each farmer of the canton paying thirty sous (a franc and a half), and the proprietors contributing such larger sums as may be expedient. The cost of the cavalcade is defrayed by a subscription amongst the towns-people, and any surplus beyond what is needed for actual expenditure is handed over to the hospital. This institution in Candé is a very useful one, and is well managed. Much to the credit of the town, it is one of their ancient establishments that has not been done away with. For although in feudal times Candé had "a salt granary, Seignorial jurisdiction, almshouse, hospital, and college of secondary instruction;" none of these exist now-a-days except the hospital.

On one day during my stay at the Château Villegontier I paid a visit to the little bourg of Chalin, six miles off, and quite close to the magnificent Château of the Rochefoucault family. The object of this was to see a Dolmen that is on a farm called La Mauxionnaie, about half a mile outside the village. There it lies imbedded in a ditch, without any of the several rich proprietors around taking the slightest interest to have it examined.

Going out of Candé on the opposite road towards Laval, we pass by the Château of Monsieur de Falloux, at Bourg d'Iré, and of Le Comte Henri d'Armaillé, at La Douve. These are almost opposite to one another near to the hamlet, which doubtless was an appanage of the old Château de la Bijotiere hard by. The mansion of Monsieur de Falloux is built in the style of the Louis XIII. period, and within a neat chapel, which it contains, are several sculptures of the fifteenth century. La Bijotiere,—of which only a few fragments remain, that are covered with ivy,—belonged to the family of Monte Clert in the fifteenth century. Afterwards it passed into the hands of the Montmorencies. To this castle often came Fénélon (of whom we have such remembrances at school with his "Telemachus"), the celebrated Archbishop of Cambray, to visit his cousin the Marquis of Laval. Between Bourg d'Iré and Segré is the college of Combré, not the least important of the educational establishments in this part of France.

Segré, one of the first baronies of Lower Anjou, and only three miles beyond Bourg d'Iré, was a fortified city in the middle-ages, belonging in A.D. 1097 to Jean de l'Espinay, who gave the church to the Abbaye of Nyoiseau, not far distant. In A.D. 1201, it passed into the hands of Berangère de Castille, widow of our English Richard Cœur de Lion. Of its chronicles in those fighting times, I learn from M. de la Bessière, that towards the end of the thirteenth century it was possessed by the Counts de La Guerche. To these succeeded the house of Creon, as holders of its feudal rights. The strong castle of Segré was almost destroyed by an attack of English marauders, headed by John de La Pouille in A.D. 1422. But it was rebuilt in 1591 by some of the Leaguers of the period in question. However, the Count of Rochefort, Governor of Anjou, very soon after had it almost entirely knocked down. So that at present very few traces of its ancient fortifications are remaining.

Situated on the river Verzée, not far distant from where that stream unites with the Oudon and the Argos, is Segré, a very quiet, pretty little town:—in every feature of its aspect, to a stranger suggestive of having seen better days. It has a quay, and its river is navigable for boats communicating with the river Mayenne, before the latter joins the Sarthe, and becomes the Maine as it passes by Angers. There are many umbrageous walks outside the town. Besides these, Segré has a savings-bank, some philanthropic societies, printing-office, newspaper, and a very handsome parish church. This last has been constructed on the ruins of St. Sauveur, which was erected in the eleventh century.

Very shortly,—perhaps in a year or two,—it will have to turn itself out of the sleep of centuries; for a railway line has been surveyed, that is to cut across the country from Laval to Angers.

CHAPTER XV.

Visit to Angers—The second capital of England in the Plantagenet period—Originally peopled by Andes tribe—Their chief Dumnacus—Roman curia—Dispute between Francs and Saxons—Expulsion of Roman paganism—The first Bishop Defensor—Visitandine Nunnery, now a barracks—Cathedral on the site of a temple of Apollo—Tradition of foundation—Solemn light inside—Chief attractive features—Presentation by King René—The Logis Barrault—Tower of St. Aubin—Museums and Library—Awe-inspiring cocked-hats—Sculptor David—Ruins of Touissant Abbey—By moonlight—Effects of age on ruins—Place de Railliement and Theatre—Château in its gloomy aspect—Birthplace of King René—His statue in the Place du Château.

SHARP and pattering shower, such as they frequently have in France during the autumnal equinox, was falling on the glass roof of the railway station at Angers as I turned myself and carpet-bag on to the platform, and out of a train (from Nantes to Paris) which I had joined at Varades.

The old city here must be considered doubly interesting to British tourists from what we are told of it in Adolphe Joanne's Itinerary; namely, that, under the Plantagenets, Angers was the second capital of England. At the death of Richard Cœur de Lion, his brother, John Lackland, usurped the rights of Arthur, seized on Angers, and with his own hand killed his nephew —the said Arthur. He did not remain long in possession of the place, for he was soon turned out by Philip Augustus, who reunited the Anjevin territory to the crown of France (A.D. 1180 to A.D. 1189).

But to me the most interesting incidents in the history of Angers are those that by more than a thousand years preceded the last mentioned. Little or nothing is known of it previous to the invasion of the Romans. Julius Cæsar mentions, without designating their cities, the tribe of the Andes, who peopled the district at that period, and of whom Dumnacus was chief. Whether Angers held a civic position in those days we are not certain. But as soon as the Romans came into possession, they gave it the name of Julio-Magus—constituted it the capital of a *Curia* (or Senate House) and surrounded the settlement with walls. Of these there remains only a trifling relic to-day, inclosed within an iron railing quite close to the Academy. They built a Capitol on the spot where now the bishop's palace stands;—they constructed a curial palace over the site where we find the Château. And on that of the existing Cathedral of St. Maurice once stood, in the Roman period, a temple sacred to Apollo. Besides these, they made walls and constructed roads, of which vestiges—in the grand style, adopted by the Romans in everything they did—are still visible in many places. "The invasion of the barbarians," as the Northmen were styled, " came to put an end to the brilliant civilization of the Romans," says Monsieur L. I. La Bessière. But he seems to have forgotten that the Christian religion came in at the same time. The Francs and Saxons disputed about the Curia of the Andes. The Saxon Odoacer took possession of it in A.D. 464. Childeric I. chief of the Francs, made himself master of it in 475, when he killed Paul, the Roman Governor. Under the domination of the Francs, the principal city of the Andes tribe took the name of Andegavi, from which we have now the modern name of Angers.

Hand in hand with the expellers of Roman paganism came the introducers of the Christian faith. The first bishop of Angers who had the excellent name of Defensor (A.D. 338), was the founder of religious establishments here. On the site of the temple of Apollo he raised a chapel in wood, the actual position of the Cathedral. Soon after he had erected two other churches, one to St. Peter, and the other to St. Maurille. Both of these were in the Place du Railliement, where to-day we find a vegetable market, with a cardboard-looking theatre hard by.

Passing from the station into the street, when the shower has ceased, I leave to my left a very large barracks, the exterior aspect of which by its architectural details, is at once recognized as having been a convent in its early days. It was, in fact, an institution of the Visitandine Nuns, erected in A.D. 1636,—spoliated by the Revolutionists in 1791,—and now secularized for the military. In its primitive condition it had room for only 500 inmates; but the War department has made considerable additions. So that it can accommodate 1000 soldiers.

Five minutes' walk brings us to the Cathedral, —so shut in by high houses, of streets and lanes around,—that it is difficult for a stranger at first sight to recognize its holy character. This refers to coming on it as I did from behind, through the Chaussée St. Pierre. For the magnificent façade at the grand entrance, with the two towers of the twelfth century, at once proclaim its sanctity. The history of its dedication is thus chronicled.[1]

It appears that St. Maurice, formerly chief of a legion of Thebans, was, under Diocletian, called into France by Maximilian to aid in fighting the men of the new faith. The Roman chiefs, whilst staying at Martigny-en-Valais, having ordered a sacrifice to the gods, Maurice and his companions declared themselves Christians, and refused to join in the pagan ceremonies. Twice their troop was decimated, but they still refused. Maximilian then ordered a general massacre. This occurred in A.D. 286, or fifty-two years previous to the Episcopacy of Bishop Defensor. All of them perished in martyrdom at Agannum, since then styled St. Maurice of Valais. The sacrifice at the time made a great noise through the Christian world, small as was the latter at the period indicated.

According to tradition this Cathedral was founded by Charlemagne (A.D. 768), or by his father Pepin the Short (A.D. 752), who was the first of the Carlovingian race that reigned over France. It was rebuilt and consecrated in A.D. 1030 by Hubert de Vendôme,—the forty-first bishop of the diocese, and who died in A.D. 1047.

[1] "Guide to Angers," p. 88.

I have rarely been inside a building where the light through the stained glass window has such a solemn and soothing influence as that in the cathedral of Angers. The chief attractive features within are—1. a most elaborately carved oak pulpit;—2. a stretch of tapestry high up on each side of the nave;—3. a very large chair, on which are allegorical figures;—4. a massive organ supported by four colossal Caryatides—and a font of green marble, supported by two lions in white. This last was presented by King René— René the Good—who was Duke of Anjou in A.D. 1434, and whose memory is held in the highest repute in his native city. For he was born in the Château, and as some say baptized in the very font now before us, at that time placed in the little chapel there, which was erected by his mother, Yolande d'Arragon. It is a chapel no longer— but is to-day converted into a fencing-room for the soldiers garrisoned in the old castle. René was the last of the hereditary sovereigns of Anjou.

Not more than two minutes' walk from the Cathedral, one of the most interesting localities of Angers is in the neighbourhood of the Logis Barrault, in the Rue Courte. Here up a street, which ought to be styled narrow as well as short, and behind the tower of St. Aubin,— built in

A.D. 1495 by Oliver Barrault, the treasurer of Brittany, I pass under a lofty archway into a courtyard, to find myself in the presence of a pair of cocked-hats, with plush knee-breeches, white stockings, coats trimmed with scarlet on the cuffs and collars—corresponding with the two majestic presences before me. I hesitated a little before proceeding in—chiefly to examine if the spurs, white gloves, and sword were there. But the last named military decorations being absent I took heart, and went on. These officials are the guardians, as well as demonstrators of the three museums, and the public library inside. The last mentioned inaugurated in A.D. 1798, at the bishop's palace, and since transferred here, contained beyond forty thousand volumes and manuscripts. There is a museum of painting as well as of sculpture. Under the latter head there is one specially devoted to the works of the celebrated Angers sculptor, J. David—consisting mainly of his own works that he willed as a legacy to his native town. There is also a Museum of Archæology, founded in 1841, which owes its origin as well as excellent organization to the good taste of Monsieur Godard. It has been enriched with many Celtic, and Roman relics turned out at the time—some few years ago—

when they were excavating for the foundations of the railway station.

Out of the David Gallery I step on to a plateau, nicely gravelled over—along the exit part and sides of which run the walls and windows of museums and library. Whilst walking in front to a distance of about twenty yards, I am stopped by a low bastion wall of about two feet in height. From this I look down into a large garden, that is flanked on the right side by the Prefecture, now domiciled in the Benedictine Abbey of St. Aubin ;—this is of the oldest religious houses, next to Le Ronceray at the other side of the river. It was founded by Childebert, whose father Theodebert was King of France in A.D. 534, when the Abbey was consecrated. The tower of this building, which I passed when coming to the Barrault Museums, is of the twelfth century, and about eighty feet high.

Round the corner from the St. Aubin cloisters are the ruins of the Toussaint Abbey—the most graceful-looking architectural *débris* it is possible to conceive. From where I am standing now is an end wall with one of those ogival stone wheel-shaped window-frames, like that of Holyrood Palace—or the same form in Holy Cross Abbey, county of Tipperary. Through the apertures of the wheel window, I can see trees growing up within the sacred precincts, and have rarely felt so much regret as at not having time to go through the broken relics. I am told that on a moonlight night the view of these is charming in the extreme.

During my single day in Angers, I have experienced more than one sight, which impressed on me a conviction, that I have frequently thought over in my five and twenty years journeying through the world. It is, that age treats castles, churches, houses, and other edifices, to a certain extent as it does men. On some the hand of time is laid with softened touch, that is gentle to the end. Whilst others are smitten down with sharp strokes, expressive of a hapless fate. We find ruins, that, in spite of the anachronism, seem as if they never had been anything but ruins. Some wrecks of buildings have about them an air of *parvenu* origin and intention. Whilst there are deserted castles, churches, and palaces, which though dating back several centuries beyond either of the last two classes, still preserve a majesty and dignity of bearing. Of this species I have seen some at Redon—at Nantes—at Quimperle. But I have observed more of them at Angers than any place else.

The same narrow Chaussée St. Pierre takes me back again behind the Cathedral, and down an incline into the Place du Railliement. This is now a market-place for the sale of fruits and vegetables sold out of baskets, which the women squat around upon the ground. On the spot where stands that gimcrack-looking theatre was the early Christian burying-ground. Is it too used-up a quotation to read in fancy on every figure outside that building the reflection: "To what base uses shall we come at last, Horatio"? From its first use as a cemetery, it was changed in King René's time to an institution called "Les grandes Écoles," where the faculties of law and medicine delivered their lectures and held their examinations. The first theatre here was erected in 1820. Amongst the stars who appeared in it were the names of Rachel and Ristori. It was burned down in December, 1865, and rebuilt between 1869 and 1871. In spite of having all its front crowded with statues—allegories of Truth, Calumny, Eloquence, Lyric Poetry, and several others, it is but a shoddy building after all. And so consulting my Guide Book I am off to see something better worth looking at.

Instead of turning up through the Rue d'Alsace to the Boulevard, I hie my way to the

Titanic Château by the water's side. Dark, frowning, and prison-like is that old building, seeming by the massiveness of its immense towers, and the depth of the fosse surrounding, that it was only meant for giants. This grand old fort was erected by Louis IX. King of France, who ascended the throne, some say in A.D. 1226, others in 1230, at the age of fifteen. He was the son of Louis VIII. who was called the Lion, and who had driven John Lackland out of France in A.D. 1203. The immense mass of masonry in this work is wonderful. The foundation is on a rock—the site of the Roman curial. Contemporaneous with the erection of this castle was erected by the young king a third inclosure of walls to protect the town. Of the last-named colossal work, the part on the left side of the Maine stretched for 2500 yards,—was supported by twenty-four round towers, from which armed men could fight,—and had six gates of entrance. Some of these are still standing. On the right side of the river, called the Doutre, the walls extended for 1500 metres, with nineteen towers and two gates. These protecting high works were furnished with small towers, and mâchicoulis (slits to fire through). The walls, being built of dark schist, gave to the town the title of " *Ville Noir*," which it held for many years. The public is not admitted into the Château;—therefore the modern visitor can see nothing of it except the walls, towers, and deep fosse, which surround it.

The entire demolition of this grand old building was ordered by Henry III., king of France, in 1574. What has been destroyed must have been restored again as I could not see any evidence of a' breach. The chronicles tell us, that all the towers were partly broken up, except that on the north side, which was respected because it had a mill on it. The complete destruction of the castle was arrested by the valiant Captain Dunnadieu Puycharic (A.D. 1587), afterwards made Seneschal, whose statue in white marble, and on his knees, is found in the Museum. He not only stopped the work of demolition, but had it restored to the condition in which it is found to-day. From this castle to the opposite side of the river there is reputed to be a subterranean passage, which in old times reached to the suburb of St. Nicholas. It is now said to be shut up. With it was also connected the chain which stretched across the river in the position at present occupied by the Bridge of La Basse Chaine. Higher up in the river was another chain put across, but these must have been placed in their respective sites long after Hastings and the barbarian Northmen had come up the river Maine with their flotilla,—subsequent to ascending the Loire, and sacking Nantes. Hastings occupied Angers for six years, and was only driven out after a long siege by Charles the Bald, helped by Solomon, king of Brittany. The grand operation by which this was achieved, was effected by turning the river Maine from its natural course, and leaving the bed of the river which flowed by the town to be perfectly dry.

"This old fortress," says a recent writer,[2] "with its towers uncrowned, its bastions overturned, its fosses filled up to half their size, still presents an aspect full of majesty and grandeur. The elevation of its black walls, which the rock sustains as well as begins—the aerial supports, which stick close to the flanks of the towers, receive on their narrow platform the sentinel, charged to survey the feet of the fortress, where the enemy could glide in silently;—the memories of so many combats, labours, splendours, and ruins, make by good right this edifice one of the

---

[2] "Angers, Ancien et Moderne, Guide de l'Étranger. Par E. L., Membre de la Société d'Agriculture, Sciences et Arts d'Angers." P. Lachesse, 13, Chaussée Saint Pierre.

most interesting in the city to attract the eyes of the stranger, and to speak to his spirit."

In the centre of the roadway outside the Château, between it and the Place de l'Académie, is a statue of the good King René, executed by the sculptor David, and put up here in 1853. There is a grace and a finish about this, joined to simplicity, that appeared to me very pleasing. It comprises a synopsis of the history of Anjou, in the small statuettes with which the basement is decorated.

The King and the Sculptor here prove exceptions to the axiom that a prophet rarely finds honour in his own country. The latter, born in 1789, and died in 1856, is held in the highest reverence. His statue holds the most prominent place in the Museum to which the town has given his name.

Since 1806, the old walls of the city have been demolished, through the solicitation of permission from the Government, under the mayoralty of Monsieur de la Besnardiere. They are now replaced by handsome boulevards.

CHAPTER XVI.

Disagreeable water of the Maine—Waterworks at Ponts de Cé—Holiday town—The bridges of Angers—First bridge in sixth century—Those made by Foulques Nerva III. and Henry II.—223 soldiers killed by falling of Suspension Bridge in 1850—Doutre side of the river—"*École des Arts et des Métiers*"—Abbey de Ronceray—Hôtel Dieu of Henry II.—Churches of St. James and La Trinité—Comfort and luxury in King Henry's Hospital—Granary and caves cut in the rock—Now used as a brewery—The Mall and its pleasures—Cleanliness of Angers city—Interesting objects of antiquity—Great field for explorers.

THE river Maine, which flows through Angers, and is here as wide as the Thames at London Bridge, joins with the Loire, near the village of La Pointe, some miles lower down, and on the way to Nantes. Yet despite of its volume in front of the city, it is of disagreeable taste, and has little power of dissolving. These bad qualities are said to proceed from much of its course being over a bed of schist hereabouts. The water used at Angers for domestic purposes is, therefore, brought from the Loire by the action at the Ponts de Cé, about three miles distant, of two engines, which send it up through large pipes to a reservoir, wherefrom the city is supplied, at the corner of the Rue Madeleine.

Ponts de Cé is the chief attractive holiday place for the people of Angers. On Sundays and feast days crowds of omnibuses and all kinds of vehicles, crammed with excursionists, are constantly on the road to and fro. I have not visited it, and therefore cannot tell of its attractions; save that it is a town of a single street, nearly three quarters of a league in length;—that it has three or four bridges, necessitated by so many divisions of the Loire, with the canal of Anthion in the neighbourhood. Relics have been found here, dating back to the period of Roman occupation. There are likewise many interesting associations, connected with its Château.

Crossing the Maine, to join both sides of the city, I find three bridges, to each of which historical recollections of very deep interest are attached.

In order to see these as well as the Hôtel Dieu and its accessory buildings, erected by our King Henry II., in A.D. 1153, I must take a coach. For I find rambling about on foot in the autumn heat to be more fatiguing to me than it was twenty-five years ago. These wonderful works of our Plantagenet monarch were done on the hillock of St. Lawrence, and chiefly through the superintendence of Etienne de Mathias, at the period Seneschal of Angers.

The renowned Archæologist, M. Godard, informs us, that so far back as the sixth century, under the temporary ruler, Count Beppolen, when the Francs were almost cut in pieces by Waroch and his Bretons; "the fugitives ran away towards Angers, in order to reach the bridge placed over the torrent of the Maine." Thus leading to the supposition, that, even at the early period indicated, there were inhabitants on the right side of the river, and communication between the two.

Those ruins sticking out of the water are relics of that which was constructed by orders of Henry, when he had caused to be made weirs for the benefit of the hospital. But this latter was not put up till the weirs and bridge were finished.

Yet before Henry's time,—indeed in A.D. 987,—a substantial bridge had been erected here by Foulques Nerra III., at the period Count of Anjou. He was founder of the Abbey of Ronceray. I find by a chart of Angers, dated 1028, which was laid before the Archæological

Congress held at this city in 1841, that certain fisheries and tolls levied on mills were made over by Foulques to the Prior of the Abbey for its use and benefit. So far as can be learned, I believe the smaller bridge, which debouches from the Rue Bourgeoisie, to be on the site of that first built by the Count. Not more than a hundred feet from this is the Pont Grand. Up to the end of last century there was a row of houses on piles at each side of the former, resembling what was on London Bridge in ages not long gone by.

The lowest down the river of these in Angers, —the position of the Basse Chaine in early days, —has very sad memories connected with its location.

Many of my readers may remember, that up to 1850 there was a chain-suspension bridge here, attached to two stone pillars—one at each side of the river, and that on the city bank, abutting from the lowest tower of the Castle. On the 15th of April, in the last mentioned year, a battalion of the 11th regiment of infantry had arrived at the Doutre side, and bivouacked there for the night. Next morning, after a pleasant breakfast and all in high spirits, they set out to march across to their barracks. Going over the bridge with a swinging step—the structure snapped in two, and the whole detachment, except the Colonel leading, fell into the river. He, escaped, as it were, only by the merest chance. For his horse's forelegs were on the solid ground, whilst the hind ones were on the broken chain. The animal's agility in jumping saved him. The men being in marching order, and with fixed bayonets, it can scarcely be wondered at, that 223 perished on the occasion. The funeral procession of all the bodies recovered was one of the most melancholy sights ever witnessed by the population of Angers. The late Emperor, who was at the period Prince President, sent down an *Aide-de-Camp* to represent him at the burial ceremonies. In a few days after Napoleon himself came, and was most solicitous in his attentions to the wounded, who had been rescued. Like all the others, the bridge across here is now of stone.

By one of the upper two the coach takes me to the Doutre side. And then through streets so narrow, there is scarcely room for a mouse to creep between the carriage wheels and the footway. This latter is barely a slice of *trottoir*. Nearly all the houses by which we pass here are "antiquest of the antique." On several I see square blocks of sand-stone in the walls, with what seems, in the rapid transit, only hieroglyphics. But I know these to be family escutcheons of the old nobility, in the days of feudalism, and of whom little or nothing is left but these and a few such-like "insubstantial pageants."

In a large open space, facing the river, I pass a grim and prim-looking mass of white-washed building, on which are painted in large letters—"*École des Arts et des Métiers.*" This was originally founded by Napoleon I. in 1807, at Beaupreau, about sixty miles to the southeast (in the same department of Maine et Loire). In 1815 it was transferred to Angers, and located where it stands to-day. It contains now beyond 300 pupils, and has turned out some very eminent men.

But it has swallowed up, or coalesced with, in the fashion of an octopus, the old Abbey of de Ronceray, of which I have already spoken as founded by Foulques Nerra, Count of Anjou at the end of the tenth century. The name is said to have been derived from a bronze gilt statue of the Virgin found amongst some roots (*au milieu des ronces*) in a crypt here. Adolphe Joanne[1] tells us these were discovered in A.D. 1527, whereas the Angers Guide[2] dates the finding of the statue to the period of Foulque's reign. From which

[1] Op. p. 122. [2] P. 24.

I am obliged to draw a pair of inferences. *First*, that if Monsieur Joanne be correct, the monastery must have had some other name during the interval between its foundation in A.D. 938 and discovery of the statue in 1527. Yet he gives no explanation of other title. *Second*, if E. L. be right, we may suppose a more ancient church to have stood here (before the Ronceray period), of which the statue in question was one of the relics.

Not having much time at my disposal, I was obliged to pass on without going inside. For my mission was to see the Plantagenet Collection, as I may entitle them;—the Hôtel Dieu, with its granaries and vaults;—the chapel of St. John which was attached to the hospital;—the churches of St. James and *La Trinité* close by. I had but a cursory glance at these solemn ruins.

The Hôtel Dieu, erected in A.D. 1153, shortly after Henry ascended the throne of England, is said by some malicious people to have been built by the monarch as an expiation for the murder of St. Thomas à Becket. But as it was finished nearly eighteen years before that event took place, such a deduction is simply preposterous.

It was not only a hospital for the aged, and

infirm of both sexes, and of all conditions, but principally for the poor. And yet, whilst chiefly designed for the destitute of this world, it was built, fitted up, and furnished in the comfort and spaciousness of a palace. The great room, in which there are twenty-four arches, supported by pillars, and divided into three large segments, is now occupied by beer vats,—for the place is desecrated by a brewery! Wandering through the chambers without a guide, it is difficult to recognize the peculiarities of its former *ménage*. But one can see what wonderful labour and expense must have been laid out in their erection. A workman at the brewery—a Barclay and Perkin's model of humanity—came with me up a narrow ladder to the granary, where we find more beer vats. Thence descending, and having obtained a light, we went into the caves. These, although cut in the solid rock, have their floors on a level with the outside road. I groped through six or seven of them, and there may be more. Beer vats here,—likewise water trickling down everywhere,—and a large spring well in the centre of one vault-chamber.

The new church of La Trinité, in connexion with, and alongside the old one, was barely looked at. Returning to the hotel in time for dinner, I afterwards spent a delightful evening, listening to a military band that played on the Mall, quite close to the Hôtel d'Angers where I was staying, and opposite to the Mayoralty. This Mall is a favourite promenade in summer evenings, and a most charming spot. It is full of flower-beds and pretty walks,—having also a profusely-showering fountain, that, in these warm evenings, spreads a delicious coolness around.

 I have left few places with greater regret at not being able to see more of it than Angers. It is a most agreeable old city, as well as one of the cleanest and freshest that I have visited in France. Of interesting subjects for the tourist, who is fond of antiquities, it is overflowing.

CHAPTER XVII.

Sablé and its marble quarries—Château of Duchesse de Chartreuse—The river Sarthe—To the Abbey of Solesmes—Famous for works of Art—Gracious courtesy—Accommodation for strangers—Thorn from our Saviour's Crown a relic here—Anachronisms and anomalies—Statue of St. Peter—Beautifully carved stalls—The Sepulture of Christ—Sepulture of Blessed Virgin—Crowning of the Virgin in Heaven—Christ amongst the Doctors—Figures of sublime Majesty—Divine aspect of the Saviour—King René lowering the winding-sheet—Prior Jean Bougler doing like office with that of the Virgin—Soldiers' faces battered and smashed—Figures of Luther and Calvin representing the Doctors in the Temple—Foundation of Abbey in eleventh century—Strange reading during dinner—Château Juigné.

IDWAY between Angers and Le Mans—or twelve leagues distant from either—again I get out of the train at Sablé—a place famous for its marble quarries. The town is about a quarter of a mile from the station, and like the greater number of those in Brittany is very old. It is built on the side of a declivity, sloping down to the river Sarthe, which falls into the Maine,—a short distance before the latter

reaches Angers, and receives into its waters the river Erne, not far above Sablé. There is not much to be seen in passing through Sablé, and it is difficult to imagine where can be stowed away the 5000 inhabitants which it is reputed to contain. As we cross the bridge, and look up to the right—although on the left bank of the stream—I see a very spacious, and solemn-looking Château, the property and residence of the Dowager Duchesse de Chartreuse. This has all the appearance of a comparatively new building.

Remnants of the old Château are still about in the shape of a few large towers behind, and one in front, surmounted by a belfry. As I get along and pass out of the town, I pass on the left a church and a considerable-sized Hôtel Dieu—both as antiquated and used-up looking as it is possible to imagine. Perhaps I should have already explained that I am mounted alongside the driver on an omnibus, which I have all to myself. For I hired it at the station to take me out to the Abbey of Solesmes—distance two miles—fare one franc.

The mining for marble,—with machineries for polishing this, as well as a few high chimneys convenient to coal-shafts,—points out the industry of the place as we go along. To the little bourg of Solesmes, in the centre whereof is the large monastery, so celebrated through France for some superb works of art, and to see which was the chief object of my visit.

Sending in my card from the *conciergerie*, I was invited to enter, and after a few minutes' waiting in the guest's room, the Hôtelier of the Abbey, the Rev. P. Fontaneau came in.

With the most gracious courtesy I was asked to remain for dinner, as well as pressed to stay for the night. The round tower detached from the main building is fitted up with from sixteen to twenty beds for strangers, who visit this place. Sometimes they are entertained here—of course gratuitously—for a week. But this only takes place when they come on retreat, or religious devotion—or are known to the community. No females are admitted inside the convent walls.

The Reverend Hôtelier sent at once for a countryman of mine, temporarily resident there,—Mr. Patrick O'Leary, of the Irish College at Paris,—who chaperoned me through the grounds, the chapel, and the monastery.

Before commencing my tour, I may explain that this Abbey was founded somewhere about the beginning of the eleventh century.[1] It was

[1] Adolphe Joanne, Op. p. 111.

consecrated in A.D. 1010, as a Priory dependent on the Benedictine Abbey of La Couture at Le Mans. On the return from the Holy Land of the first crusade in the twelfth century, there was brought here as a gift one of the thorns, taken from the crown, that was put on our Saviour's head by the Jews before His crucifixion. Towards the end of the fifteenth century, a silver-gilt case was procured for it by the Prior Cheminart, and it is still preserved in the church as a highly-prized relic. When the Revolutionists came here in A.D. 1791, the Abbey was sold, and the sacred thorn stolen, but it was again restored in 1801. It is sometimes exposed for devotional purposes; but I do not know on what occasions.

Much as this place is spoken of for its famous works of Art, in my whole progress through it, I could not avoid being impressed with what seemed to me their anachronisms and anomalies. Here in the Square Arcade—on one side of which is the dinner room—I find Indian corn, and scarlet oleander flowers, springing up amongst cabbages and potatoes. On the side buttresses are several broken statues—one of a saint on horseback, and the rider having but a single leg—venerable-looking bearded figure with nose smashed—and a general aspect of dislocation amongst them all.

Entering the church, in front of the door is a statue of St. Peter, wearing the tiara, and the bunch of keys at his side. On the basement of this is an inscription of something Greek—though done in Roman alphabet. The upper end of the nave, where the great altar stands, is quite new —as if the plaster were scarcely dry upon it. Yet on either side, between the altar and transept, are beautifully-carved oak stalls, of the sixteenth century. On these the genealogy of our Saviour's parents is demonstrated.

In the transept, and at both sides, we see the works of Art, for which Solesmes has attained a celebrity. Of these the chief are the Sepulture of Christ, and the Sepulture of the Blessed Virgin—the former being on the right side, and the latter on the left. On the side where the Saviour's monument exists, there is no other. But over that of the Virgin, there is one group representing her in the moments of dying, and our Saviour administering to her the Sacraments —with St. John and St. Peter supporting. Six of the Apostles are also present, together with St. Hierothée. The crowning of the Blessed Virgin in Heaven is another group—whilst a fourth represents the Holy Mother and St. Joseph finding our Saviour disputing with the Doctors in the Temple.

Several of the figures in these scenes are expressive of the most sublime majesty of outline, and finish of Art. In the first-mentioned we view the wonderfully impressive and Divine appearance of our Saviour, recumbent on the winding-sheet as He is about to be lowered into the tomb. The woe-stricken attitude and expression of the Virgin mother, supported by St. John, are very fine. At her left we see two women, dressed in the costume of the fifteenth century, one of whom holds in her hands a vase of incense. These are known to be likenesses of persons who were benefactors to the Abbey. The figure of Mary Magdalen, seated at the side of the sepulchre, is considered—and with justice —to be the pearl of the monument. But amongst the personages holding on the shroud, and lowering the Saviour into the grave, we notice the figure of Joseph of Arimathea, dressed in a costume of the period of Louis XI., and a collar of some order of chivalry round his neck. The two soldiers, guarding the tomb, have had their lances taken away—noses battered so that not a vestige of nasal appendage remains—arms broken off—

helmets smashed—and presenting a general mutilation. This was done from time to time, by the peasantry, who came on pilgrimages to the tomb, and who would not recognize that soldiers had any right to be on their desecrating watch.

In the group at the burial of the Blessed Virgin there are fifteen figures. Of those four are posed like these at the Saviour's—each holding a corner of the winding-sheet to lower the body recumbent on it into the tomb. The face of the dead Virgin is as the mother of God may be supposed to have appeared—mild, placid, angelic, divine, and resigned. St. Peter, with his hands clasped in an agony of grief, is a very striking figure. St. John holds one corner of the shroud, and near him, to the right of St. Peter is St. James the Less, leaning downwards as if in an attitude of grief, towards the Virgin. Another corner of the winding-sheet is held by a priest in the garb of a Benedictine monk. This is the portrait statue of Jean Bougler, who was Prior here about A.D. 1550 when the work of this Sepulture was executed. That of our Saviour had been accomplished under the Priorship of Bougler's predecessor nearly fifty years previously. One of the figures seated near the tomb of the Virgin

O

is fearfully mutilated by the country people. They supposed it to represent the Devil searching in a book for the sins of the blessed Virgin and disconcerted at not finding any. The group, representing the crowning of the Virgin in Heaven, is too high to permit me to get a good view of it. Opposite to it we see ten personages, representing the scene of our Saviour found in the Temple disputing with the Doctors. There can be no doubt that in these last named are put portrait figures of Luther, Calvin, and the principal leaders of the Reformation; for the likenesses are said to be life-like.

I hope I shall not be considered a vulgarian in taste, or a know-nothing in the Fine Arts, for confessing that these works did not impress me very favourably. I look upon Art to be most sublime when it is most truthful. Therefore putting King René—though he was René the Good—in the position of holding the mortuary sheet at the burial of our Saviour, or placing Prior Jean Bougler, to perform the same office at the burial of the Blessed Virgin, seemed to discord with my ideas of the truth of Art. So that I left them much disappointed.

It was in A.D. 1833 that this Abbey came into the possession of its present occupants, the

Benedictine Monks. There is a statue of St. Benoit at the end of the garden, and where the recreation promenade is made, under shelter from the rays of the sun by a row of beech-trees. Through a brief of Pope Gregory XVI. in 1837 this was created an Abbey of Benedictines. At the present time its community consists of forty priests, fifteen novices, some of whom are priests, and fifteen brothers, a total of seventy, under the charge of the Abbé Dom Couturier, who was absent on the day of my visit. In the chapel I was curious enough to go down into a crypt, where repose the remains of the last Abbé, Dom Gueranger, who was a native of Sablé—held in high friendship by Pope Pius IX.—and who died on 31st January last, 1875.

On the opposite side of the road, and a few hundred yards distant, is a convent of Benedictine Nuns, to which is attached a very large church.

The bell now rings for dinner, and I accompany Mr. O'Leary to the Refectory, where I am presented by the Rev. Hôtelier to the Rev. P. Piolin, acting Prior in the absence of Dom Couturier. After the introduction, the Prior, *locum tenens*, poured water on the hands of each of the strangers — of whom there were four beside myself—whilst an attendant held a basin and towel for us. The dinner was an excellent one. During its progress one of the priests was up in a pulpit reading a lesson from a book. This after some time grated upon my ears; as the words " Oligarchy," " Aristocracy," Democracy," and " Bourgeoisie," were repeated over and over again, and had the changes rung upon them to a most distressing extent. After dinner on inquiring what the reading was, I learned it was an extract from a famous work, of which a chapter is read every day at meal times : " Les Lois de la Société Chrétienne, par Charles Perin ;" one of the Professors at Louvaine.

The Abbey is quite close to the left bank of the Sarthe, and overhanging the river, On the opposite side are some marble quarries, and polishing houses for the stone that is taken from them. Looking up the stream we can see the woods and ruins of the old Château Juigné. In this neighbourhood was a Roman settlement. For there still remain ruins of a church and vestiges of a camp, both Roman. The thick woods hide the view from the Abbey, of the new Château, which is rich in family portraits. The last eventful occurrence connected with this place was the visit of President Le Maréchal Mac-

Mahon, to it in August 1874, when he was received in Royal State by the authorities of Sablé, as well as by the Marquis de Juigné at the mansion of the latter.

CHAPTER XVIII.

To Notre Dame du Chêne – Miraculous statue of A.D. 1494 – Charming prospect – Valley of Sarthe – Shops at the Church door – Scaffolding around the building – *Ex voto* offerings and bannerets – Ancient traditions – Of wild pigeons as of starry lights – Statue placed in an oak-tree – Miracle subsequently occurring – Crick in the neck – Other prodigies – Oak held in veneration after it fell down – Preservative against thunder and lightning – Large pilgrimages in 1515 – Results of the Calvin heresy – The Huguenots laying the country waste – Sablé pillaged – Farms despoliated – Monasteries destroyed – Pilgrimages suspended – New miracles – Reign of Terror here – Sale of church of Notre Dame – Purchaser broke his leg – Statue concealed by Mayor of Vion – Restoration in 1866 – New chapel and new wonders – Latest of those in October 1874.

HAVING engaged a one-horse phaeton to come out for me from Sablé at two o'clock, I directed the driver to take me over to the Church of Notre Dame du Chêne, a distance of six kilometres, or about four miles from Solesmes. All I had previously known about this spot was that it had been at one time a place of large pilgrimages, and wonderful miracles in connexion with a statue of the blessed Virgin, dating back to A.D. 1494.

There is a charming prospect over the valley of the Sarthe as we drive down a sloping road in view of the chapel of Vion to our destination. I find Notre Dame du Chêne situated in a wild camp district, and not yet finished; as the tower is covered over with scaffolding. There is no house in the neighbourhood save the spacious dwelling of the priests. Save also—I should say—half a dozen wooden structures, evidently for shop-py purposes. In those I see exposed for sale small statues, rosaries, medals, and such things as are generally used in their devotions by the peasantry. Strangers coming to these shrines are always importunately solicited to buy something before entering the chapel;—not so much for a sort of toll-rate, as that every one is accredited to travel hither with the same intention, i. e. of devotion. Several large blocks of cut stone are about, though no workmen are visible either below or on the scaffolding. Only one woman was in the chapel when I entered, and a priest passed through on his way out from the Sanctuary, during the quarter of an hour that I sat there making my observations.

The building is a very ordinary one, with a scant and unfinished appearance about the in- side as well as the outside. Not more than half a dozen *ex voto* bannerets are on the walls. But a considerable quantity of offerings, in the shape of silver crucifixes, medals, and small pictures, was nailed up on each side of the nave at its upper end. These all seemed very trifling compared to what I had seen at St. Anne d'Auray. On the altar, amidst a quantity of new-looking candlesticks and ecclesiastical furnishings, I recognize the statue—brown and discoloured with age, and its vicissitudes—about which we are told an extraordinary story by the Père Dom Paulo Piolin,[1]—the acting Abbé of the Solesmes Priory,—and by whom I have had the honour of having water poured over my hands before dinner a few hours ago.

Nearly as far as tradition or history records of the spot where the Chapel of Notre Dame du Chêne now stands, it has been always considered a place worthy of veneration. For here the shepherds, looking after their sheep, and the labourers, cultivating the soil, used frequently see flocks of wild pigeons careering about the locale. Nobody knew the whereabouts of their

---

[1] "La Miraculeuse Chapelle de Notre Dame du Chêne." Par le R. P. Dom Paul Piolin, Bénédictin de la Congrégation de France. (Sixième Edition.) Le Mans. Imprimerie Lechigeux-Gallienne, 1875.

nests or abiding-places; and they were so timid, they would fly away if any one attempted to approach them. Often too during the night time did the people observe flames in the form of stars rising up from the earth, and remaining for some time suspended in the air, when they vanished like the light of a candle on blowing it out. To such a simple people as the Breton peasantry of this part, these signs were not only awe-inspiring, but unintelligible. At length, in the year 1494, a holy priest named James Buret placed in an oak, which was growing in the vicinity, a small statue of the Blessed Virgin carrying the Divine infant in her arms. We are not told,—but we may suppose from the simple act of the holy man,—that there was no house of God—no edifice of church or chapel in the neighbourhood. This sacred effigy was not long in its place, before the cottagers for miles around congregated to pray before the statue in the tree. Soon they became imbued with the spirit of pouring out their prayers and supplications to Notre Dame du Chêne, whilst the trunk of the oak was adorned with flowers, and branches of trees brought there in reverence by the devotees. One day a poor woman had deposited a bouquet at the feet of the statue. A young man, who was shortly after passing by, took it away with irreverent gestures. But at the moment that he removed it he felt burdened with his larceny, and was almost instantaneously seized by a violent crick in the neck. Though suffering fearful torture he nevertheless reached the house of his parents. His father and mother, on hearing of the circumstances, at once insisted on his returning with the flowers, and accompanied him to the tree. On arrival, and restoring them to the spot whence they were taken, he was at once relieved of his pains.

Trifling as this incident was, it soon spread round the district, and was looked on as a miracle. Shortly after a modest oratory was constructed quite close to the oak, and the service of the mass was begun to be performed. Prodigies were now becoming frequent in their occurrence. The faithful poured in their offerings; but the holy priest who had put up the statue did not live long enough to see much of its wonderful effects. His name, however, was held in veneration for many centuries all through the district of Sablé; and the Benedictine monk, Jean Baptiste Muret, tells us that, after a chapel was built, and the statue was placed beneath its roof, the oak was held in veneration. Even subsequent to its coming down, in the seventeenth century, many families preserved fragments of the old tree, to which they attributed the faculty of protecting its possessors from the effects of thunder and lightning.

During the whole of the sixteenth century, more especially in the year 1515, large numbers of persons came here soliciting to be cured. The larger portion of these was from the neighbouring diocese of Le Mans and Angers. Of the successes of their pilgrimages scores of instances are recorded by Father Piolin. Amongst others Marguerite of Lorraine, Duchess of Alençon, and great grand-mother of Henry IV., visited the shrine of Notre Dame du Chene. She afterwards died in a convent, to which she was attached as a religious.

All around Sablé, in the parishes of Vion, La Flèche, and Louailles, the country was desolated by the civil wars, supervening on the Calvin heresy in the latter half of the fifteenth century. Even the farm of La Jarriaye, on which the holy oak was growing, suffered in the general spoliation. Stately châteaux, and comfortable farms gave place to shattered ruins, and waste lands—producing nothing but weeds and briars. In A.D. 1562, the small village of Parcé, beyond the Château Juigné, and near to which are some Druidical grottoes, was sacked by the Huguenots, who were afraid to attack Sablé, because it was well fortified by the Guises. But in 1567, they returned, headed by Rohan Pontivay, took Sablé, pillaged and spread ruin everywhere in the town as the environs. "Had it not been for the courage of the inhabitants of Solesmes," says Rev. P. Piolin, "they would have burned the monastery, and destroyed the *chefs-d'œuvre* of its sculptors, which are the glory of the country." In fact, from 1562 to 1598, the departments of Sarthe and of Maine et Loire, were despoliated to the utmost by Calvinists and Huguenots; several chapels and monasteries were destroyed; and the pilgrimage to Notre Dame du Chêne was temporarily suspended.

In the beginning of the seventeenth century, a revival of religious sentiment grew up in France; and this was palpably evident in the dioceses of Le Mans and Angers. A poor woman discovered under a mass of rubbish near the site of the old chapel, which had fallen into ruin during the raids last mentioned, the statue of the Virgin. The ancient Notre Dame du Chêne revealed itself, through a brilliant light which surrounded it. This finding, though it created some sensation, led to nothing practical in regard to rebuilding of the church, till a new miracle occurred in 1621. The deformed child of a rich man was committed to the charge of a woman—very pious, although in the lowest ranks of life—to be taken care of. One day, the nurse felt urged, as she considered it, by some holy inspiration, to enter the ruins wherein the statue was again replaced. When she fell on her knees, and with hands clasped, said in her simplicity, and amongst her solicitations that she would not cease praying till the child was cured. For six weeks she continued, making every day the same prayer. As she was one morning in the chapel, supplicating with all her energy, she could scarcely believe her eyes, the whole figure as well as the face of the child underwent a change, and all its distortions were dissipated. Other miracles succeeded this, and so rapidly, that within the ensuing six months, there were ten of them—all equally wonderful. These being verified, brought fresh crowds to the place; and soon a new chapel sprung up on the ruins of the old. The devotions here had much to do with the religious spirit that called the Benedictines of both sexes to their respective cloisters at Solesmes.

Once again in the Reign of Terror period, misfortune came to Notre Dame du Chêne, as it did to every religious community, or institution in France. Despite of the humble but fervent appeals of the clergy and people to the authorities, the chapel was sold at the end of 1793 to a slater in Sablé, named Lefevre. With the sale was the indispensable condition, that it should be entirely destroyed. The sacred vessels, and silver ornaments of the chapel were taken possession of by the district authorities of Sablé. In the sixth year of the Republic (1798), the furniture was disposed of for a little over seventy francs, or a trifle under three pounds. But in the meantime, Monsieur Lebailleul, Mayor of Vion, managed to get the statue out of the church during some period, when the mob was not watching, and kept it concealed in his house in the Faubourg St. Nicholas. Soon, however, another miracle was accomplished. For on Monsieur Lefevre going with a lot of workmen to demolish the chapel,—he was so ready to keep up to the terms of his contract as to its destruction,—he got on the roof to have the satisfaction of giving it the first blows with his own hand. He had only struck twice, when he fell to the ground and broke his leg. No one cared to venture after this, and so the chapel was not pulled down after all. To the time of his death at Sablé in 1840, Monsieur Lefevre was under the impression, that the fall and breaking of his leg were effected by some supernatural agency. Shortly after the occurrence, he re-sold the edifice to Monsieur Jean Dolbeau, who, eight years after, conceded to the wishes of the people to have it restored to its former and proper pious uses. Then the statue was removed from the pious care of Monsieur Lebailleul to its old position in the chapel, at the time semi-ruined from neglect.

Through the influence and money of the Dowager Countess of St. Sauveur, the holy house passed again in 1816 into the hands of the clergy. During 1819 and 1820, the pilgrimage revival once more sprung up with great energy. On one occasion, ten thousand persons came to this shrine. Since 1857, the brothers of St. Vincent de Paul from Le Mans, Laval, and Château-gontier make annual pilgrimages in the month of May—the month which is specially devoted to services for the Blessed Virgin. Whilst people of all classes, not only the poor peasantry, but bishops, counts, marquises, and the highest of the land, with their families, come hither in crowds. The good Benedictines of Solesmes still have records of miracles performed at Notre-Dame du Chêne;—even some of them so recent as October, 1874.

PARDON DANCE AT LARMOOR, NEAR L'ORIENT.

CHAPTER XIX.

Pardóns and pilgrimages in Brittany—Universality of the ceremonies—Half fair, half festival—Hereditary sentiment in religious devotions—Statues and fountains—Guingamp—Wrestling matches, and Armorican bagpipes—Martyrdom of St. Lawrence—Muscular Christianity—Old Breton costume—The *Bragou-bras*—*Pardón des Oiseaux*—*Danse Macabre*—Mixture of Druidical with Christian ruins—*St. Jean du Doigt*—Legend of Notre Dame de Folgoët—The idiot Salaun—The *Ave Maria* lily—Highest Druidical Menhir—Strange superstition connected with it—Pagan cemetery—Bread turned into stones—Setting dogs at the Virgin—Punishment for this offence—Church of St. Herbot—Showers of coins and ox's tails thrown in as offerings—*Les Vies des Saints de Bretagne*—Canonized in the hearts of the people.

N no part of France is the principle of religious pilgrimages so assiduously and extensively practised as in Brittany. This is more especially so in *Basse* Bretagne, which includes the departments of Finisterre and Morbihan. Nearly every village here has a fountain, a church, or a miraculous statue at which an annual gathering is held. To this the title *Pardón* is given. It is half fair, half religious

festival ; and is frequently the scene of merry-makings. Such as dancing to the music of the bagpipes, and wrestling matches between the young men of different parishes. Truly has it been said of the Bretons by a recent writer :[1]—
" The people seem to be influenced by hereditary sentiment on the subject of Divine Providence and the temples of the Most High. They are not more enlightened in respect of education than their class in provinces far distant ; but the bent of their mind is meditative, and favourable to pious culture."

The most remarkable feature of this hereditary sentiment, is exemplified in the devotion to traditions of holy statues, miracle-working fountains, and legends of supernatural appearances. Of these I shall adduce a few instances, which I believe to be new to many English readers, who have never visited this part of the Continent.

At Guingamp (which is on the line of railway from Rennes to Brest, and about twenty-two miles to the west of St. Brieuc), we find the *Pardón* or pilgrimage of the *Bon Secours*, which

[1] "A Ramble into Brittany," by the Rev. George Musgrave, M.A. London: Hurst and Blackett, 1870. Vol. ii. p. 203.

M. Joanne tells us [2] "is one of the most celebrated and best frequented of any through Brittany. It is held annually on the Saturday before the first Sunday of July." This it may be scarcely to need add is a town, once famous for its cotton manufactures, and whence the title of our Gingham is derived. The chief characteristics of the function here are the immense crowds of people—clattering and getting entangled amongst the thousands of fair stalls that fill the streets—drinking the consecrated water of the fountain—and making their homages to the statue of the Virgin. The last-named enrobed in silk, and surrounded by archangels on a platform covered by ermine, is placed at the church door.

As night comes on, begins the dancing to the music of the Armorican bagpipes; and at 9 p.m. the statue of the Virgin is conducted in solemn procession to the principal square of the town, where three immense bonfires are lighted, and dancing is again commenced. At midnight a solemn mass is celebrated; the *Pardón* for the year is terminated; and the pilgrims return to their homes.

As a proof of the importance of the celebra-

[2] "Guide Diamant de Bretagne." Hachette and Co., Paris, 1874, p. 61.

tion here, it appears [3] that "On the 8th of September, 1857, the great feast of the Virgin's nativity, the Madonna of Guingamp received the particular homage of a crown of gold, offered by the Chapter of St. Peter's at Rome, in the name of the sovereign Pontiff, to such images of the Virgin as conjoined the triple conditions of antiquity, popularity, and miracles."

Not far from Guingamp, and nearer to the village of *Plonégat-Moisan* is held another annual *Pardón* at the chapel of St. Lawrence of Pouldour. Here the devotees crawl into a heated oven, to recall the martyrdom of St. Lawrence, They kiss the scorched stone, and after rubbing their hands and bodies at the feet of the saint's statue, they wash themselves in the sacred fountain which is hard by. From time immemorial, wrestling matches form portion of the programme at the function of Poldoun—so that muscular Christianity is not the invention of the Kingsley school of clericals after all.

At the distance of about fifteen or twenty minutes' walk from the station at Plougastel—after passing Morlaix on the way to Brest—is the chapel of St. Languy, to which a pilgrimage is

[3] Adolphe Joanne. Op. cit., p. 61.

BRETON PEASANTS—WOMAN, WITH QUENOUILLE IN HAND, AND MAN WEARING THE BRAGOU-BRAS.

made. Close to this is a fountain, whereto the country people come in order to wash therein the inner garments of children suffering from debility.

As the traveller approaches Brest, he can see on the left-hand side of the river of Landerneau and above the Passage, the chapel of St. John of Plougastel. This, on the feast day, the 24th day of June, attracts a large number of pilgrims. Steam-boats on that occasion ply every hour between Brest and St. John's, up and down the river. Here we can see some of the visitors, dressed in the old Breton costume of the *Bragou-bras*, the short red breeches, reaching to the knees, and bound at the edges with thick cords, that hang in knots over the legs. This is part of the toilet of Louis XIII. period. One portion of the festivity on this celebration is dancing of the peasantry to the music of the bagpipes, and continuing this saltatory action in a "fast and furious" manner, without ever exchanging a word. As soon as the first mass is finished, a fair for the sale of birds is carried on. These are brought in by young boys, who have gone the rounds of the country on the previous day, and whose success in pillaging birds' nests is displayed by the numbers they have to sell in rough cages made of osier twigs. The traffic, instituted by these ornithological brigands, gives to the festival the name of the "*Pardón des Oiseaux.*"

There is a fountain of St. Nonne, on the road between Châteaulin and Brest, to which some miraculous legend of the fifth century is attached. A few hundred yards distant is another fountain of St. Divy, son of St. Nonne. To both of these pilgrimages are made

At the chapel of Kermaria-an-Isquit, between St. Brieuc and Paimpol, is another famous pilgrimage. Besides the statue of the Virgin, and those of the Twelve Apostles, there was discovered in 1856, on the walls of the vault in which are buried the founders of the chapel, a painting representing forty figures engaged in a dance (M. Joanne entitles it *une danse macabre*[4]). Beneath each group of these is an inscription in verse, describing a dialogue between the dead and the living.

Mixed up, almost everywhere, with these fountains, chapels, and pilgrim shrines, we find scattered over Brittany, innumerable Druidical remains of Dolmens, Menhirs, and Cromlechs.

[4] Adolphe Joanne. Op. cit., p. 256.

From Paimpol to Morlaix, and about five miles outside the little village of Lanmeur, is the chapel of St. Jean du Doigt, so called because the first joint from index finger and right hand of St. John the Baptist is kept here in a small crystal case mounted in gold. In this place the ceremony of the *Pardôn* is celebrated on the Eve of the saint's day, the 23rd of June. A lengthened account of it is given by M. Pol de Courcy in Joanne's Itinerary.[5]

Near the town of Lesneven is the small bourg of Folgoët—of which the Church of Notre Dame has attached to its foundation[6] a pretty story, which runs as follows :—" Towards the middle of the fourteenth century, and during the existence of one of the most bloody civil wars that desolated Brittany, there lived in a forest, in the neighbourhood of Lesneven, a poor idiot, named Salaun, better known under the title of the Fool of the Woods (Folgoët)." There, like a solitary sparrow (wrote one of his panegyrists of 1684, in language worthy of St. Francis de Sales), he chanted in his own fashion the praises of the adorable Virgin, to whom after God he had consecrated his heart. And at night, like the

[5] Op. cit., p. 267.   [6] Op. cit., p. 281.

gracious nightingale, perched on the thorn of harsh discipline (*sur l'épine de l'austérité*) he sung the Ave Maria.

He was miserably clad; always barefooted; with the earth for his bed, and a stone for his pillow. His only covering during the hours of night rest being a crooked-tree, that grew near a fountain, surrounded by a green grass border. He went every day to beg his poor bread, to the village of Lesneven or its environs—importuning nobody at the doors, except with two or three little words. These were *Ave Maria*, and in the Breton dialect—*Salaun a Zebré bara*—(i.e. Salaun will eat some bread). He took all they gave him —returning calmly to his rude hermitage near the fountain. In this he steeped his crusts, without any other seasoning than the holy name of Mary.

Such manner of life he led for thirty-nine or forty years—without ever having offended anybody. At last he fell ill, but could not be persuaded to change his dwelling. He was found dead not far from the fountain—near the trunk of the tree, which had been his retreat. They interred him without noise and without parade.

In a short time nothing was spoken of Salaun, and even the remembrance of him seemed to be as effectually buried in oblivion, as his body was deposited in the earth; when, one morning it was seen that there had sprung up on his grave, a white lily, which was not only beautiful exceedingly to look at, but spread around, on all sides, a most agreeable odour. Yet more wonderful still, when the flower was examined, they found written on the leaves, in characters of gold, the words 'Ave Maria!' The report of this miracle ran in less than no time over all Brittany. And soon immense crowds flocked to the spot to see the wonderful flower, which lasted in blossom for more than six weeks. Then it commenced to fade. Advice was therefore given by the ecclesiastics, nobles, and officers of the Duke, that they should dig all around the body to find out where the plant had taken root. The digging was at once procceded with—and to their astonishment they found the stalk growing out of the mouth of the dead Salaun. The wonder was of course very great, and the discovery was at once recognized as a grand testimony of the sanctity and innocence of him, whom but a short time previous they regarded as a fool. Dom Juan de Langoneznou, Abbé of Landevennes—one of the witnesses of the miracle—wrote a relation of it in Latin, from which all the authors who have written about Folgoët have quoted. "The people, who have organized a pilgrimage to the place, continuing year after year to renew the *Fleur-de-lys* at the tomb of Salaun," as the Chronicle says, "they determined to erect a church to Notre Dame over the fountain of the poor mendicant, whose faith had been recompensed. Such is the origin of one of the most beautiful monuments of Finisterre.'

Contiguous to the farm of Kerloas is to be found the highest Druidical Menhir in Finisterre.[7] This is twelve metres, or nearly forty feet in height. At the distance of about a yard from the ground, and at opposite sides of the Menhir, are observed two projecting lumps of stone—each a foot in diameter. To these a very whimsical superstition is attached. "Now and then, on the approach of night," observes Monsieur de Fremmville, "a newly-married couple may be seen coming devoutly to the foot of this Menhir. They strip off their clothes, and rub their bodies against the stony lumps—the woman on one side, and the man on the other. After this ceremony is accomplished in the most perfect gravity, and seriousness, the happy

---

[7] Adolphe Joanne. Op. cit., p. 287.

pair return joyfully to their home. The man feeling confident that he is always to have male infants born to him—and the woman contented in believing, that she will never fail to keep her husband in leading-strings."

About fifteen miles further on, we come to Laurivoaré—a small village of a few hundred inhabitants. This derives its name from St. Rivoaré—one of the Apostles of Armorica—and its celebrity from a cemetery; of which latter tradition relates, that a whole tribe of people out of Rivoaré's district, were buried here—after being massacred by a neighbouring horde of Pagans. This necropolis, in which nobody has been interred since its first use, is separated from the ordinary Christian burying-ground of the parish. The latter has spacious arcades, in the centre of which is a statue of the blessed Virgin. On the day of the *Pardôn*, the faithful make the tour of the funereal sanctuary on their knees—first entering therein barefooted. At one end of the cemetery are seven large round stones—ranged on the steps of the cross. These, the inhabitants say, are loaves of bread, changed into stone by St. Hervé (nephew of St. Rivoaré), to punish a man who kept a public oven, and who had refused to give him alms.

Again between Rennes and Vannes—at Josselin, the ancient capital of the county of Porhoel—another *Pardón* is held on the Tuesday of Pentecost, at the Chapel of Notre Dame de Roncier. The last named is the title of the village in the neighbourhood—and the legend about the miraculous statue is to the following effect :[8] That on one occasion, in remote times, the Virgin of Roncier, hidden under the rags of a mendicant, had not only been refused a glass of water by some washerwomen, but they set the dogs at her. Whereupon they and their families—for generations subsequent—were afflicted with epilepsy, accompanied by barking and convulsions. Those always came on strongly at or about the feast of Pentecost—and were only subdued by carrying the sufferers to the shrine,— accompanied by holding them to kiss, with the foam on their lips, the sacred relics. In the present day there are but the remains of the miraculous statue, which was burned by the Revolutionists in 1795.

On another route, which is a carriage road between Carhaix and Landerneau, and about four miles from Huelgoat, is the chapel of St.

---

[8] Adolphe Joanne. Op. cit., p. 301.

Herbot. To this in the month of May a curious pilgrimage is made. St. Herbot was the patron saint of all horned beasts. During the three days of this *Pardón* all the oxen hereabouts in Cornouailles,[2]—Cornus Galliæ, or the Horn of Brittany,—are allowed to rest from labour. But the visitors to the chapel bring large quantities of cow and ox tails,[1] " qu'on fait pleuvoir sur les autels de St. Herbot, en sa qualité de patron des bêtes à cornes." The quantity of hair given to this chapel every year, realizes a revenue of 1500 to 1800 francs, which is doubled whenever there exists any epizootic disease amongst the cattle.

In fact there is scarcely a single square mile in Brittany, more especially in Basse Bretagne, where one does not find these simple religious festivals of visiting holy wells—shrines sacred by miracles—and statues of which legends are handed down through father and son, as mother to daughter—from generation to generation. To know all about the many saints of this part of the world, the reader should consult "*Les Vies des Saints de Bretagne*," by Albert Le Grand, who was a native of Morlaix. Together with having been canonized in Rome, they are sanctified in

---

[2] No doubt the *alter et ego* of our Cornwall.
[1] Adolphe Joanne, p. 323.

the pious devotional spirit, which is racy of the people—and which is exemplified in the simple legends, as in the solemn processions—everywhere recognizable as the "outward and visible signs" of an intensely pure faith in Brittany.

CHAPTER XX.

Cathedral of St. Pol—Deep religious feeling—Seriousness and sincerity *versus* Irreligion and impiety—From Quimper to Vannes—So-called "trashy" legend—Nature's nobility—*Les prix de Vertu*—The locksmith of Rennes—His wonderful charities—Madame Besnard—Remarkable self-denial—Rescuing unfortunates—In the field of battle—Madlle. Prudhomme—Nursing the cancer patient—Cancer developed in the Nurse—Stinted resources—Marie Grosbois of Paimbœuf—Noble sacrifice to self-imposed duty—Rosin Cherin, the sempstress—Supporting three families by her needlework—Great privations—Assiduous industry—The Paris locksmith—Extraordinary filial piety—Yearly prizes through French Academy—M. Montyon and philanthropic confrères—Such deeds need to be exalted—High-souled development—Deficiency in organic laws.

A PRIMARY result of the educational influence, effected by the practices and devotions detailed in the last chapter, joined perhaps to the hereditary sentiment previously spoken of, may be inferred from what is recorded by a Church of England clergyman, of the things he saw at the Cathedral of St. Pol.[1]

[1] Rev. G. Musgrave's "Ramble into Brittany," before quoted, vol. ii. p. 201.

There, in a congregation of about 500, the men of whom mounted to nearly 300, and many boys at their sides, "It was the first occasion in life," he says, "of my beholding a whole multitude testifying, without any exception, deep religious feeling. Those who were not kneeling stood. None sate—still less lounged, or lolled, or slumbered. Their eyes wandered not; they were intent on worship, in silence, in all seriousness and sincerity."

Yet these were of the same class and condition in life with the common people in England, whom the writer, himself a minister of the Established Church, describes after thirty years' acquaintance with them, "frequently indulging in practices of irreligion, and impiety in the house of God, long continued talk, giggling, laughing, cutting names on pew-panels, cracking nuts, or peeling chestnuts, and winking and nodding to female acquaintances during the sermon."

Still although the reverend author never saw anything of such impropiety of behaviour as that last mentioned amongst French congregations, and believes "such scandalous conduct to be exclusively English," he cannot attribute to the former any sincerity, whatever may be underneath. For he tells us,[2] when passing

[2] Op. cit., vol. ii. p. 257.

from Quimper to Vannes,—" There is a trashy legend also in connexion with Auray, and the miracle-working well or spring of St. Anne, which for two hundred years has been the resort of the Bretons and their neighbours suffering under rheumatism and scrofula."

He ignores the fact that from such like "trash" have proceeded the "deep religious feeling,"— the "hereditary sentiment of religion,"—the "sincerity and seriousness of worship,"—described at the Cathedral of St. Pol.

Whilst from the same source we see springing up these illustrations of Nature's nobility, whereof, here in this historic land, we have so many examples during the past year.[3] Besides the case of Anne Tessier previously recorded by me,[4] I find the following receiving in 1874, the prizes of virtue. All of them are resident, and have been brought up in Brittany.

1. At Rennes dwells Marie Joseph Besnard, a humble locksmith, the produce of whose workshop barely sufficed to supply the ordinary wants of his household. Yet even these scanty

[3] "Discours prononcé par M. Cuviller Fleury, Directeur de l'Académie Française, dans la Séance publique du 13 Août, 1874, sur les prix de Vertu." Didot Frères, 56, rue de Jacob, 1874.

[4] Chap. xiii., p. 150.

resources he distributed amongst such of his neighbours as were poorer than himself. Every Sunday he gave away in charity the gains of the preceding week, to the sick, the orphan, the destitute, and the prisoners : in fact, to all who were suffering and in distress. His wife had been engaged in the same work of charity with him for thirty years. She, like her husband, was patient, assiduous, vigilant, without display or ostentation, and always ready for anything good.

One day Madame Besnard was walking along the street for the first time after a prolonged and serious illness. She met four children who had been abandoned by their parents. The body of each was covered with a hideous leprosy, and was in a state of disgusting filth. Madame Besnard brought them home with her,—devoting herself to the care of their cleanliness, and medical treatment, whilst indifferent to the contagion which they carried with them, and had brought under her roof. To accommodate this increase to his family, Besnard had to enlarge his house. He therefore deprived himself of everything, in the shape of comfort, to accomplish this object.

On another occasion Madame Besnard encountered in the streets, a poor wandering and half-naked girl. The good *Samaritaine* covered the shoulders of this unfortunate with her cloak, and conducted her to the Refuge of St. Cyr, where her youth and honour were in safety. According to report made by the authorities of the city of Rennes, Madame Besnard has been instrumental in saving and reforming more than a hundred depraved women, chiefly young girls, the infamous dens of whose residences she had visited frequently.

When the war broke out, this valiant woman heard that the camp of Conlie was full of wounded and dying. She went to it at once, devoting herself to the service of the afflicted. Her husband remained at Rennes, like a soldier on duty: ready at any hour of the day or night, or at the first cry of agony, to cure the soldiers stricken down by small-pox, and when they succumbed, to bury the dead.

2. In the good old city of Nantes, once the chief stronghold of Breton power, lives Emilie Prudhomme, fifty years of age. Her life consists of one work, but this she has followed almost since her infancy. When very young, and an orphan, Mdlle. Prudhomme was adopted by a honest workman, poor like herself, and who soon after was struck with a fearful misfortune. A

horrible cancer broke out in his face. To stop the progress of this calamity, as well as to support not only his courage, but that of his wife, Emilie was their only solace. She never faltered a step, either in presence of the disgusting duty of daily dressings, or before the dread of contagion. One day the disgusting malady became developed on her countenance. But its progress is arrested by sharp and efficacious remedies, which after a few weeks enable her to return to her post, "Bearing on her face," as the author of a most touching letter addressed to the Academy says, "a wound as glorious as that gained on the field of battle." If we inquire how she obtains resources for her inexhaustible, though unknown charity, we find that she works in a cotton manufactory for wages of twenty-five sous (or about one shilling) per day. One of her relatives, wishing to free her from the trials of this hard life, offered her an asylum in his house. She refused. The old workman, who had in early days adopted her, now needs her care more than ever. So she remains. Death alone will subdue the persistency of her gratitude.

3. In the year 1834 Marie Grosbois was engaged as a servant in a grocer's establishment at Paimbœuf. She lived with the family without

anything remarkable occurring till 1859, when they became embarrassed in circumstances. Not only were they compelled to break up their establishment, but were unable to pay Marie for any future wages as their servant. Far from abandoning them in their distress she insisted on continuing with them, refusing to leave even when her mistress proposed going into an alms-house. Now she expended all her little savings in contributing to the comfort of her old employers. And when her former benefactor fell ill, she imposed on herself the greatest privations in order to conduce to her comfort.

4. Rose Cherin, who dwells at Briollay, not far from Candé, is a sempstress. For twelve years she had been caring in the tenderest manner her sister, who was left a young widow with two children; her helpless old mother, who was paralyzed; her brother, a widower, and with a family likewise. She spends all she can earn in supporting them. For she is, in fact, their only sustenance. She cares them all as if they were her children, not flinching a step before the heaviest sacrifice, whilst imposing on herself the greatest privations, and the most assiduous industry.

Several instances of similar, and in some cases of loftier, domestic heroism are related by M.

Fleury from other and various parts of France, where the same influences hold good as those in Brittany, thus proving—

> "There are homesteads which have witness'd deeds
> That battle-fields with all their banner'd pomp
> Have little to compare with."

Amongst them we are told of an honest and intelligent locksmith in Paris, named Henri-Charles-Emille—Bisilliat—Murat, on whom was bestowed one of the prizes. He is thirty years of age, and for the last fifteen years has devoted himself with the most exemplary filial piety to the care of his mother. She, although only forty-eight years of age, is completely paralyzed. "Whilst I have arms to work, my dear mother shall not leave me; nor shall I desert her!" he replied to those who proposed to get her into an alms-house. He also declines to get married, fearing that step might bring up obstacles to the object of his life's cares and attentions. In the morning before going to work he helps his mother to dress herself—in fact, he arranges all her clothes upon her. Then he cleans up the house, brings in provisions, cooks and leaves them within reach of his stricken parent. On Sundays he lifts her into a little carriage, purchased out of his savings, and draws the vehicle himself to the houses of friends, to whom she pays a weekly visit. Thus for fifteen years he has sacrificed to filial love the pleasures and enjoyments of youth and manhood.

Every year the French Academy awards the prizes left by Monsieur Montyon and his fellow-philanthropists for such virtuous deeds.

The most interesting feature of these distributions consists in the fact, that the premiums are never sought for by the people to whom they are awarded, the greater portion of them being those who

> "—— do good by stealth,
> And blush to find it fame."

For the names of persons considered to be worthy of the reward are generally found out by the neighbours,—communicated by them to the *Curé*,—thence to the Prefect or some civil authority; after which a report of the circumstances testified by the Mayor of the *locale* is forwarded to the Secretary of the Academy in Paris. Whereupon the decree is passed for the prize, and such an opportunity as the public gathering at an Agricultural Exhibition, like that we had at Candé, is generally made available to enhance the honours of the award by bestowing it in presence of the recipient's compatriots, and fellow-parishioners.

This is as it should be. Special instances of social and domestic heroism like these,—particularly when they are based on the divine principle of filial love, ought to be exalted and translated into every language. For they manifest more sublime courage than many feats on the battle-field.

But unfortunately we see in the world every day a disposition to snub, or disparage whatever evidences of high-souled accomplishments may come before us.

It is, therefore, full time to lend even the humblest aid,—not only to stamp out what Carlyle calls the "abominable and damnable cesspool of lies, shoddies, and shams" that are found amongst so many parts of the globe in this nineteenth century of our Christianity;—but to help in making public these holy deeds that are scarcely known outside the Academy or beyond the village. By doing this we may hope to neutralize the quasi-natural deficiency in part of our organic laws, lamented many years ago by the poet Gray:—

> " Full many a gem of purest ray serene,
> The dark unfathom'd caves of ocean bear,
> Full many a flower is born to blush unseen,
> And waste its sweetness on the desert air."

THE END.

GILBERT AND RIVINGTON, PRINTERS, ST. JOHN'S SQUARE, LONDON.

Catalogues of American and Foreign Books Published or Imported by MESSRS. S. LOW & CO. *can be had on application.*

Crown Buildings, 188, *Fleet Street, London.*
January, 1876.

A List of Books

PUBLISHING BY

SAMPSON LOW, MARSTON, SEARLE, & RIVINGTON.

ALPHABETICAL LIST.

 CLASSIFIED Educational Catalogue of Works Published in Great Britain. Demy 8vo. Cloth extra. Second edition, greatly revised. 5s. [*Nearly ready.*

Ablett (H.) Reminiscences of an Old Draper. 1 vol. small post 8vo. 2s. 6d.

About in the World, by the author of "The Gentle Life." Crown 8vo. bevelled cloth, 4th edition. 6s.

Adamson (Rev. T. H.) The Gospel according to St. Matthew, expounded. 8vo. 12s.

Adventures of Captain Magon. A Phœnician's Explorations 1000 years B.C. By LEON CAHUN. Numerous illustrations. Crown 8vo. Cloth.

Adventures of a Young Naturalist. By LUCIEN BIART, with 117 beautiful Illustrations on Wood. Edited and adapted by PARKER GILLMORE. Post 8vo. cloth extra, gilt edges, new edition, 7s. 6d.

Adventures on the Great Hunting Grounds of the World, translated from the French of Victor Meunier, with engravings, 2nd edition. 5s.

"The book for all boys in whom the love of travel and adventure is strong. They will find here plenty to amuse them and much to instruct them besides."—*Times.*

Alcott, (Louisa M.) Aunt Jo's Scrap-Bag. Square 16mo. 2s. 6d.

——— Cupid and Chow-Chow. Small post 8vo. 3s. 6d.

——— Little Men: Life at Plumfield with Jo's Boys. By the author of "Little Women." Small post 8vo. cloth, gilt edges, 2s. 6d. (Rose Library, 1s.)

A

Alcott (Louisa M.) Little Women. 2 vols., 2s. 6d. each. (Rose Library, 2 vols. 1s. each.)

—— **Old Fashioned Girl,** best edition, small post 8vo. cloth extra, gilt edges, 2s. 6d. (Rose Library, 1s.)

—— **Work. A Story of Experience.** New Edition. In One volume, small post 8vo., cloth extra. 6s. Several Illustrations. Also, Rose Library, "Work," Part I. 1s.

—— **Beginning Again.** A Sequel to "Work." 1s.

—— **Shawl Straps.** Small post 8vo. Cl. extra, gilt, 3s. 6d.

—— **Eight Cousins, or the Aunt Hill.** Small post 8vo. with illustrations. 5s. [*Ready.*

"Miss Alcott's stories are thoroughly healthy, full of racy fun and humour . . . exceedingly entertaining . . . . We can recommend the 'Eight Cousins.'"—*Athenæum.*

Alexander (Sir James E.) Bush Fighting. Illustrated by Remarkable Actions and Incidents of the Maori War. With a Map, Plans, and Woodcuts. 1 vol. demy 8vo. pp. 328, cloth extra, 16s.

Alexander (W. D. S.) The Lonely Guiding Star. A Legend of the Pyrenean Mountains and other Poems. Fcap. 8vo. cloth. 5s.

Amphlett (John). Under a Tropical Sky: a Holiday Trip to the West Indies. Small post 8vo., cloth extra. 7s. 6d.

—— **Warnton Kings.** Crown 8vo. cloth. 10s. 6d.

Andersen (Hans Christian). Fairy Tales, with Illustrations in Colours by E. V. B. Royal 4to. cloth. 1l. 5s.

Andrews (Dr.) Latin-English Lexicon. 13th edition. Royal 8vo. pp. 1,670, cloth extra. Price 18s.

"The best Latin Dictionary, whether for the scholar or advanced student."—*Spectator.*
"Every page bears the impress of industry and care."—*Athenæum.*

Anecdotes of the Queen and Royal Family, collected and edited by J. G. HODGINS, with Illustrations. New edition, revised by JOHN TIMBS. 5s.

Anglo-Scottish Year Book, The, for 1875. By ROBERT KEMPT. Fcap. 8vo. 1s.

Arctic Regions (The). Illustrated. *See* **Bradford.**

—— **German Polar Expedition.** *See* **Koldewey.**

—— **Explorations.** *See* **Markham.**

Art, Pictorial and Industrial. New Series, vols. 1 to 3, 18s. each. In numbers, 1s. each.

Assollant (A.) The Fantastic History of the Celebrated Pierrot. Written by the Magician ALCOFRIBAS, and translated from the Sogdien by ALFRED ASSOLLANT, with upwards of One Hundred humorous Illustrations by Van' Dargent. Square crown 8vo., cloth extra, gilt edges, 7s. 6d.

Atmosphere (The). *See* Flammarion.

Auerbach (Berthold). Waldfried. Translated from the German. 3 vols. crown 8vo. 31s. 6d.

Australian Tales, by the "Old Boomerang." Post 8vo. 5s.

"**B**" an Autobiography. By FENTON. 3 vols. 8vo. 31s. 6d.

BACK-LOG Studies. *See* Warner.

Backward Glances. Edited by the Author of "Episodes in an Obscure Life." Small post 8vo., cloth extra. 5s.

Bancroft's History of America. Library edition, vols. 1 to 10, 8vo. 6l.

Barnes's (Rev. A.) Lectures on the Evidences of Christianity in the 19th Century. 12mo. 7s. 6d.

Barrington (Hon. and Rev. L. J.) From Ur to Macpelah; the Story of Abraham Crown 8vo., cloth, 5s.

Barton (J. A. G.) Shunkur. A tale of the Indian Mutiny. Crown 8vo., cloth. 5s.

Bryant (W. C., assisted by S. H. Gay.) A Popular History of the United States. About 4 vols., to be profusely Illustrated with numerous Engravings on Steel and Wood, after designs by the best Artists. [*Vol. I. now in the Press.*

THE BAYARD SERIES. Comprising Pleasure Books of Literature produced in the Choicest Style as Companionable Volumes at Home and Abroad.

"We can hardly imagine better books for boys to read or for men to ponder over."—*Times.*

Price 2s. 6d. each *Volume, complete in itself, printed at the Chiswick Press, bound by Burn, flexible cloth extra, gilt leaves, with silk Headbands and Registers.*

The Story of the Chevalier Bayard. By M. DE BERVILLE.

De Joinville's St. Louis, King of France.

The Essays of Abraham Cowley, including all his Prose Works.

Abdallah; or, the Four Leaves. By EDOUARD LABOULLAYE.

Table-Talk and Opinions of Napoleon Buonaparte.

Vathek: An Oriental Romance. By WILLIAM BECKFORD.

The King and the Commons: a Selection of Cavalier and Puritan Song. Edited by Prof. MORLEY.

Words of Wellington: Maxims and Opinions of the Great Duke.

Dr. Johnson's Rasselas, Prince of Abyssinia. With Notes.

Hazlitt's Round Table. With Biographical Introduction.

The Religio Medici, Hydriotaphia, and the Letter to a Friend. By Sir THOMAS BROWNE, Knt.

Ballad Poetry of the Affections. By ROBERT BUCHANAN.

Coleridge's Christabel, and other Imaginative Poems. With Preface by ALGERNON C. SWINBURNE.

Lord Chesterfield's Letters, Sentences and Maxims. With Introduction by the Editor, and Essay on Chesterfield by M. De Ste.-Beuve, of the French Academy.

Essays in Mosaic. By THOS. BALLANTYNE.

My Uncle Toby; his Story and his Friends. Edited by P. FITZGERALD.

Reflections; or, Moral Sentences and Maxims of the Duke de la Rochefoucauld.

Socrates, Memoirs for English Readers from Xenophon's Memorabilia. By EDW. LEVIEN.

Prince Albert's Golden Precepts.

"We can hardly imagine better books for boys to read or for men to ponder over."—*Times.*

The New Volumes in the Bayard Series in preparation are:—

Swift's Lighter Miscellanies. Curious and quaint. [*Preparing.*

Walpole's Reminiscenses and Ana. [*Preparing.*

A suitable Case containing 12 volumes, price 31s. 6d.; or the Case separate, price 3s. 6d.

Beauty and the Beast. An Old Tale retold, with Pictures. By E. V. B. Demy 4to. cloth extra, novel binding. 10 Illustrations in Colours (in same style as those in the First Edition of "Story Without an End"). 12s. 6d.

Beecher (Henry Ward, D. D.) Life Thoughts. 12mo. 2s. 6d.

List of Publications.

Beecher (Dr. Lyman) Life and Correspondence of. 2 vols. post 8vo. 1*l*. 1*s*.

Bees and Beekeeping. By the Times' Beemaster. Illustrated. Crown 8vo. New Edition, with additions. 2*s*. 6*d*.

Bell (Rev. C. D.) Faith in Earnest. 18mo. 1*s*. 6*d*.

———— **Blanche Nevile.** Fcap. 8vo. 6*s*.

Better than Gold. By Mrs. ARNOLD, Author of "His by Right," &c. In 3 volumes, crown 8vo., 31*s*. 6*d*.

Benedict (F. L.) Miss Dorothy's Charge. 3 vols. 31*s*. 6*d*.

Beumer's German Copybooks. In six gradations at 4*d*. each.

Bickersteth's Hymnal Companion to Book of Common Prayer.

The following Editions are now ready:—

			s.	d
No. 1. A Small-type Edition, medium 32mo. cloth limp			0	6
No. 1. B	ditto	roan limp, red edges	1	0
No. 1. C	ditto	morocco limp, gilt edges	2	0

No. 2. Second-size type, super-royal 32mo. cloth limp			1	0
No. 2. A	ditto	roan limp, red edges	2	0
No. 2. B	ditto	morocco limp, gilt edges	3	0

No. 3. Large-type Edition, crown 8vo. cloth, red edges			2	6
No. 3. A	ditto	roan limp, red edges	3	
No. 3. B	ditto	morocco limp, gilt edges		

No. 4. Large-type Edition, crown 8vo. with Introduction and Notes, cloth, red edges			3	6
No. 4. A	ditto	roan limp, red edges	4	6
No. 4. B	ditto	morocco, gilt edges	6	6

No. 5. Crown 8vo. with accompanying Tunes to every Hymn, New Edition			3	0
No. 5. A	ditto	with Chants	4	0
No. 5. B The Chants separately			1	6
No. 5. C Large Edition. Tunes and Chants.			7	

No. 6. Penny Edition.

Fcap. 4to. Organists' edition. Cloth, 7*s*. 6*d*.

The Church Mission Hymn Book has been recently issued: it contains 120 Hymns for Special Missions and Schoolroom Services, selected, with a few additions, from the Hymnal Companion. Price 8*s*. 4*d*. per 100, or 1½*d*. each.

*** *A liberal allowance is made to Clergymen introducing the Hymnal.*

An 8 pp. prospectus sent post free on application.

☞ THE BOOK OF COMMON PRAYER, bound with THE HYMNAL COMPANION. 32mo. cloth, 9*d*. And in various superior bindings.

The Hymnal Companion is also sold, strongly bound with a Sunday School Liturgy, in two sizes, price 4*d*. and 8*d*.

Bickersteth (Rev. E. H., M.A.) The Reef, and other Parables. One Volume square 8vo., with numerous very beautiful Engravings, uniform in character with the Illustrated Edition of Heber's Hymns, &c., price 7s. 6d.

—— **The Master's Home-Call; Or, Brief Memorials of Alice Frances Bickersteth.** 3rd Edition. 32mo. cloth gilt. 1s.

"They recall in a touching manner a character of which the religious beauty has a warmth and grace almost too tender to be definite."—*The Guardian.*

—— **The Shadow of the Rock. A Selection of Religious Poetry.** 18mo. Cloth extra. 2s. 6d.

—— **The Clergyman in his Home.** Small Post 8vo. 1s.

—— **The Shadowed Home and the Light Beyond.** By the Rev. EDWARD HENRY BICKERSTETH. Third Edition. Crown 8vo, cloth extra, 5s.

Bida, The Authorized Version of the Four Gospels. With the whole of the magnificent etchings on steel, after the drawings by M. Bida.

The Gospels of St. Matthew, St. John, and St. Mark, appropriately bound in cloth extra, price £3 3s. each, are now ready. (St. Luke in preparation.)

"Bida's Illustrations of the Gospels of St. Matthew and St. John have already received here and elsewhere a full recognition of their great merits. To these is now added the Gospel of St. Mark, which is in every respect a fitting pendant to its predecessors. By next season we are promised the complete series."—*Times.*

Bidwell (C. T.) The Balearic Isles. Illustrations and a Map. [*Shortly.*

Bits of Talk about Home Matters. By H. H. Fcap. 8vo. cloth gilt edges. 3s.

Black (Wm.) Three Feathers. 3 vols. 31s. 6d.

—— —— —— Small post 8vo. cloth extra. 6s. Sixth Edition.

—— **Lady Silverdale's Sweetheart, and other Stories.** 1 vol. Crown 8vo. 10s. 6d.

—— **Kilmeny: a Novel.** Small Post 8vo. cloth. 6s.

—— **In Silk Attire.** 3rd and cheaper edition, small post 8vo. 6s.

"A work which deserves a hearty welcome for its skill and power in delineation of character."—*Saturday Review.*

—— **A Daughter of Heth.** 11th and cheaper edition, crown 8vo., cloth extra. 6s. With Frontispiece by F. Walker, A.R.A.

"If humour, sweetness, and pathos, and a story told with simplicity and vigour, ought to insure success, 'A Daughter of Heth' is of the kind to deserve it."—*Saturday Review.*

List of Publications.

Black (C. B.) New Continental Route Guides.

—— Guide to the North of France, including Normandy, Brittany, Touraine, Picardy, Champagne, Burgundy, Lorraine, Alsace, and the Valley of the Loire; Belgium and Holland; the Valley of the Rhine to Switzerland; and the South-West of Germany, to Italy by the Brenner Pass. Illustrated with numerous Maps and Plans. Crown 8vo., cloth limp. 9s. 6d.

—— Guide to Normandy and Brittany, their Celtic Monuments, Ancient Churches, and Pleasant Watering-Places. Illustrated with Maps and Plans. Crown 8vo., cloth limp, 2s. 6d.

—— Guide to Belgium and Holland, the North-East of France, including Picardy, Champagne, Burgundy, Lorraine, and Alsace; the Valley of the Rhine, to Switzerland; and the South-West of Germany, to Italy, by the Brenner Pass, with Description of Vienna. Illustrated with Maps and Plans. Crown 8vo., cloth limp, 5s.

—— Paris, and Excursions from Paris. Illustrated with numerous Maps, Plans, and Views. Small post 8vo., cloth limp, price 3s.

—— Guide to the South of France and to the North of Italy: including the Pyrenees and their Watering-Places; the Health Resorts on the Mediterranean from Perpignan to Genoa; and the towns of Turin, Milan, and Venice. Illustrated with Maps and Plans. Small post 8vo., cloth limp, 5s.

—— Switzerland and the Italian Lakes. Small post 8vo. price 3s. 6d.

—— Guide to France, Corsica, Belgium, Holland, the Rhine, the Moselle, the South-West of Germany, and the North of Italy. With numerous Maps and Plans. Complete in One Volume. Limp cloth, price 15s.

—— Railway and Road Map of Switzerland, West Tyrol, and the Italian Lake Country. Boards, price 1s.

Blackburn (H.) Art in the Mountains: the Story of the Passion Play, with upwards of Fifty Illustrations. 8vo. 12s.

—— Artists and Arabs. With numerous Illustrations. 8vo. 7s. 6d.

—— Harz Mountains: a Tour in the Toy Country. With numerous Illustrations. 12s.

—— Normandy Picturesque. Numerous Illustrations. 8vo. 16s.

—— Travelling in Spain. With numerous Illustrations. 8vo. 16s.

—— Travelling in Spain. Guide Book Edition. 12mo. 2s. 6d.

—— The Pyrenees. Summer Life at French Watering-Places. 100 Illustrations by Gustave Doré, Royal 8vo. 18s.

8   *Sampson Low and Co.'s.*

Blackmore (R. D.) Lorna Doone. New edition. Crown, 8vo. 6s.

> "The reader at times holds his breath, so graphically yet so simply does John Ridd tell his tale."—*Saturday Review.*

———— **Alice Lorraine.** 3 vols. 1l. 11s. 6d.

———— ———— ———— 1 vol. small post 8vo. 6s. Sixth Edition.

———— **Cradock Nowell.** New Edition. 6s.

———— **Clara Vaughan.** Revised edition. 6s.

———— **Georgics of Virgil.** Small 4to. 4s. 6d.

Blackwell (E.) Laws of Life. New edition. Fcp. 3s. 6d.

Boardman's Higher Christian Life. Fcp. 1s. 6d.

Bombaugh (C. C.) Gleanings for the Curious from the Harvest Fields of Literature. 8vo. cloth, 12s.

Bonwick (J.) Last of the Tasmanians. 8vo. 16s.

———— **Daily Life of the Tasmanians.** 8vo. 12s. 6d.

———— **Curious Facts of Old Colonial Days.** 12mo. 2s. 6d.

Book of Common Prayer with the Hymnal Companion. 32mo. cloth. 9d. And in various bindings.

Books suitable for School Prizes and Presents. (Fuller description of each book will be found in the alphabet.)

    Adventures of a Young Naturalist. 7s. 6d.
    ———— on Great Hunting Grounds. 5s.
    Allcott's Aunt Jo's Scrap-bag. 3s. 6d.
    ———— Cupid and Chow Chow. 3s. 6d.
    ———— Old Fashioned Girl. 3s. 6d.
    ———— Little Women. 3s. 6d.
    ———— Little Men. 3s. 6d.
    ———— Shawl Straps. 3s. 6d.
    ———— Eight Cousins. 5s.
    Anecdotes of the Queen. 5s.
    Atmosphere (The). By FLAMMARION. 30s.
    Backward Glances. 5s.
    Bayard Series (*See* Bayard.)
    Bickersteth (Rev. E. H.) Shadow of the Rock. 2s. 6d.
    Bida's Gospels. (*See* Bida.)
    Black (Wm.) Novels. (*See* Black.)
    Blackmore (R. D.) Novels. (*See* Blackmore.)

List of Publications.

Books for School Prizes and Presents, *continued*—

Burritt's Ten Minutes Talk on all sorts of Topics. Sm. 8vo. 6s.
Butler's Great Lone Land. 7s. 6d.
—— Wild North Land. 7s. 6d.
—— Akim-foo. 7s. 6d.
Changed Cross (The). 2s. 6d.
Child's Play. 7s. 6d.
Choice Editions of Choice Books. (*See* Choice Editions.)
Christ in Song. 5s.
Craik (Mrs.) Adventures of a Brownie. 5s.
Dana's Corals and Coral Islands. 21s. Cheaper Edition. 8s. 6d.
—— Two Years before the Mast. 6s.
Davies's Pilgrimage of the Tiber. 18s.
—— A Fine Old English Gentleman. 6s.
D'Avillier's Spain. Illustrated by Doré. £3 3s.
Erkmann-Chatrian's The Forest House. 3s. 6d.
Faith Gartney. 3s. 6d. cloth; boards, 1s. 6d.
Favell Children (The). 4s.
Fogg's Arabistan. 14s.
Forbes (J. G.) Africa: Geographical Exploration and Christian Enterprise. Crown 8vo. cloth. 7s. 6d.
Franc's Emily's Choice. 5s.
—— John's Wife. 4s.
—— Marian. 5s.
—— Silken Cord. 5s.
—— Vermont Vale. 5s.
—— Minnie's Mission. 4s.
Friswell (Laura) The Gingerbread Maiden. 3s. 6d.
Gayworthys (The). 3s. 6d.
Gentle Life Series. (*See* Alphabet).
Getting on in the World. 6s.
Glover's Light of the Word. 2s. 6d.
Hans Brinker. 7s. 6d.
Healy (Miss) The Home Theatre. 3s. 6d.
Holland (Dr.) Mistress of the Manse. 2s. 6d.
House on Wheels. By Madame STOLZ. 2s. 6d.
Hugo's Toilers of the Sea. 10s. 6d.
" " " 6s.
Kingston's Ben Burton. 3s. 6d.
King's Mountaineering in the Sierra Nevada. 6s.
Low's Edition of American Authors. 1s. 6d. and 2s. each.
Vols. published. *See* Alphabet under Low.
Lyra Sacra Americana. 4s. 6d.
Macgregor (John) Rob Roy Books. (*See* Alphabet.)

Books for School Prizes and Presents, *continued*—
   Maury's Physical Geography of the Sea. 6s.
   Phelps (Miss) The Silent Partner. 5s.
   Picture Gallery British Art. 18s.
   Picture Gallery Sacred Art. 12s.
   Read's Leaves from a Sketch Book. 25s. (*See* Read.
   Reynard the Fox. 100 Exquisite Illustrations. 7s. 6d.
   Sea-Gull Rock. 79 Beautiful Woodcuts. 7s. 6d. and 2s. 6d.
   Stanley's How I Found Livingstone. 7s. 6d.
   Stowe (Mrs.) Pink and White Tyranny. 3s. 6d.
   —— Dred. 1s.
   —— Old Town Folks. Cloth extra 6s. and 2s. 6d.
   —— Minister's Wooing. 5s. ; boards, 1s. 6d.
   —— Pearl of Orr's Island. 5s., 2s. 6d. and 1s.
   —— My Wife and I. 6s.
   Tauchnitz's German Authors. *See* Tauchnitz.
   Tayler (C. B.) Sacred Records. 2s. 6d.
   Thompson's Old English Homes. 2l. 2s. (*See* Thompson.
   Titcomb's Letters to Young People. 1s. 6d. and 2s.
   Under the Blue Sky. 7s. 6d.
   Verne's Books. (*See* Verne.)
   Whitney's (Mrs.) Books. *See* Alphabet.
   Wilson's Rambles in Northern India. 1l. 1s. (*See* Wilson.)

Bowles (T. G.) The Defence of Paris, narrated as it was seen. 8vo. 14s.

Bowker (G.) St. Mark's Gospel. With Explanatory Notes. For the Use of Schools and Colleges. By GEORGE BOWKER, late Second Master of the Newport Grammar School, Isle of Wight. 1 vol. foolscap, cloth.

Bradford (Wm.) The Arctic Regions. Illustrated with Photographs, taken on an Art Expedition to Greenland. With Descriptive Narrative by the Artist. In One Volume, royal broadside, 25 inches by 20, beautifully bound in morocco extra, price Twenty-five Guineas.

Bremer (Fredrika) Life, Letters, and Posthumous Works. Crown 8vo. 10s. 6d.

Brett (E.) Notes on Yachts. Fcp. 6s.

Bristed (C. A.) Five Years in an English University. Fourth Edition, Revised and Amended by the Author. Post 8vo. 10s. 6d.

Broke (Admiral Sir B. V. P., Bart., K.C.B.) Biography of. 1l.

Brothers Rantzau. *See* Erckmann-Chatrian.

Brown (Colin Rae). Edith Dewar. 3 vols. Cr. 8vo. 1l. 11s. 6d.

Browning (Mrs. E. B.) The Rhyme of the Duchess May. Demy 4to. Illustrated with Eight Photographs, after Drawings by Charlotte M. B. Morrell. 21s.

Burritt (E.) The Black Country and its Green Border Land. Second edition. Post 8vo. 6s.

—— **Lectures and Speeches.** Fcap. 8vo. cloth, 6s.

——— **Ten-Minutes Talk on all sorts of Topics.** With Autobiography of the Author. Small post 8vo., cloth extra. 6s.

Burton (Captain R. F.) Two Trips to Gorilla Land and the Cataracts of the Congo. By Captain R. F. BURTON. 2 vols., demy 8vo., with numerous Illustrations and Map, cloth extra 28s.

Bushnell's (Dr.) The Vicarious Sacrifice. Post 8vo. 7s. 6d.

—— **Sermons on Living Subjects.** Crown 8vo. cloth. 7s. 6d.

——— **Nature and the Supernatural.** Post 8vo. 3s. 6d.

—— **Christian Nurture.** 3s. 6d.

—— **Character of Jesus.** 6d.

——— **The New Life.** Crown 8vo. 3s. 6d.

Butler (W. F.) The Great Lone Land; an Account of the Red River Expedition, 1869-1870, and Subsequent Travels and Adventures in the Manitoba Country, and a Winter Journey across the Saskatchewan Valley to the Rocky Mountains. With Illustrations and Map. Fifth and Cheaper Edition. Crown 8vo. cloth extra. 7s. 6d. (The first 3 Editions were in 8vo. cloth. 16s.).

——— **The Wild North Land: the Story of a Winter Journey with Dogs across Northern North America.** Demy 8vo. cloth, with numerous Woodcuts and a Map. Fourth Edition. 18s. (See also Low's Library of Travel.)

——— **Akim-foo: the History of a Failure.** Demy 8vo. cloth. 16s. Second Edition. Also in a Third and Cheaper edition. 7s. 6d.

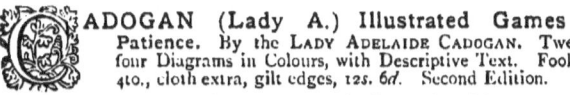**ADOGAN (Lady A.) Illustrated Games of Patience.** By the LADY ADELAIDE CADOGAN. Twenty-four Diagrams in Colours, with Descriptive Text. Foolscap 4to., cloth extra, gilt edges, 12s. 6d. Second Edition.

Cahun (Leon). Adventures of Captain Magon. See Adventures.

California. See **Nordhoff.**

Carlisle (Thos.) The Unprofessional Vagabond. Fcap. 8vo. Fancy boards. 1s.

Case of Mr. Lucraft, and other Stories. By the author of "Ready-Money Mortiboy." 3 vols. crown. 31s. 6d.

Ceramic Art. See **Jacquemart.**

Changed Cross (The) and other Religious Poems. 2s. 6d.

Chefs-d'œuvre of Art and Master-pieces of Engraving, selected from the celebrated Collection of Prints and Drawings in the British Museum. Reproduced in Photography by STEPHEN THOMPSON. Imperial folio, Thirty-eight Photographs, cloth gilt. 4l. 14s. 6d.

Child's Play, with 16 coloured drawings by E. V. B. An entirely new edition, printed on thick paper, with tints, 7s. 6d.

China. *See* **Illustrations of.**

Choice Editions of Choice Books. 2s. 6d. each. Illustrated by C. W. COPE, R.A., T. CRESWICK, R.A., E. DUNCAN, BIRKET FOSTER, J. C. HORSLEY, A.R.A., G. HICKS, R. REDGRAVE, R.A., C. STONEHOUSE, F. TAYLER, G. THOMAS, H. J. TOWNSHEND, E. H. WEHNERT, HARRISON WEIR, &c.

Blomfield's Farmer's Boy.
Campbell's Pleasures of Hope.
Coleridge's Ancient Mariner.
Goldsmith's Deserted Village.
Goldsmith's Vicar of Wakefield.
Gray's Elegy in a Churchyard.
Keat's Eve of St. Agnes.
Milton's L'Allegro.
Poetry of Nature. Harrison Weir.
Rogers' (Samuel) Pleasures of Memory.
Shakespeare's Songs and Sonnets.
Tennyson's May Queen.
Elizabethan Poets.
Wordsworth's Pastoral Poems.

[*All now ready.*]

" Such works are a glorious beatification for a poet."—*Athenæum*.

N.B.—This is not a mere reduction in price of the 5s. volumes, it is an entire *Reprint from Type specially cast for the purpose*, including also the whole of the beautiful Woodcuts. Each volume is complete in itself, and will be sold separately. Small post 8vo., printed on the finest cream white paper and choicely bound, cloth extra. 2s. 6d. each.

Christ in Song. Hymns of Immanuel, selected from all Ages, with Notes. By PHILIP SCHAFF, D.D. Crown 8vo. toned paper, beautifully printed at the Chiswick Press. With Initial Letters and Ornaments and handsomely bound. New Edition. 5s.

Christabel. *See* **Bayard Series.**

Christmas Presents. *See* **Illustrated Books.**

Chronicles of the Castle of Amelroy. 4to. With Photographic Illustrations. 2l. 2s.

Chronicles of Sir Harry Earlsleigh, Bart. A Novel. 3 vols., crown 8vo. 31s.

Clara Vaughan. *See* **Blackmore.**

Clark (R. W.) The Work of God in Great Britain under Messrs. Moody and Sankey. 1873 to 1875. With Portraits, and with Biographical Sketches by RUFUS W. CLARK, D.D. Second edition, over 300 pages. 2s., cloth cover.

Coffin (G. C.) Our New Way Round the World. 8vo. 12s.

Conquered at Last; from Records of Dhu Hall and its Inmates; A Novel. 3 vols. Crown; cloth. 31s. 6d.

Constantia. By the Author of "One Only." 2 vols. crown 8vo. 21*s*.

Cook (D.) Young Mr. Nightingale. A Novel. 3 vols. Crown 8vo., cloth. 31*s*. 6*d*.

—— **The Banns of Marriage.** 2 vols. crown 8vo. 21*s*.

Courtship and a Campaign; a Story of the Milanese Volunteers of 1866, under Garibaldi. By M. DALIN. 2 vols. cr. 8vo. 21*s*.

Cradock Nowell. *See* **Blackmore.**

Craik (Mrs.) The Adventures of a Brownie, by the Author of "John Halifax, Gentleman." With numerous Illustrations by Miss PATERSON. Square cloth, extra gilt edges. 5*s*.

A Capital Book for a School Prize for Children from Seven to Fourteen.

Craik (Miss G.) Without Kith or Kin. 3 vols. crown 8vo. 31*s*. 6*d*.

—— **Hero Trevelyan.** 2 Vols. Post 8vo. 21*s*.

Cumming (Miss C. F. G.) From the Hebrides to the Himalayas; Eighteen Month's Wanderings in Western Isles and Eastern Highlands. By Miss CONSTANCE F. GORDON CUMMING, with very numerous Full-page and other Woodcut Illustrations, from the Author's own Drawings. 2 vols., medium 8vo., cloth extra. 42*s*.

Cummins (Maria S.) Haunted Hearts (Low's Copyright Series). 16mo. boards. 1*s*. 6*d*.; cloth, 2*s*.

Curley (E. A.) Nebraska; its Advantages, Resources, and Drawbacks. With Maps and Illustrations. 8vo., cloth extra. 12*s*. 6*d*.

ANA (R. H.) Two Years before the Mast and Twenty-four years After. New Edition, with Notes and Revisions. 12mo. 6*s*.

Dana (Jas. D.) Corals and Coral Islands. Numerous Illustrations, charts, &c. New and Cheaper Edition, with numerous important Additions and Corrections. Crown 8vo. cloth extra. 8*s*. 6*d*.

"Professed geologists and zoologists, as well as general readers, will find Professor Dana's book in every way worthy of their attention."—*The Athenæum.*

Daughter (A) of Heth, by WM. BLACK. Thirteenth and Cheaper edition. 1 vol. crown 8vo. 6*s*.

Davies (Wm.) The Pilgrimage of the Tiber, from its Mouth to its Source; with some account of its Tributaries. 8vo., with many very fine Woodcuts and a Map, cloth extra. Second Edition. 18*s*.

—— **A Fine Old English Gentleman**, Exemplified in the Life and Character of Lord Collingwood: a Biographical Study. By WILLIAM DAVIES, Author of "The Pilgrimage of the Tiber," &c. 1 vol. crown 8vo., cloth extra. 6*s*. [*Ready.*

N.B.—This little volume is enriched by a very fine Portrait, engraved by C. H. Jeens, after a mezzotint by Charles Turner from a painting in the possession of Lady Collingwood in 1811.

*** A few Engraver's proofs of the Portrait printed on large paper, suitable for the portfolio or for framing. 5*s*.

De Witt (Madame Guizot). An Only Sister. Vol. V. of the "John Halifax" Series of Girls' Books. With Six Illustrations. Small post 8vo. cloth. 4s.

Dodge (Mrs. M.) *See* Hans Brinker.

Doré's Spain. *See* Spain.

Dougall's (J. D.) Shooting; its Appliances, Practice, and Purpose. *See* Shooting.

Duer's Marine Insurance. 2 vols. 3*l*. 3*s*.

Duplessis (G.) Wonders of Engraving. With numerous Illustrations and Photographs. 8vo. 12*s*. 6*d*.

CHOES of the Heart. *See* Moody.

English Catalogue of Books (The). Published during 1863 to 1871 inclusive, comprising also the Important American Publications.

This Volume, occupying over 450 Pages, shows the Titles of 32,000 New Books and New Editions issued during Nine Years, with the Size, Price, and Publisher's Name, the Lists of Learned Societies, Printing Clubs, and other Literary Associations, and the Books issued by them; as also the Publisher's Series and Collections—altogether forming an indispensable adjunct to the Bookseller's Establishment, as well as to every Learned and Literary Club and Association. 30*s*. half-bound.

*** The previous Volume, 1835 to 1862, of which a very few remain on sale, price 2*l*. 5*s*.; as also the Index Volume, 1837 to 1857, price 1*l*. 6*s*.

—— Supplements, 1863, 1864, 1865, 3*s*. 6*d*. each; 1866, 1867 to 1874, 5*s*. each.

English Writers, Chapters for Self-improvement in English Literature; by the author of "The Gentle Life." 6*s*.

—— Matrons and their Profession; With some Considerations as to its Various Branches, its National Value, and the Education it requires. By M. L. F., Writer of "My Life, and what shall I do with it." "Battle of the Two Philosophies," and "Strong and Free." Crown 8vo., cloth, extra, 7*s*. 6*d*.

English Painters of the Georgian Era. Hogarth to Turner. Biographical Notices. Illustrated with 48 permanent Photographs, after the most celebrated Works. Demy 4to., cloth extra. 18*s*.
[*Ready*.

Erckmann-Chatrian. Forest House and Catherine's Lovers. Crown 8vo. 3*s*. 6*d*.

—— The Brothers Rantzau: A Story of the Vosges. 2 vols. crown 8vo. cloth. 21*s*. New Edition. 1 vol., profusely illustrated. Cloth extra. 5*s*.

Evans (C.) Over the Hills and Far Away. By C. EVANS, Author of "A Strange Friendship." One Volume, crown 8vo., cloth extra, 10*s*. 6*d*.

—— A Strange Friendship. Crown 8vo., cloth. 5*s*.

Evans (T. W.) History of the American Ambulance,
established in Paris during the Siege of 1870-71. Together with the Details of its Method and its Work. By THOMAS W. EVANS, M.D., D. D. S. Imperial 8vo., with numerous illustrations, cloth extra, price 35s.

E. V. B.'s Beauty and the Beast. See Beauty and the Beast.

FAITH GARTNEY'S Girlhood, by the Author of "The Gayworthys." Fcap. with Coloured Frontispiece. 3s. 6d.

Favell (The) Children. Three Little Portraits. Crown 12mo. Four Illustrations. Cloth gilt. 4s.
"A very useful and clever story."—*John Bull.*

Few (A) Hints on Proving Wills. Enlarged Edition, sewed. 1s.

Field (M. B.) Memories of Many Men and of some Women. Post 8vo., cloth. 10s. 6d.

Fields (J. T.) Yesterdays with Authors. Crown 8vo. 10s. 6d.

Flammarion (C.) The Atmosphere. Translated from the French of CAMILLE FLAMMARION. Edited by JAMES GLAISHER, F.R.S., Superintendent of the Magnetical and Meteorological Department of the Royal Observatory at Greenwich. With 10 beautiful Chromo-Lithographs and 81 woodcuts. Royal 8vo. cloth extra, bevelled boards. 30s.

Fleming's (Sandford) Expedition. See Ocean to Ocean.

Flemish and French Pictures. With Notes concerning the Painters and their Works by F. G. STEPHENS, Author of "Flemish Relics," "Memoirs of Sir Edwin Landseer," &c. Small 4to. cloth extra, bevelled boards, gilt sides, back, and edges. 1l. 8s.

Fletcher and Kidder's Brazil and the Brazilians. Entirely new edition. [*In the press.*

Fogg's (W. P.) Arabistan; or, the Land of "The Arabian Nights." Being Travels through Egypt, Arabia, and Persia to Bagdad. By WILLIAM PERRY FOGG, M.A. Demy 8vo., with numerous Illustrations, cloth extra. 14s.

Fool of the Family, and other Tales. By JOHN DANGERFIELD. 2 vols., crown 8vo. 21s.

Forbes (J. G.) Africa: Geographical Exploration and Christian Enterprise, from the Earliest Times to the Present. By J. GRUAR FORBES. Crown 8vo., cloth extra, 7s. 6d.

Forrest (John) Explorations in Australia; being Mr. John Forrest's Personal Accounts of his Journeys: 1st. In Search of Dr. Leichardt and Party. 2nd. From Perth or Adelaide, around the Great Australian Bight. 3rd. From Champion Bay across the Desert to the Telegraph and to Adelaide. 1 vol. demy 8vo., cloth, with several Illustrations from the Author's Sketches, drawn on wood by G. F. Angas, and 3 Maps. 16s.

Forrest's (R. W.) Gleanings from the Pastures of Tekoa.
By ROBERT WILLIAM FORREST, M.A., Vicar of St. Jude's, South Kensington. Contents:—The Words of Amos—National Evils—National Privileges—Serious Questions—The Great Meeting—At Ease in Zion—Intercessory Prayer—Summer Fruit—The Word of the Lord—Hearing the Word—Last Words. 1 vol. small post 8vo., 260 pp., cloth extra. 6s.

Franc (Maude Jeane) Emily's Choice, an Australian Tale.
1 vol. small post 8vo. With a Frontispiece by G. F. ANGAS. 5s.

—— **Hall's Vineyard.** Small post 8vo., cloth. 4s.

—— **John's Wife.** A Story of Life in South Australia.
Small post 8vo., cloth extra. 4s.

—— **Marian, or the Light of Some One's Home.** Fcp.
3rd Edition, with Frontispiece. 5s.

—— **Silken Cords and Iron Fetters.** 4s.

—— **Vermont Vale.** Small post 4to., with Frontispiece. 5s.

—— **Minnie's Mission.** Small post 8vo., with Frontispiece. 4s.

Friswell (J. H.) *See* Gentle Life Series.

—— **One of Two.** 3 vols. 1l. 11s. 6d.

Friswell (Laura.) The Gingerbread Maiden; and other Stories. With Illustration. Square cloth. 3s. 6d.

GARVAGH (Lord) The Pilgrim of Scandinavia.
By LORD GARVAGH, B.A., Christ Church, Oxford, and Member of the Alpine Club. 8vo., cloth extra, with Illustrations. 10s. 6d.

"Although of late there has been no lack of works on Iceland, this little volume is written with so much freshness and vivacity that it will be read with interest and pleasure."—*Standard.*

Gayworthys (The), a Story of New England Life. Small post 8vo. 3s. 6d.

Gems of Dutch Art. Twelve Photographs from finest Engravings in British Museum. Sup. royal 4to. cloth extra. 25s.

Gentle Life (Queen Edition). 2 vols. in 1. Small 4to. 10s. 6d.

THE GENTLE LIFE SERIES. Printed in Elzevir, on Toned Paper, handsomely bound, forming suitable Volumes for Presents. Price 6s. each; or in calf extra, price 10s. 6d.

The Gentle Life. Essays in aid of the Formation of Character of Gentlemen and Gentlewomen. Tenth Edition.

"Deserves to be printed in letters of gold, and circulated in every house."—*Chambers' Journal.*

About in the World. Essays by the Author of "The Gentle Life."

"It is not easy to open it at any page without finding some handy idea."—*Morning Post.*

Like unto Christ. A New Translation of the "De Imitatione Christi" usually ascribed to Thomas à Kempis. With a Vignette from an Original Drawing by Sir Thomas Lawrence. Second Edition.

"Could not be presented in a more exquisite form, for a more sightly volume was never seen."—*Illustrated London News.*

Familiar Words. An Index Verborum, or Quotation Handbook. Affording an immediate Reference to Phrases and Sentences that have become embedded in the English language. Second and enlarged Edition.

"The most extensive dictionary of quotation we have met with."—*Notes and Queries.*

Essays by Montaigne. Edited, Compared, Revised, and Annotated by the Author of "The Gentle Life." With Vignette Portrait. Second Edition.

"We should be glad if any words of ours could help to bespeak a large circulation for this handsome attractive book."—*Illustrated Times.*

The Countess of Pembroke's Arcadia. Written by Sir PHILIP SIDNEY. Edited, with Notes, by the Author of "The Gentle Life." Dedicated, by permission, to the Earl of Derby. 7s. 6d.

"All the best things in the Arcadia are retained intact in Mr. Friswell's edition.—*Examiner.*

The Gentle Life. Second Series. Seventh Edition.

"There is not a single thought in the volume that does not contribute in some measure to the formation of a true gentleman."—*Daily News.*

Varia: Readings from Rare Books. Reprinted, by permission, from the *Saturday Review, Spectator,* &c.

"The books discussed in this volume are no less valuable than they are rare, and the compiler is entitled to the gratitude of the public." —*Observer.*

The Silent Hour: Essays, Original and Selected. By the Author of "The Gentle Life." Third Edition.

"All who possess the 'Gentle Life' should own this volume."—*Standard.*

Essays on English Writers, for the Self-improvement of Students in English Literature.

"To all (both men and women) who have neglected to read and study their native literature we would certainly suggest the volume before us as a fitting introduction."—*Examiner.*

Other People's Windows. By J. HAIN FRISWELL. Second Edition.

"The chapters are so lively in themselves, so mingled with shrewd views of human nature, so full of illustrative anecdotes, that the reader cannot fail to be amused."—*Morning Post.*

A Man's Thoughts. By J. HAIN FRISWELL.

German Primer; being an Introduction to First Steps in German. By M. T. PREU. 2*s.* 6*d.*

Getting On in the World; or, Hints on Success in Life. By WILLIAM MATHEWS, LL.D. Small post 8vo., cloth extra, bevelled edges. 6*s.*

Girdlestone (C.) Christendom. 12mo. 3*s.*

────── **Family Prayers.** 12mo. 1*s.* 6*d.*

Glover (Rev. R.) The Light of the Word. Third Edition. 18mo. 2*s.* 6*d.*

Goethe's Faust. With Illustrations by Konewka. Small 4to. Price 10*s.* 6*d.*

Gospels (Four), with Bida's Illustrations. *See* Bida.

Gouffé: The Royal Cookery Book. By JULES GOUFFÉ; translated and adapted for English use by ALPHONSE GOUFFÉ, head pastrycook to Her Majesty the Queen. Illustrated with large plates, printed in colours. 161 woodcuts. 8vo, cloth extra, gilt edges. 2*l.* 2*s.*

────── Domestic Edition, half-bound. 10*s.* 6*d.*

"By far the ablest and most complete work on cookery that has ever been submitted to the gastronomical world."—*Pall Mall Gazette.*

────── **The Book of Preserves;** or, Receipts for Preparing and Preserving Meat, Fish salt and smoked, Terrines, Gelatines, Vegetables, Fruits, Confitures, Syrups, Liqueurs de Famille, Petits Fours. Bonbons, &c. &c. 1 vol. royal 8vo., containing upwards of 500 Receipts and 34 Illustrations. 10*s.* 6*d.*

────── **Royal Book of Pastry and Confectionery.** By JULES GOUFFÉ, Chef-de-Cuisine of the Paris Jockey Club. Royal 8vo. Illustrated with 10 Chromo-lithographs and 137 Woodcuts, from Drawings from Nature by E. Monjat, cloth extra, gilt edges, 35*s.*

List of Publications. 19

Gouraud (Mdlle.) Four Gold Pieces. Numerous Illustrations. Small post 8vo., cloth. 2s. 6d. *See also* Rose Library.

Gower (Lord Ronald). Hand-book to the Art Galleries, Public and Private, of Belgium and Holland. 18mo., cloth. 5s.

—— The Castle Howard Portraits. 2 vols. Folio, cloth extra. £6 6s.

Greek Testament. *See* Novum Testament.

Guizot's History of France. Translated by ROBERT BLACK. Royal 8vo. Numerous Illustrations. Vols. I. II. III. and IV., cloth extra, each 24s.; in Parts, 2s. each (to be completed in one more volume). *Will be completed about May,* 1876.

Guyon (Mad.) Life. By Upham. Sixth Edition. Crown 8vo. 6s.

—— A Short Method of Prayer and Spiritual Torrents. Translated from the French original of Madame DE LA MOTHE GUYON. 12mo., cloth extra. 2s. [*Now ready*.

Guillemin. Comets. Translated and Edited by JAMES GLAISHER. Numerous Chromos and other Illustrations. [*In Press*.

Guyot (A.) Physical Geography. By ARNOLD GUYOT, Author of "Earth and Man." In 1 volume, large 4to., 128 pp., numerous coloured Diagrams, Maps and Woodcuts, price 10s. 6d., strong boards.

HACKLANDER (F. W.) Bombardier H. and Corporal Dose; or, Military Life in Prussia. First Series. The Soldier in Time of Peace. Translated (by permission of the Author) from the German of F. W. Hackländer. By F. E. R. and H. E. R. Crown 8vo., cloth extra, 5s.

Hale (E. E.) In His Name; a Story of the Dark Ages. Small post 8vo., cloth, 3s. 6d.

Half-Length Portraits. Short Studies of Notable Persons. By OLIVER ST. JAMES. Small Post 8vo., cloth extra. 6s. [*Shortly*.

Hall (S. P.) Sketches from an Artist's Portfolio. *See* Sketches.

Hall (W. W.) How to Live Long; or, 1,408 Health Maxims, Physical, Mental, and Moral. By W. W. HALL, A.M., M.D. Small post, 8vo., cloth. 2s. Second Edition. [*Ready*.
"We can cordially commend it to all who wish to possess the *mens sana in corpore sano.*"—*Standard.*

Hans Brinker; or, the Silver Skates. An entirely New Edition, with 59 Full-page and other Woodcuts. Square crown 8vo., cloth extra. 7s 6d. [*Ready*.
N.B.—This is an Edition *de Luxe* of an old favourite.

Harper's Handbook for Travellers in Europe and the East. New Edition, 1875. Post 8vo. Morocco tuck, 1l. 11s. 6d

Hawthorne (Mrs. N.) Notes in England and Italy. Crown 8vo. 10s. 6d.

Hayes (Dr.) Cast Away in the Cold; an Old Man's Story of a Young Man's Adventures. By Dr. I. ISAAC HAYES, Author of "The Open Polar Sea." With numerous Illustrations. Gilt edges, 6s.

—— **The Land of Desolation;** Personal Narrative of Adventures in Greenland. Numerous Illustrations. Demy 8vo., cloth extra. 14s.

Hazard (S.) Santo Domingo, Past and Present; With a Glance at Hayti. With upwards of One Hundred and Fifty beautiful Woodcuts and Maps, chiefly from Designs and Sketches by the Author. Demy 8vo. cloth extra. 18s.

Hazard (S.) Cuba with Pen and Pencil. Over 300 Fine Woodcut Engravings. New edition, 8vo. cloth extra. 15s.

Hazlitt (William) The Round Table. (Bayard Series.) 2s. 6d.

Healy (M.) Lakeville. 3 vols. 1l. 11s. 6d.

—— **A Summer's Romance.** Crown 8vo., cloth. 10s. 6d.

—— **The Home Theatre.** Small post 8vo. 3s. 6d.

—— **Out of the World.** A Novel. Three Volumes, crown 8vo, cloth extra. 1l. 11s. 6d.

Hearth Ghosts. By the Author of "Gilbert Rugge." 3 Vols. 1l. 11s. 6d.

Heber's (Bishop) Illustrated Edition of Hymns. With upwards of 100 Designs engraved in the first style of art under the superintendence of J. D. COOPER. Small 4to. Handsomely bound, 7s. 6d.

Henderson (A.) Latin Proverbs and Quotations; with Translations and Parallel Passages, and a copious English Index. By ALFRED HENDERSON. Fcap. 4to., 530 pp. 10s. 6d.

Higginson (T. W.) Atlantic Essays. Small post 8vo. 6s.

—— **Young Folks' History of the United States.** Small post 8vo., cloth. 6s.

Hitherto. By the Author of "The Gayworthys." New Edition. cloth extra. 3s. 6d. Also in Low's American Series. Double Vol. 2s. 6d.

Hofmann (Carl) A Practical Treatise on the Manufacture of Paper in all its Branches. Illustrated by One Hundred and Ten Wood Engravings, and Five large Folding Plates. In One Volume, 4to, cloth ; about 400 pages. 3l. 13s. 6d.

Holland (Dr.) Kathrina and Titcomb's Letters. *See* Low's American Series.

—— **Mistress of the Manse.** 2s. 6d. *See also* Rose Library.

Holmes (Oliver W.) The Guardian Angel; a Romance. 2 vols. 16s.

—— **(Low's Copyright Series.)** Boards, 1s. 6d.; cloth, 2s.

—— **Songs in Many Keys.** Post 8vo. 7s. 6d.

—— **Mechanism in Thought and Morals.** 12mo. 1s. 6d.

Horace (Works of). Translated literally into English Prose. By C. Smart, A.M. New edition. 18 mo., cloth. 2s.

How to Live Long. *See* Hall.

Hugo (Victor) "Ninety-Three." Translated by Frank Lee Benedict and J. Hain Friswell. New Edition. Illustrated. One vol. crown 8vo. 6s.

—— **Toilers of the Sea.** Crown 8vo. 6s.; fancy boards, 2s.; cloth, 2s. 6d.; Illustrated Edition, 10s. 6d.

Hunt (Leigh) and S. A. Lee, Elegant Sonnets, with Essay on Sonneteers. 2 vols. 8vo. 18s.

—— **Day by the Fire.** Fcap. 6s. 6d.

Hutchinson (Thos.) Summer Rambles in Brittany. Illustrated. [*Shortly*.

Hymnal Companion to Book of Common Prayer. *See* Bickersteth.

ILLUSTRATIONS of China and its People. By J. Thomson, F.R.G.S. Being Photographs from the Author's Negatives, printed in permanent Pigments by the Autotype Process, and Notes from Personal Observation.

*** The complete work embraces 200 Photographs, with Letter-press Descriptions of the Places and People represented. Four Volumes, imperial 4to., each £3 3s.

Illustrated Books, suitable for Christmas, Birthday, or Wedding Presents. (The full titles of which will be found in the Alphabet.)

Adventures of a Young Naturalist. 7s. 6d.
Alexander's Bush Fighting. 16s.

Illustrated Books, *continued*—

Andersen's Fairy Tales. 25*s*.
Arctic Regions. Illustrated. 25 guineas.
Art, Pictorial and Industrial. New Series, Vols. I. to III., 18*s*. each.
Bida's Gospels. 3*l*. 3*s*. each.
Blackburn's Art in the Mountains. 12*s*.
—— Artists and Arabs. 7*s*. 6*d*.
—— Harz Mountains. 12*s*.
—— Normandy Picturesque. 16*s*.
—— Travelling in Spain. 16*s*.
—— The Pyrenees. 18*s*.
Butler's Great Lone Land. 7*s*. 6*d*.
—— Wild North Land. 7*s*. 6*d*.
—— Akim-foo. 7*s*. 6*d*.
Cadogan (Lady) Games of Patience. 12*s*. 6*d*.
Chefs-d'oeuvre of Art. 4*l*. 14*s*. 6*d*.
China. Illustrated. 4 vols. 3*l*. 3*s*. each vol.
Choice Books. 2*s*. 6*d*. each. *See* Choice Editions.
Davies's Pilgrimage of the Tiber. 18*s*.
D'Avillier's Spain. Illustrated by DORÉ. 3*l*. 3*s*.
Dream Book, by E. V. B. 21*s*. 6*d*.
Flammarion's The Atmosphere. 30*s*.
Goethe's Faust, illustrations by P. KONEWKA. 10*s*. 6*d*.
Goufté's Royal Cookery Book. Coloured plates. 42*s*.
—— Ditto. Popular edition. 10*s*. 6*d*.
—— Book of Preserves. 10*s*. 6*d*.
Hans Brinker. 7*s*. 6*d*.
Hazard's Santa Domingo. 18*s*.
—— Cuba. 15*s*.
Heber (Bishop) Hymns. Illustrated edition. 7*s*. 6*d*.
How to Build a House. By VIOLLET-LE-DUC. 8vo. 12*s*.
Jacquemart's History of the Ceramic Art. 42*s*.
Koldewey's North German Polar Expedition. 1*l*. 15*s*.
MacGahan's Campaigning on the Oxus. 7*s*. 6*d*.
Markham (Capt.) Whaling Cruise to Baffin's Bay. 7*s*. 6*d*.
Markham (Clements) Threshold of the Unknown Region. 10*s*. 6*d*.
Markham's Cruise of the Rosario. 16*s*.
Masterpieces of the Pitti Palace. 3*l*. 13*s*. 6*d*.
Milton's Paradise Lost. (Martin's plates). 3*l*. 13*s*. 6*d*.
My Lady's Cabinet. 21*s*.
Palliser (Mrs.) History of Lace. 21*s*.
—— Historic Devices, &c. 21*s*.
Pike's Sub-Tropical Rambles. 18*s*.
Read's Leaves from a Sketch Book. 25*s*.
Red Cross Knight (The). 25*s*.
Schiller's Lay of the Bell. 14*s*.
Stanley's How I Found Livingstone. 7*s*. 6*d*.
—— Coomassie and Magdala. 16*s*.
Sullivan's Dhow Chasing. 16*s*.
Thompson's Old English Homes. 2*l*. 2*s*.
Thomson's Straits of Malacca. 21*s*.
Verne (Jules) Books. 12 vols. *See* Alphabet.
Werner (Carl) Nile Sketches. 2 Series, each 3*l*. 10*s*.
Wilson's Rambles in Northern India. 21*s*.

In the Isle of Wight. Two volumes, crown 8vo., cloth. 21*s*.

ACK HAZARD, a Story of Adventure by J. T. TROWBRIDGE. Numerous illustrations, small post. 3s. 6d.

Jackson (H.) Argus Fairbairne; or, a Wrong Never Righted. By HENRY JACKSON, Author of "Hearth Ghosts," &c. Three volumes, crown 8vo., cloth, 31s. 6d.

Jacquemart (J.) History of the Ceramic Art: Descriptive and Analytical Study of the Potteries of all Times and of all Nations. By ALBERT JACQUEMART. 200 Woodcuts by H. Catenacci and J. Jacquemart. 12 Steel-plate Engravings, and 1,000 Marks and Monograms. Translated by Mrs. BURY PALLISER. In 1 vol., super royal 8vo., of about 700 pp., cloth extra, gilt edges, 42s. [*Ready.*

"This is one of those few gift books which, while they can certainly lie on a table and look beautiful, can also be read through with real pleasure and profit."—*Times*.

Jessup (H. H.) The Women of the Arabs. With a Chapter for Children. By the Rev. HENRY HARRIS JESSUP, D.D., seventeen years American Missionary in Syria. Crown 8vo., cloth extra, 10s. 6d.

Jilted. A Novel. 3 vols. Second Edition. 1l. 11s. 6d.

John Holdsworth, Chief Mate. By the Author of "Jilted." 3 vols., crown 8vo. Second Edition. 31s. 6d.

Johnson (R. B.) Very Far West Indeed. A few rough Experiences on the North-West Pacific Coast. Cr. 8vo. cloth. 10s. 6d. New Edition—the Fourth, fancy boards. 2s.

ENNAN (G.) Tent Life in Siberia. 3rd edition. 6s.

Kennaway (L. J.) Crusts. A Settler's Fare due South; or, Life in New Zealand. Illustrations by the Author. Crown 8vo., cloth extra. 5s.

Kennedy's (Capt. W. R.) Sporting Adventures in the Pacific. With Illustrations. [*Shortly.*

King (Clarence) Mountaineering in the Sierra Nevada. Crown 8vo. Third and Cheaper Edition, cloth extra. 6s.

The *Times* says:—"If we judge his descriptions by the vivid impressions they leave, we feel inclined to give them very high praise."

Koldewey (Capt.) The Second North German Polar Expedition in the Year 1869-70, of the Ships "Germania" and "Hansa," under command of Captain Koldewey. Edited and condensed by H. W. BATES, Esq., and Translated by LOUIS MERCIER, M.A. (Oxon.) Numerous Woodcuts, Maps, and Chromo-lithographs. Royal 8vo, cloth extra. 1l. 15s.

LANE (Laura C. M.) Gentleman Verschoyle.
3 vols. 1*l*. 11*s*. 6*d*.

Lang (Dr. J. D.) An Historical and Statistical Account of New South Wales, from its Founding of the Colony in 1788 to the present day, including details of the remarkable discoveries of Gold, Copper, and Tin in that Colony. By JOHN DUNMORE LANG, D.D., A.M., Senior Minister of the Scotch Church, Sydney. Fourth Edition. In 2 vols., crown 8vo, cloth extra. 1*l*. 1*s*.

Lang (Dr. J. D.) The Coming Event. 8vo. 12*s*.

Leared (A.). Morocco and the Moors. Being an Account of Travels, with a general Description of the Country and its People. By ARTHUR LEARED, M.D., Member of the Royal Irish Academy, and of the Icelandic Literary Society. With Illustrations, 8vo., cloth extra, 18*s*.

Leavitt's (Professor J. M.) New World Tragedies.

Le Duc (V.) How to Build a House. By VIOLLET LE DUC, Author of "The Dictionary of Architecture," &c. Numerous Illustrations, Plans &c. One vol., medium 8vo, cloth, gilt edges. Second Edition. 12*s*.

—— **Annals of a Fortress.** Numerous Illustrations and Diagrams. Demy 8vo, cloth extra. 15*s*.

—— **The Habitations of Man in all Ages.** By E. VIOLLET-LE-DUC. Illustrated by 103 Woodcuts. Translated by BENJAMIN BUCKNALL, Architect. 8vo., cloth extra. 16*s*.

—— **Lectures on Architecture.** By VIOLLET-LE-DUC. Translated from the French by BENJAMIN BUCKNALL, Architect. In 2 vols., royal 8vo., 3*l*. 3*s*. [*In the Press.*

—— **On Restoration.** By VIOLLET-LE-DUC, and a Notice of his Works in connection with the Historical Monuments of France. By CHARLES WETHERED. Crown 8vo., with a Portrait on Steel of VIOLLET-LE-DUC, cloth extra, 2*s*. 6*d*. [*Ready.*

Lessing's Laocoon: an Essay upon the Limits of Painting and Poetry, with remarks illustrative of various points in the History of Ancient Art. By GOTTHOLD EPHRAIM LESSING. A New Translation by ELLEN FROTHINGHAM, crown 8vo. cloth extra. 5*s*.

L'Estrange (Sir G. B.) Recollections of Sir George B. L'Estrange. With Heliotype reproductions. 8vo. cloth extra. 14*s*.

Lindsay (W. S.) History of Merchant Shipping and Ancient Commerce. Over 150 Illustrations, Maps, and Charts. In 4 vols., demy 8vo. cloth extra. Vols. 1 and 2, 21*s*. each; vols. 3 and 4, 24*s*. each; 4 vols. £4 10*s*.
"Another standard work."—*The Times.*

Little Preacher. 32mo. 1*s*.

Locker (A.) The Village Surgeon. A Fragment of Autobiography. By ARTHUR LOCKER, Author of "Sweet Seventeen." Crown 8vo., cloth. New Edition. 3*s*. 6*d*.

Low's German Series.

The attention of the Heads of Colleges and Schools is respectfully directed to this New Series of German School Books, which has been projected with a view to supply a long-felt want, viz.: thoroughly reliable Text-Books, edited by German scholars of the highest reputation, and at a price which will bring them within the reach of all. The Series will comprise:—

1. **The Illustrated German Primer.** Being the easiest introduction to the study of German for all beginners. 1s.
2. **The Children's Own German Book.** A Selection of Amusing and Instructive Stories in Prose. Edited by Dr. A. L. MEISSNER, Professor of Modern Languages in the Queen's University in Ireland. Small post 8vo., cloth. 1s. 6d.
3. **The First German Reader, for Children from ten to fourteen.** Edited by Dr. A. L. MEISSNER. Small post 8vo., cloth. 1s. 6d.
4. **The Second German Reader.** Edited by Dr. A. L. MEISSNER. Small post 8vo., cloth. 1s. 6d. [*In preparation.*

Buchheim's Deutsche Prosa. Two volumes, sold separately:—

5. **Schiller's Prosa.** Containing Selections from the Prose Works of Schiller, with Notes for English Students. By Dr. BUCHHEIM, Professor of the German Language and Literature, King's College, London. Small post 8vo. 2s. 6d. [*Ready.*
6. **Goethe's Prosa.** Containing Selections from the Prose Works of Goethe, with Notes for English Students. By Dr. BUCHHEIM. Small post 8vo. [*In preparation.*

Low's Half-Crown Series, choicely bound, cloth, gilt edges, small post 8vo.

1. **Sea-Gull Rock.** By JULES SANDEAU. Numerous Illustrations.
2. **The House on Wheels.** By Madame STOLZ. Numerous Illustrations.
3. **The Mistress of the Manse.** By Dr. HOLLAND.
4. **Undine, and the Two Captains.** By FOUQUÉ. Illustrations.
5. **Draxy Miller's Dowry and the Elder's Wife.**
6. **The Four Gold Pieces.** By Madame GOURAUD. Numerous Illustrations.
7. **Picciola; or, The Prison Flower.** By X. B. SAINTINE. Numerous Illustrations.
8. **Robert's Holidays.** Profusely Illustrated.
9. **The Two Children of St. Domingo.** Profusely Illustrated.
10. **The Pearl of Orr's Island.**
11. **The Minister's Wooing.**
12. **Aunt Jo's Scrap Bag.**

Low's Copyright and Cheap Editions of American Authors, comprising Popular Works, reprinted by arrangement with their Authors:—

1. **Haunted Hearts.** By the Author of "The Lamplighter."
2. **The Guardian Angel.** By "The Autocrat of the Breakfast Table."
3. **The Minister's Wooing.** By the Author of "Uncle Tom's Cabin."
4. **Views Afoot.** By BAYARD TAYLOR.
5. **Kathrina, Her Life and Mine.** By J. G. HOLLAND.
6. **Hans Brinker: or, Life in Holland.** By Mrs. DODGE.
7. **Men, Women, and Ghosts.** By Miss PHELPS.
8. **Society and Solitude.** By RALPH WALDO EMERSON.
9. **Hedged In.** By ELIZABETH PHELPS.

Low's Copyright and Cheap Editions, *continued—*

11. Faith Gartney.
12. Stowe's Old Town Folks. 2s. 6d.; cloth, 3s.
13. Lowell's Study Windows.
14. My Summer in a Garden. By CHARLES DUDLEY WARNER.
15. Pink and White Tyranny. By Mrs. STOWE.
16. We Girls. By Mrs. WHITNEY.
17. Other Girls. By Mrs. WHITNEY. 2s.
20. Back-Log Studies. By CHARLES DUDLEY WARNER, Author of "My Summer in a Garden."
   "This is a delightful book."—*Atlantic Monthly.*
22. Hitherto. By Mrs. T. D. WHITNEY. Double Volume, 2s. 6d. fancy flexible boards.
23. Farm Ballads. by Will. Carleton. 1s.

Low's Standard Library of Travel and Adventure.
Crown 8vo. Bound uniformly in cloth extra.

1. The Great Lone Land. By W. F. BUTLER. With Illustrations and Map. Fifth Edition. 7s. 6d.
2. The Wild North Land: the Story of a Winter Journey with Dogs across Northern North America. By W. F. BUTLER. With numerous Woodcuts and a Map. Fifth Edition. 7s. 6d.
3. How I Found Livingstone. By H. M. STANLEY. Introductory Chapter on the Death of Livingstone, with a Brief Memoir. 7s. 6d.
4. The Threshold of the Unknown Region. By C. R. MARKHAM. With Maps and Illustrations. Fourth Edition, with Additional Chapters. 10s. 6d.
5. A Whaling Cruise to Baffin's Bay and the Gulf of Boothia. By A. H. MARKHAM. New Edition. Two Maps and several Illustrations. 7s. 6d.
6. Campaigning on the Oxus. By J. A. MACGAHAN. Fourth Edition. 7s. 6d. [*Shortly.*
7. Akim-foo: the History of a Failure. By MAJOR W. F. BUTLER. New edition. 7s. 6d.
   ⁎ *Other volumes in preparation.*

Low's Standard Novels. Crown 8vo. 6s. each, cloth extra.

Three Feathers. By WILLIAM BLACK.
A Daughter of Heth. Thirteenth Edition. By W. BLACK. With Frontispiece by F. WALKER, A.R.A.
Kilmeny. A Novel. By W. BLACK.
In Silk Attire. By W. BLACK.
Alice Lorraine. By R. D. BLACKMORE.
Lorna Doone. By R. D. BLACKMORE. Eighth Edition.
Cradock Nowell. By R. D. BLACKMORE.
Clara Vaughan. By R. D. BLACKMORE.
Innocent. By Mrs. OLIPHANT. Eight Illustrations.
Work: a Story of Experience. By LOUISA M. ALCOTT. Illustrations. (*See also* "Rose Library.")
Mistress Judith: a Cambridgeshire Story. By C. C. FRAZER-TYTLER.
Ninety-Three. By VICTOR HUGO. Numerous illustrations.

Low's Handbook to the Charities of London for 1874.
Edited and Revised to February, 1875, by CHARLES MACKESON, F.S.S., Editor of "A Guide to the Churches of London and its Suburbs," &c Price 1s.

Lunn (J. C.) Only Eve. 3 vols. 31s. 6d.

Lyne (A. A.) The Midshipman's Trip to Jerusalem.
With illustration. Third Edition. Crown 8vo., cloth. 10s. 6d.

Lyra Sacra Americana. Gems of American Poetry, selected and arranged, with Notes and Biographical Sketches, by C. D. CLEVELAND, D. D. author of the " Milton Concordance." 18mo. 4s. 6d.

AC GAHAN (J. A.) Campaigning on the Oxus and the Fall of Khiva. With Map and numerous Illustrations. Fourth Edition. Small post 8vo., cloth extra, 7s. 6d. *See also* Low's Library of Travel and Adventure.

―――― **Under the Northern Lights**; or, The Cruise of the Pandora to Peel's Straits in Search of Sir John Franklin's Papers. With Illustrations by Mr. DE WYLDE, who accompanied the Expedition. Demy 8vo., cloth extra. [*Shortly.*

Macgregor (John,) "Rob Roy" on the Baltic. Third Edition, small post 8vo. 2s. 6d.

―――― **A Thousand Miles in the "Rob Roy" Canoe.** Eleventh Edition. Small post, 8vo. 2s. 6d.

―――― **Description of the "Rob Roy" Canoe,** with plans, &c. 1s.

―――― **The Voyage Alone in the Yawl "Rob Roy."** Second Edition. Small post, 8vo. 5s.

Mahony (M. F.) A Chronicle of the Fermors; Horace Walpole in Love. By M. F. MAHONY. 2 vols. demy 8vo., with steel portrait. 24s.

Manigault, The Maid of Florence; or, a Woman's Vengeance. 3s. 6d.

March (A.) Anglo-Saxon Reader. 8vo. 7s. 6d.

―――― **Comparative Grammar of the Anglo-Saxon Language.** 8vo. 12s.

Marigold Manor. By Miss WARING. With Introduction by Rev. A. SEWELL. With Illustrations. Small post 8vo. 4s.

Markham (A. H.) The Cruise of the "Rosario." By A. H. MARKHAM, Commander, R.N. 8vo. cloth extra, with Map and Illustrations. 16s.

―――― **A Whaling Cruise to Baffin's Bay and the Gulf of Boothia.** With an Account of the Rescue, by his Ship, of the Survivors of the Crew of the "Polaris;" and a Description of Modern Whale Fishing. Third and Cheaper Edition. Crown 8vo. 2 Maps and several Illustrations. Cloth extra. 7s. 6d.

Markham (C. R.) The Threshold of the Unknown Region.
Crown 8vo. with Four Maps. Fourth Edition. With additional chapters, giving the history of our present expedition as far as known, and an account of the cruise of the Pandora. Cloth extra. 10s. 6d.

Marlitt (Miss) The Princess of the Moor. Tauchnitz Translations.

Marsh (G. P.) Origin and History of the English Language. 8vo. 16s.

―― **The Earth, as modified by human action,** being a New Edition of "Man and Nature." Royal 8vo., cloth, 18s.

―― **Lectures on the English Language.** 8vo. 15s.

Martin's Vineyard. By Agnes Harrison. Crown 8vo. cloth. 10s. 6d.

Mason (C. W.) The Rape of the Gamp. 3 vols. 31s. 6d.

Masterpieces of the Pitti Palace, and other Picture Galleries of Florence, with some Account of the Artists and their Paintings. Atlas 4to. handsomely bound in cloth extra, gilt edges. 3l. 13s. 6d.

Maury (Commander) Physical Geography of the Sea and its Meteorology. Being a Reconstruction and Enlargement of his former Work; with illustrative Charts and Diagrams. New Edition. Crown 8vo. 6s.

Price 1s 6d., a New Monthly Periodical. (See also page 47.)
Men of Mark; a Gallery of Contemporary Portraits (taken from Life of the most eminent men of the day). Printed in Permanent Photography. With brief Biographical Notices. A specimen of the Photographs, mounted complete, will be forwarded on receipt of six penny stamps.

"The miniatures now before us retain the personal characteristics, the expression peculiar to each face, and the air of the sitter, with *great good fortune*. The book is sure to succeed as a serious companion to 'Vanity Fair.'"—*Athenæum*.

"It contains three splendid photographs, rendered permanent by the Woodbury process, and is got up in faultless style."—*Globe*.

Mercier (Rev. L.) Outlines of the Life of the Lord Jesus Christ. 2 vols. crown 8vo. 15s.

Michell (N.) The Heart's Great Rulers, a Poem, and Wanderings from the Rhine to the South Sea Islands. Fcap. 8vo. 3s. 6d.

Milton's Complete Poetical Works; with Concordance by W. D. CLEVELAND. New Edition. 8vo. 12s.; morocco 1l. 1s.

Miss Dorothy's Charge. By FRANK LEE BENEDICT, Author of "My Cousin Elenor." 3 vols. crown 8vo. 31s. 6d.

List of Publications. 29

Missionary Geography (The); a Manual of Missionary Operations in all parts of the World, with Map and Illustrations. Fcap. 3s. 6d.

Mistress Judith. A Cambridgeshire Story. By C. C. FRASER-TYTLER, Author of "Jasmine Leigh." A New and Cheaper Edition. In one volume, small post 8vo., cloth extra. 6s.

Mohr (E.). To the Victoria Falls of the Zambesi. By EDWARD MOHR. Translated by N. D'ANVERS. Numerous Full-page and other Woodcut Illustrations, and four beautiful Chromolithographs and a Map. 1 vol., demy 8vo., cloth extra. 24s.

Mongolia, Travels in. *See* Prejevalsky.

Monk of Monk's Own. 3 vols. 31s. 6d.

Montaigne's Essays. *See* Gentle Life Series.

Moody (Emma). Echoes of the Heart. A Collection of upwards of 200 Sacred Poems. 16mo. cloth, gilt edges, price 3s. 6d.

Morocco, Adventures in. *See* ROHLFS.

—— and the Moors. *See* LEARED.

Mountain (Bishop) Life of. By his Son. 8vo. 10s. 6d.

Mundy (D. L.) Rotomahana, or the Boiling Springs of New Zealand. Sixteen large Permanent Photographs, with descriptive Letterpress. By D. L. MUNDY. Edited by Dr. F. VON HOCHSTETTER. Imperial 4to. cloth extra. 42s. Second Edition.

My Cousin Maurice. A Novel. 3 vols. Cloth, 31s. 6d.

My Lady's Cabinet. Charmingly Decorated with Lovely Drawings and Exquisite Miniatures. Contains Seventy-five Pictures. Royal 4to., and very handsomely bound in cloth. 1l. 1s.

NAPOLEON I., Recollections of. By Mrs. ABELL. Third Edition. Revised with additional matter by her daughter, Mrs. CHARLES JOHNSTONE. Demy 8vo. With Steel Portrait and Woodcuts. Cloth extra, gilt edges, 10s. 6d.

Napoleon III. in Exile: The Posthumous Works and Unpublished Autographs. Collected and arranged by COUNT DE LA CHAPELLE. 8vo., cloth extra. 14s.

Narrative of Edward Crewe, The. Personal Adventures and Experiences in New Zealand. Small post 8vo., cloth extra. 5s.

Never Again: a Novel. By Dr. MAYO, Author of "Kaloolah." New and Cheaper Edition, in One Vol., small post 8vo. 6s. Cheapest edition, fancy boards, 2s.

New Testament. The Authorized English Version; with the various Readings from the most celebrated Manuscripts, including the Sinaitic, the Vatican, and the Alexandrian MSS., in English. With Notes by the Editor, Dr. TISCHENDORF. The whole revised and carefully collected for the Thousandth Volume of Baron Tauchnitz's Collection. Cloth flexible, gilt edges, 2s. 6d.; cheaper style, 2s.; or sewed, 1s. 6d.

Noel (Hon. Roden) Livingstone in Africa; a Poem. By the Hon. RODEN NOEL, Author of "Beatrice," &c. Post 8vo., limp cloth extra, 2s. 6d.

Nordhoff (C.) California: for Health, Pleasure, and Residence. A Book for Travellers and Settlers. Numerous Illustrations. 8vo., cloth extra. 12s. 6d.

—— **Northern California, Oregon, and the Sandwich Islands.** Square 8vo., cloth extra, price 12s. 6d.

Nothing to Wear, and Two Millions. By WILLIAM ALLEN BUTLER. 1s.

Novum Testamentum Græce. Edidit OSCAR DE GEBHARDT. 18mo. cloth. 3s. 6d.

LD **English Homes.** *See* Thompson.

Old Fashioned Girl. See Alcott.

Old Masters. Da Vinci, Bartolomeo, Michael Angelo, Romagna, Carlo Dolci, &c., &c. Reproduced in Photography from the Celebrated Engravings by Longhi, Anderloni, Garavaglia, Toschi, and Raimondi, in the Collection of Prints and Drawings in the British Museum, with Biographical Notices. By STEPHEN THOMPSON. Imperial folio, cloth extra. 3l. 13s. 6d.

Oleographs. *See* page 45.

Oliphant (Mrs.) Innocent. A Tale of Modern Life. By Mrs. OLIPHANT, Author of "The Chronicles of Carlingford," &c., &c. With Eight full-page Illustrations. Small post 8vo., cloth extra. 6s.

On the Rock. *See* Whitall.

One Only; A Novel. By Eleanor C. PRICE. 2 vols. Crown 8vo., cloth, 21s.

Only Eve. By Mrs. J. CALBRAITH LUNN. Three Vols. post 8vo. cloth. 31s. 6d.

Our American Cousins at Home. By VERA, Author of "Under the Red Cross." Illustrated with Pen and Ink Sketches, by the Author, and several fine Photographs. Crown 8vo, cloth. 9s.

Our Little Ones in Heaven. Edited by Rev. H. ROBBINS. With Frontispiece after Sir JOSHUA REYNOLDS. Fcap. cloth extra. New Edition, the Third, with Illustrations. Price 5s. About March, 1876.

List of Publications. 31

ALLISER (Mrs.) A History of Lace, from the Earliest Period. A New and Revised Edition, with additional cuts and text, with upwards of 100 Illustrations and coloured Designs. 1 vol. 8vo. 1*l*. 1*s*. Third Edition.

" One of the most readable books of the season ; permanently valuable, always interesting, often amusing, and not inferior in all the essentials of a gift book."—*Times.*

―――― Historic Devices, Badges, and War Cries. 8vo. 1*l*. 1*s*.

―――― The China Collector's Pocket Companion. With upwards of 1,000 Illustrations of Marks and Monograms. Second Edition, with Additions. Small post 8vo., limp cloth, 5*s*.

" We scarcely need add that a more trustworthy and convenient handbook does not exist, and that others besides ourselves will feel grateful to Mrs. Palliser for the care and skill she has bestowed upon it."—*Academy.*

The first attempt at a full and connected military history of the whole war.

Paris (Comte de). History of the Civil War in America. By the COMTE DE PARIS. Translated, with the approval of the Author, by LOUIS F. TASISTRO. Edited by HENRY COPPÉE, LL.D. Volume I. (Embracing, without abridgment, the First Two Volumes of the French Edition). With Maps faithfully engraved from the Originals, and printed in three colours. 8vo., cloth, 18*s*.

Parisian Family. From the French of Madame GUIZOT DE WITT. Fcap. 5*s*.

Phelps (Miss) Gates Ajar. 32mo. 6*d*.

―――― Men, Women, and Ghosts. 12mo. Sd. 1*s*.6*d*. ; cl. 2*s*.

―――― Hedged In. 12mo. Sewed, 1*s*. 6*d*. ; cloth, 2*s*.

―――― Silent Partner. 5*s*.

―――― Trotty's Wedding Tour. Small post 8vo. 3*s*. 6*d*.

―――― What to Wear. Foolscap 8vo., fancy boards. 1*s*.

Phillips (L.) Dictionary of Biographical Reference. 8vo. 1*l*. 11*s*. 6*d*.

Photography (History and Handbook of). *See* Tissandier.

Picture Gallery of British Art (The). Thirty-eight beautiful and Permanent Photographs after the most celebrated English Painters. With Descriptive Letterpress. Vols. 1 to 4, cloth extra, 18*s*. each. Each parate and complete in itself.

*** *For particulars of the Monthly Parts, see page* 46.

Pike (N.) Sub-Tropical Rambles in the Land of the Aphanapteryx. In 1 vol. demy 8vo. 18s. Profusely Illustrated from the Author's own Sketches, also with Maps and valuable Meteorological Charts.

Plutarch's Lives. An Entirely New and Library Edition. Edited by A. H. Clough, Esq. 5 vols. 8vo., 2l. 10s.; half morocco, top gilt, 3l.

—— **Morals.** Uniform with Clough's Edition of " Lives of Plutarch." Edited by Professor Goodwin. 5 vols. 8vo. 3l. 3s.

Poe (E. A.) The Works of. 4 vols. 2l. 2s.

Poems of the Inner Life. A New Edition, Revised, with many additional Poems, inserted by permission of the Authors. Small post 8vo., cloth. 5s.

Polar Expedition. *See* **Koldeway and Markham.**

Portraits of Celebrated Women. By C. A. Ste.-Beuve. 12mo. 6s. 6d.

Preces Veterum. Collegit et edidit Joannes F. France. Crown 8vo., cloth, red edges. 5s.

Prejevalsky (N. M.). Travels in Mongolia. By N. M. Prejevalsky, Lieutenant-Colonel, Russian Staff. Translated by E. Delmar Morgan, F.R.G.S., and Annotated by Colonel Yule, C.B. 2 vols., demy 8vo., cloth extra, with numerous Illustrations and Maps.

Preu (M. T.) German Primer. Square cloth. 2s. 6d.

Prime (I.) Fifteen Years of Prayer. Small post 8vo., cloth. 3s. 6d.

—— **(E. D. G.) Around the World.** Sketches of Travel through Many Lands and over Many Seas. 8vo., Illustrated. 14s.

—— **(W. C.) I go a-Fishing.** Small post 8vo., cloth. 5s.

Publishers' Circular (The), and General Record of British and Foreign Literature; giving a transcript of the title-page of every work published in Great Britain, and every work of interest published abroad, with lists of all the publishing houses.
Published regularly on the 1st and 15th of every Month, and forwarded post free to all parts of the world on payment of 8s. per annum.

(*See also* page 48.)

Purdy (W.) The City Life, a Review of Finance and Commerce. Crown 8vo., cloth.

Ralston (W. R. S.) Early Russian History. Four Lectures delivered at Oxford by W. R. S. Ralston, M.A. Crown 8vo., cloth extra. 5s.

Randolph (Mrs.) Clarice Adair. 3 vols. 1l. 11s. 6d. Second Edition.

Rasselas, Prince of Abyssinia. By Dr. JOHNSON. With Introduction by the Rev. WILLIAM WEST, Vicar of Nairn. (Bayard Series.) 2s. 6d.

Read (S.) Leaves from a Sketch Book: Pencillings of Travel at Home and Abroad. By SAMUEL READ. Royal 4to. containing about 130 Engravings on Wood, cloth extra. 25s.

"We do not think that the season is likely to yield a more artistic, suggestive, and beautiful gift-book than this."—*Nonconformist*.

Reminiscences of America in 1869, by Two Englishmen. Crown 8vo. 7s. 6d.

Retzsch (M.) Outlines to Burger's Ballads. Etchings by MORITZ RETZSCH. With Text, Explanations, and Notes. Designs. Oblong 4to., cloth extra. 10s 6d.

——— **Outlines to Goethe's Faust.** Etchings by MORITZ RETZSCH. 26 Etchings. Oblong 4to., cloth extra. 10s. 6d.

——— **Outlines to Schiller's "Fight with the Dragon,"** and "Fredoline." Etchings by MORITZ RETZSCH. 26 Etchings. Oblong 4to., cloth extra. 10s. 6d.

——— **Outlines to Schiller's "Lay of the Bell."** Comprising 42 Etchings, after Designs engraved by MORITZ RETZSCH. With Lord Lytton's Translation. New Edition. Oblong 4to., cloth extra. 10s. 6d.

Reynard the Fox. The Prose Translation by the late THOMAS ROSCOE. With about 100 exquisite Illustrations on Wood, after designs by A. J. ELWES. Imperial 16mo. cloth extra, 7s. 6d.

Richardson (A. S.) Stories from Old English Poetry. Small post 8vo., cloth. 5s.

Rivington's (F.) Life of St. Paul. With map. 5s.

Rochefoucauld's Reflections. Flexible cloth extra. 2s. 6d. (Bayard Series.)

Rogers (S.) Pleasures of Memory. See "Choice Editions of Choice Books." 2s. 6d.

Rohlfs (Dr. G.) Adventures in Morocco and Journeys through the Oases of Draa and Tafilet. By Dr. GERHARD ROHLFS, Gold Medallist of the Royal Geographical Society. Translated from the German. With an Introduction by WINWOOD READE. Demy 8vo. Map, and Portrait of the Author, cloth extra, 12s.

Rose Library (The). Popular Literature of all countries. 1s. each volume. Many of the volumes are Illustrated. The following volumes are now ready:—

1. **Sea-Gull Rock.** By JULES SANDEAU. Illustrated. 1s.
2. **Little Women.** By LOUISA M. ALCOTT. 1s.
3. **Little Women Wedded.** (Forming a Sequel to "Little Women." 1s.
4. **The House on Wheels.** By MADAME DE STOLZ. Illustrated. 1s.
5. **Little Men.** By LOUISA M. ALCOTT. 1s.
6. **The Old-Fashioned Girl.** By LOUISA M. ALCOTT. 1s.
7. **The Mistress of the Manse.** By J. G. HOLLAND. 1s.
8. **Timothy Titcomb's Letters to Young People, Single and Married.** 1s.

Rose Library (The), *continued—*

9. **Undine, and the Two Captains.** By Baron DE LA MOTTE FOUQUE. A new Translation by F. E. BUNNETT. Illustrated. 1s.
10. **Draxy Miller's Dowry and the Elder's Wife.** By SAXE HOLM. 1s.
11. **The Four Gold Pieces.** By Madame GOURAUD. Numerous Illustrations. 1s.
12. **Work: a Story of Experience.** First Portion. By LOUISA M. ALCOTT. 1s.
13. **Beginning Again**: being a continuation of "Work." By LOUISA M. ALCOTT. 1s.
14. **Picciola ; or, The Prison Flower.** By X. B. SAINTINE. Numerous graphic Illustrations. 1s.
15. **Robert's Holidays.** Illustrated. 1s.
16. **The Two Children of St. Domingo.** Numerous Illustrations. 1s.
17. **Aunt Jo's Scrap Bag.** 1s.
18. **Stowe (Mrs. H. B.) The Pearl of Orr's Island.** 1s
19. —— **The Minister's Wooing.** 1s.
20. —— **Betty's Bright Idea.** 1s.
21. —— **The Ghost in the Mill.** 1s.
22. —— **Captain Kidd's Money.** 1s.
23. —— **We and Our Neighbours.** (Double vol.), 2s.
24. —— **My Wife and I.** (Double vol.), 2s.
25. **Hans Brinker, or the Silver Skates.** 1s.
26. **Lowell's My Study Window.** 1s.
27. **Holmes (O. W.) The Guardian Angel.**
28. **Warner (C. D.) My Summer in a Garden.**

Notice.—The Volumes in this Series are also published in a more expensive form on fine toned paper, cloth extra, gilt edges, at 2s. 6d. or 3s. 6d. each, according to size, &c. *See* LOW's Half-Crown Series.

Ruth and Gabriel. A Novel. By LAURENCE CHENY.
"The reader's interest is sustained from the first page to the last."— *Scotsman.*

SANTO DOMINGO, Past and Present. *See* Hazard.

Sauer's (E.) Handbook of European Commerce. What to Buy and Where to Buy it, &c. By GEORGE SAUER, for many years Correspondent of the "New York Herald." Crown 8vo., cloth. 5s. [*In the press.*

Schiller's Lay of the Bell, translated by Lord Lytton. With 42 illustrations after Retsch. Oblong 4to. 10s. 6d.

School Prizes. *See* Books.

Schuyler (E.) Turkistan. *See* Turkistan.

Schweinfurth (Dr. G.) The Heart of Africa; or, Three Years' Travels and Adventures in the Unexplored Regions of the Centre of Africa. By Dr. GEORG SCHWEINFURTH. Translated by ELLEN E. FREWER. Two volumes, 8vo., upwards of 500 pages each, with 130 Woodcuts from Drawings made by the Author, and 2 Maps. 42s. [*Second Edition.*

—— **Artes Africanæ.** Illustrations and Descriptions of Productions of the Natural Arts of Central African Tribes. With 26 Lithographed Plates. Imperial 4to., boards. 28s. [*Ready.*

Sea-Gull Rock. By Jules Sandeau, of the French Academy. Translated by ROBERT BLACK, M.A. With Seventy-nine very beautiful Woodcuts. Royal 16mo., cloth extra, gilt edges. 7s. 6d. Cheaper Edition, cloth gilt, 2s. 6d. *See also* Rose Library.

"It deserves to please the new nation of boys to whom it is presented."
—*Times.*

Shooting: its Appliances, Practice, and Purpose. By JAMES DALZIEL DOUGALL, F.S.A., F.Z.A., Author of "Scottish Field Sports," &c. Crown 8vo., cloth extra. 10s. 6d.

"The book is admirable in every way . . . . We wish it every success."—*Globe.*

"A very complete treatise . . . Likely to take high rank as an authority on shooting."—*Daily News.*

Silent Hour (The). *See* Gentle Life Series.

Simson (W.) A History of the Gipsies, with specimens of the Gipsy Language. 10s. 6d. New Edition.

Sketches from an Artist's Portfolio. By SYDNEY P. HALL. Folio, cloth extra. 3l. 3s.

N. B.—This volume contains about 60 Facsimiles of the original Sketches by this well-known Artist during his travels in various parts of Europe.

"A portfolio which any one might be glad to call their own."—*Times.*

Sketches of Life and Scenery in Australia. By a Twenty five Years' Resident. 1 vol., demy 8vo., cloth extra. 14s.

Smith (G.) Assyrian Explorations and Discoveries. By GEORGE SMITH (of the British Museum). Illustrated by Photographs and numerous Woodcut Illustrations of his recent Discoveries. Demy 8vo. 18s. Fifth edition.

—— **The Chaldean Account of Genesis.** Containing the description of the Creation, the Fall of Man, the Tower of Babel, the Times of the Patriarchs, and Nimrod; Babylonian Fables, and Legends of the Gods; from the Cuneiform Inscriptions. By GEORGE SMITH, of the Department of Oriental Antiquities, British Museum, Author of "History of Assurbanipal," "Assyrian Discoveries," &c., &c. With many Illustrations. Demy 8vo., cloth extra. 16s. Third Edition.

Smith and Hamilton's French Dictionary. 2 vols. Cloth, 21s.; half roan, 22s.

Spain. Illustrated by GUSTAVE DORÉ. Text by the BARON CH. D'AVILLIER. This fine work contains over 240 wood engravings, half of them being full-page size. All after drawings by the celebrated artist. Imperial 4to., elaborately bound in cloth, gilt extra, gilt edges. £3 3s. [*Now ready.*

"In the summer of 1872 the Baron Charles D'Avillier and M. Gustave Doré set out on a long projected tour through Spain. What they saw and heard on that tour is now reproduced in a large and handsome volume, the office of translator being ably filled by Mr. J. Thomson, F.R.G.S. . . . They seem certainly to have made good use of their time these two gentlemen, and have seen pretty nearly everything worth seeing."—*Times.*

Socrates. Memoirs, from Xenophon's Memorabilia. By
E. LEVIEN. Flexible cloth. 2s. 6d. Bayard Series.

Spooner (Very Rev. E.) St. Oswald's Sunday School.
Small post 8vo., cloth. [*In the press.*

Stanley (H. M.) How I Found Livingstone. Crown 8vo.,
cloth extra. 7s. 6d.

*** This Edition has been revised most carefully from beginning to end and all matters of a personal or irrelevant character omitted.

—— "**My Kalulu," Prince, King, and Slave.** A Story from Central Africa. Crown 8vo., about 430 pp., with numerous graphic Illustrations, after Original Designs by the Author. Cloth, 7s. 6d.

—— **Coomassie and Magdala**: A Story of Two British Campaigns in Africa. Demy 8vo., with Maps and Illustrations, 16s. Second Edition.

Steele (Thos.) Under the Palms. A Volume of Verse. By THOMAS STEELE, translator of "An Eastern Love Story." Fcap. 8vo. Cloth, 5s.

Stewart (D.) Outlines of Moral Philosophy, by Dr. McCosh.
New edition. 12mo. 3s. 6d.

—— **Mental Philosophy.** 12mo. 2s. 6d.

Stolz (Madame) The House on Wheels. Small post 8vo.
2s. 6d. *See also* Rose Library.

Stone (J. B.) A Tour with Cook Through Spain. Illustrated by Photographs. Crown 8vo., cloth. 6s.

Storey's (Justice) Works. *See* Low's American Catalogue.

Story without an End, from the German of Carové, by the late Mrs. SARAH T. AUSTIN, crown 4to. with 15 exquisite drawings by E. V. B., printed in colours in facsimile of the original water colours, and numerous other illustrations. New edition. 7s. 6d.

—— square, with illustrations by HARVEY. 2s. 6d.

—— **of the Great March,** a Diary of General Sherman's Campaign through Georgia and the Carolinas. Numerous illustrations. 12mo. cloth, 7s. 6d.

Stowe (Mrs. Beecher). Dred. Tauchnitz edition. 12mo. 3s. 6d.,
also in boards, 1s.

—— **Geography,** with 60 illustrations. Square cloth, 4s. 6d.

—— **Little Foxes.** Cheap edition, 1s.; library edition, 4s. 6d.

List of Publications. 37

Stowe (Mrs. Beecher). Minister's Wooing. 5s.; copyright series, 1s. 6d.; cloth, 2s.

—— Old Town Folk. 6s. Cheap Edition, 2s. 6d.

—— Old Town Fireside Stories. Cloth extra. 3s. 6d.

—— My Wife and I; or, Harry Henderson's History. Small post 8vo, cloth extra. 6s.

—— We and Our Neighbours. 1 vol., small post 8vo., 6s. Sequel to "My Wife and I."

—— Pink and White Tyranny. Small post 8vo. 3s. 6d. Cheap Edition, 1s. 6d. and 2s.

—— Queer Little People. 1s.; cloth, 2s.

—— Chimney Corner. 1s.; cloth, 1s. 6d.

—— The Pearl of Orr's Island. Crown 8vo. 5s.

—— Little Pussey Willow. Fcap. 2s.

—— Woman in Sacred History. Illustrated with 15 chromo-lithographs and about 200 pages of letterpress, forming one of the most elegant and attractive volumes ever published. Demy 4to. cloth extra, gilt edges, price 1l. 5s.

Studies from Nature. Four Plates, with Descriptive Letterpress. By STEPHEN THOMPSON. Imperial 4to., 4s. 6d. each part. Parts 1, 2, 3, and 4. (Complete in 6 parts.) [Now ready.
"Altogether the style of the work is excellent."—British Journal of Photography.

Sub-Tropical Rambles. See Pike (N.)

Suburban Sketches, by the Author of "Venetian Life." Post 8vo. 6s.

Sullivan (G. C.) Dhow Chasing in Zanzibar Waters and on the Eastern Coast of Africa; a Narrative of Five Years' Experiences in the suppression of the Slave Trade. With Illustrations from Photographs and Sketches taken on the spot by the Author. Demy 8vo, cloth extra. 16s. Second Edition.

Summer in Leslie Goldthwaite's Life, by the Author of "The Gayworthys," Illustrations. Fcap. 8vo. 3s. 6d.

Sweet not Lasting. A Novel, by ANNIE B. LEFURT. 1 vol. crown 8vo., cloth. 10s. 6d.

Swiss Family Robinson. 12mo. 3s. 6d.

**AUCHNITZ'S English Editions of German Authors.** Each volume cloth flexible, 2s.; or sewed, 1s. 6d. The following are now ready:—

On the Heights. By B. AUERBACH. 3 vols.
In the Year '13. By FRITZ REUTER. 1 vol.
Faust. By GOETHE. 1 vol.
L'Arrabiata. By PAUL HEYSE. 1 vol.
The Princess, and other Tales. By HEINRICH ZSCHOKKE. 1 vol.
Lessing's Nathan the Wise, and Emilia Galotti.
Hackländer's Behind the Counter, translated by MARY HOWITT. 2 vols.
Three Tales. By W. HAUFF.
Joachim v. Kammern; Diary of a Poor Young Lady. By M. NATHUSIUS.
Poems by Ferdinand Freiligrath. Edited by his daughter.
Gabriel. From the German. By ARTHUR MILMAN.
The Dead Lake, and other Tales. By P. HEYSE.
Through Night to Light. By GUTZKOW.
Flower, Fruit, and Thorn Pieces. By JEAN PAUL RICHTER. 2 vols.
The Princess of the Moor. By Miss MARLITT. 2 vols.
An Egyptian Princess. By G. EBERS. 2 vols.
Ekkehard. By J. V. SCHEFFEL. 2 vols.
Barbarossa and other Tales. By PAUL HEYSE. From the German. By L. C. S.
Wilhelm Meister's Apprenticeship. By GOETHE. 2 vols.
Prince Bismarck, a Biographical Sketch by WILHELM GÖRLACH. 1 vol.
Doubtful Plays of Shakespeare.

Tauchnitz (B.) German and English Dictionary, Paper, 1s.; cloth, 1s. 6d.; roan, 2s.

—————— **French and English.** Paper 1s. 6d.; cloth, 2s.; roan, 2s. 6d.

—————— **Italian and English.** Paper, 1s. 6d.; cloth, 2s.; roan, 2s. 6d.

—————— **Spanish and English.** Paper, 1s. 6d.; cloth, 2s.; roan, 2s. 6d.

—————— **New Testament.** Cloth, 2s.; gilt, 2s. 6d.

Tayler (C. B.) Sacred Records, &c., in Verse. Fcap. 8vo, cloth extra, 2s. 6d.

—————— **Persis. A Narrative of the Seventeenth Century.** Small post 8vo., cloth, 5s.

List of Publications.

Taylor (Bayard) The Byeways of Europe; Visits by Unfrequented Routes to Remarkable Places. By BAYARD TAYLOR, author of "Views Afoot." 2 vols. post 8vo. 16s.

―――― **Travels in Greece and Russia.** Post 8vo. 7s. 6d.

―――― **Northern Europe.** Post 8vo. Cloth, 8s. 6d.

―――― **Egypt and Iceland.** 8s. 6d.

―――― **Beauty and the Beast.** Crown 8vo. 10s. 6d.

―――― **A Summer in Colorado.** Post 8vo. 7s. 6d.

―――― **Joseph and his Friend.** Post 8vo. 10s. 6d.

―――― **Views Afoot.** Enamelled boards, 1s. 6d.; cloth, 2s. *See* Low's Copyright Edition.

Tennyson's May Queen; choicely Illustrated from designs by the Hon. Mrs. BOYLE. Crown 8vo. *See* Choice Series. 2s. 6d.

The Banns of Marriage. By DUTTON COOK, Author of "Hobson's Choice," &c. 2 vols., crown 8vo., 21s.

The Fool of the Family, and other Tales. By JOHN DANGERFIELD. 2 vols., crown 8vo., 21s.

This Indenture Witnesseth. By Mrs. ALFRED HUNT, Author of "Under Seal of Confession," &c. 3 vols., crown 8vo., 31s. 6d.

Thomson (J.) The Straits of Malacca, Indo-China, and China; or, Ten Years' Travels, Adventures, and Residence Abroad. By J. THOMSON, F.R.G.S., Author of "Illustrations of China and its People." Upwards of 60 Woodcuts, from the Author's own Photographs and Sketches. Demy 8vo, cloth extra. 21s.

Thompson (Stephen). Old English Homes: a Summer's Sketch-Book. By STEPHEN THOMPSON, Author of "Swiss Scenery," &c. 25 very fine Permanent Photographs by the Author. Demy 4to., cloth extra, gilt edges, 2l. 2s. [*Ready.*

Thorne (E.) The Queen of the Colonies; or, Queensland as I saw it. 1 vol., with Map. [*Shortly.*

Thornwell Abbas. 2 vols. 21s.

Timothy Titcomb's Letters to Young People, Single and Married. Cloth, 2s. (See also Rose Library.)

Tinne (J. E.) The Wonderland of the Antipodes: Sketches of Travel in the North Island of New Zealand. Illustrated with numerous Photographs. Demy 8vo., cloth extra. 16s.

Tischendorf (Dr.) The New Testament. *See* New Testament.

Tissandier (Gaston). A History and Handbook of Photography. Translated from the French of GASTON TISSANDIER; edited by J. THOMPSON, F.R.G.S. Imperial 16mo., over 300 pages, and 75 Wood Engravings and a Frontispiece, cloth extra, 6s.

" This work should find a place on the shelves of every photographer's library."—*The British Journal of Photography.*

" This capital handbook will tend to raise photography once more to its true position as a science, and to a high place amongst the fine arts." *The Spectator.*

Tolhausen (A.) The Technological Dictionary in the French, English, and German Languages. Containing the Technical Terms used in the Arts, Manufactures, and Industrial Affairs generally. Revised and Augmented by M. Louis Tolhausen, French Consul at Leipzig.

The First Part, containing French-German-English, crown 8vo. 2 vols. sewed, 8s.; 1 vol. half roan, 9s.

The Second Part, containing English-German-French, crown 8vo. 2 vols. sewed, 8s.; 1 vol. bound, 9s.

The Third Part, containing German-English-French. Crown 8vo., 2 vols. sewed, 8s.; 1 vol. bound, 9s.

Trollope (A.) Harry Heathcote of Gangoil. A Story of Bush Life in Australia. With graphic Illustrations. In 1 vol. Small post, cloth extra, 5s. Second Edition.

Trowbridge (A. C.). The Young Surveyor. 1 vol., small post 8vo., cloth extra, with numerous Illustrations, 5s. [*Ready.*

Tuckermann (C. K.) The Greeks of To-day. Crown 8vo. cloth. 7s. 6d.

Turkistan. Notes of a Journey in the Russian Provinces of Central Asia and the Khanates of Bokhara and Kokand. By EUGENE SCHUYLER, Secretary to the American Legation, St. Petersburg. Numerous illustrations. Demy 8vo., cloth extra. [*Nearly ready.*

Turner (Rev. F. S.) British Opium Policy. [*In the press.*

Twining (Miss). Illustrations of the Natural Orders of Plants, with Groups and Descriptions. By ELIZABETH TWINING. Reduced from the folio edition, splendidly illustrated in colours from nature. 2 vols. Royal 8vo. 5l. 5s.

Under Seal of Confession. By AVERIL BEAUMONT, Author of "Thornicroft's Model." 3 vols. crown 8vo., cloth. 31s. 6d.

VANDENHOFF'S (George), Clerical Assistant. Fcap. 3s. 6d.

——— **Ladies' Reader (The).** Fcap. 5s.

List of Publications. 41

VERNE'S (JULES) WORKS.

Five Weeks in a Balloon. New Edition. Numerous Illustrations, printed on Toned Paper, and uniformly with "Around the World," &c. Square crown 8vo. 7s. 6d.

Meridiana : Adventures of Three Englishmen and Three Russians in South Africa. Translated from the French. With Numerous Illustrations. Royal 16mo., cloth extra, gilt edges. 7s. 6d.

The Fur Country. Crown 8vo. With upwards of 80 Illustrations. Cloth extra. 10s. 6d.

Twenty Thousand Leagues Under the Sea. Translated and Edited by the Rev. L. P. MERCIER, M.A. With 113 very Graphic Woodcuts. Large post 8vo., cloth extra, gilt edges. 10s. 6d.

Around the World in Eighty Days. Numerous Illustrations. Square crown 8vo. 7s. 6d.

From the Earth to the Moon, and a Trip Round It. Numerous Illustrations. Crown 8vo., cloth, gilt edges. 10s. 6d. New Edition.

A Floating City and the Blockade Runners. Containing about 50 very fine Full-page Illustrations. Square crown 8vo. Cloth, gilt edges. 7s. 6d.

Dr. Ox's Experiment; Master Zacharius; A Drama in the Air; A Winter Amid the Ice, &c. Numerous full-page Illustrations. Cloth, gilt edges. 7s. 6d.

The Mysterious Island. In 3 Vols., all Illustrated. Square crown 8vo., cloth extra. 7s. 6d. each.

The Titles of the Volumes are :—
1. Dropped from the Clouds.
2. Abandoned.
3. The Secret of the Island.

The Survivors of the Chancellor. 1 vol., square crown 8vo., with many Illustrations. 7s. 6d.

SPECIAL NOTICE.—Messrs. SAMPSON LOW & Co. beg to inform the public, in reply to many inquiries with reference to an announcement of Cheap Editions of JULES VERNE'S WORKS by other houses, that they are the Sole Proprietors of the Copyright in all the Translations of the Works by this Author published by themselves.

The English Copyright of French Works, under the International Copyright Law, being of limited duration, they wish to intimate that, as the original Copyrights fall in by lapse of time (or in anticipation thereof), it is their intention, with a view to meet the requirements of those readers who wish to possess these interesting books, but who are unwilling to purchase the more elaborately illustrated editions, to issue their Copyright Translations in the cheapest possible form. Accordingly, they have prepared and have now ready—

1. Adventures of Three Englishmen and Three Russians in South Africa. Illustrated. 1s.

Verne's (Jules) Works, *continued*—

2. Five Weeks in a Balloon. Illustrated. 1s.
3. A Floating City. Illustrated. 1s.
4. The Blockade Runners. Illustrated. 1s.
5. From the Earth to the Moon. Illustrated. 1s.
6. Around the Moon. Illustrated. 1s.
7. Twenty Thousand Leagues under the Sea. Vol. I. 1s.
8. Ditto ditto Vol. II. 1s.

These volumes are printed in large type, on good paper, contain several Illustrations, and are published at ONE SHILLING EACH, in a very handsome and attractive cover.

N.B.—These works will continue to be sold in the original form, and at the usual prices.

⁎⁎* The remaining and forthcoming works, having yet many years of Copyright to run, and having been produced at an immense expense, both as to Author's Copyright and Illustration, will not yet be brought out in any other form than as at present.

The Public must kindly be careful to order LOW'S AUTHOR'S EDITIONS.

Vincent (F.) The Land of the White Elephant : Sights and Scenes in South-Eastern Asia. With Maps, Plans, and Illustrations. 8vo. cloth extra. 18s.

WALLER (Rev. C. H.) The Names on the Gates of Pearl, and other Studies. By the Rev. C. H. WALLER, M.A. Crown 8vo, cloth extra. 6s.

Warburton's (Col. Egerton) Journey across Australia. An Account of the Exploring Expedition sent out by Messrs. Elder and Hughes, under the command of Colonel Egerton Warburton; giving a full Account of his Perilous Journey from the centre to Roebourne, Western Australia. With Illustrations and a Map. Edited, with an Introductory Chapter, by H. W. BATES, Esq., of the Royal Geographical Society. Demy 8vo. cloth. 16s.

Warner (C. D.) My Summer in a Garden. Boards, 1s. 6d.; cloth, 2s. (Low's Copyright Series.)

—— **Back-log Studies.** Boards 1s. 6d.; cloth 2s. (Low's Copyright Series.)

—— **Mummies and Moslems.** [*In the press.*

Weppner (M.) The Northern Star and Southern Cross. Being the Personal Experiences, Impressions, and Observations of Margaretha Weppner, in a Voyage Round the World. 2 vols. Crown 8vo, cloth. 24s.

Werner (Carl), Nile Sketches, Painted from Nature during his travels through Egypt. Imperial folio, in Cardboard Wrapper. Complete in Five Parts. The four first at £3 10s. each; Part V. at £2 5s.

Westropp (H. M.) A Manual of Precious Stones and Antique Gems. By HODDER M. WESTROPP, Author of "The Traveller's Art Companion," "Pre-Historic Phases," &c. Numerous Illustrations. Small post 8vo, cloth extra. 6s.

Wheaton (Henry) Elements of International Law. New edition. [*In the press.*

When George the Third was King. 2 vols., post 8vo. 21s.

Whitall (Alice B.) On the Rock. A Memoir of Alice B. Whitall, by Mrs. PEARSALL SMITH. Small post, cloth. 2s.

White (J.) Te Rou; or, The Maori at Home. Exhibiting the Social Life, Manners, Habits, and Customs of the Maori Race in New Zealand prior to the introduction of civilization amongst them. Crown 8vo. cloth extra. 10s. 6d.

White (R. G.) Memoirs of the Life of William Shakespeare. Post 8vo. Cloth. 10s. 6d.

Whitney (Mrs. A. D. T.) The Gayworthys. Small post 8vo. 3s. 6d.

——— **Faith Gartney.** Small post 8vo. 3s. 6d. And in Low's Cheap Series, 1s. 6d. and 2s.

——— **Real Folks.** 12mo. crown. 3s. 6d.

——— **Hitherto.** Small post 8vo. 3s. 6d. and 2s. 6d.

——— **Sights and Insights.** 3 vols. crown. 31s. 6d.

——— **Summer in Leslie Goldthwaite's Life.** Small post 8vo. 3s. 6d.

——— **The Other Girls.** Small post 8vo., cloth extra. 3s. 6d.

——— **We Girls.** Small post 8vo. 3s. 6d. Cheap Edition. 1s. 6d. and 2s.

Whyte (J. W. H.) A Land Journey from Asia to Europe. Crown 8vo. 12s.

Wikoff (H.) The Four Civilizations of the World. An Historical Retrospect. Crown 8vo., cloth. 6s.

Wills, A Few Hints on Proving, without Professional Assistance. By a PROBATE COURT OFFICIAL. Fourth Edition, revised and considerably enlarged, with Forms of Wills, Residuary Accounts, &c. Fcap. 8vo., cloth limp. 1s.

Wilson (F. H.). Rambles in Northern India; with Incidents and Descriptions of the many scenes of the Mutiny, including Allahabad, Cawnpore, Delhi, Lucknow, &c., with permanent Photographic Views. By FRANCESCA H. WILSON, Author of "Truth Better than Fiction." 4to., cloth extra, gilt edges. £1 1s.

Winter at the Italian Lakes. With Frontispiece View of Lake Como. Small post 8vo., cloth extra. 7s. 6d.

44 *Sampson Low and Co.'s List of Publications.*

Woman's (A) Faith. A Novel. By the Author of "Ethel."
3 vols. Post 8vo. 31s. 6d.

Wonders of Sculpture. *See* **Viardot.**

Woolsey (C. D., LL.D.). Introduction to the Study of International Law; designed as an Aid in Teaching and in Historical Studies. Reprinted from the last American edition, and at a much lower price. Crown 8vo., cloth extra. 8s. 6d.

Worcester's (Dr.), New and Greatly Enlarged Dictionary of the English Language. Adapted for Library or College Reference, comprising 40,000 Words more than Johnson's Dictionary. 4to. cloth, 1,834 pp. Price 31s. 6d. well bound; ditto, half mor. 2l. 2s.

" The volumes before us show a vast amount of diligence; but with Webster it is diligence in combination with fancifulness,—with Worcester in combination with good sense and judgment. Worcester's is the soberer and safer book, and may be pronounced the best existing English Lexicon."—*Athenæum*.

Words of Wellington, Maxims and Opinions, Sentences and Reflections of the Great Duke, gathered from his Despatches, Letters, and Speeches (Bayard Series). 2s. 6d.

Young (L.) Acts of Gallantry; giving a detail of every act for which the Silver Medal of the Royal Humane Society has been granted during the last Forty-one years. Crown 8vo., cloth. 7s. 6d.

Young (J. F.) Five Weeks in Greece.

Xenophon's Anabasis; or, Expedition of Cyrus. A Literal Translation, chiefly from the Text of Diadorf, by GEORGE B. WHEELER. Books I to III. Crown 8vo. boards. 2s.

——— **Books I. to VII.** Boards. 3s. 6d.

LONDON:

SAMPSON LOW, MARSTON, SEARLE, & RIVINGTON,

CROWN BUILDINGS, 188, FLEET STREET, E.C.

OLEOGRAPHS.

THESE wonderful reproductions *in oil-colours* of the original Oil Paintings of the great masters, and best modern painters, have met with great and well-deserved success wherever they have been introduced. Nothing succeeds like success; and no sooner were these beautiful works of art (produced only at great cost by one or two firms of high standing on the Continent) introduced to the British public by Messrs. SAMPSON LOW and Co., and well advertised by them, than the market was flooded by a host of most inferior Chromo-Lithographs, all sailing under the new name of Oleographs, and at once bringing these new productions into disrepute.

In order as much as possible to counteract this unmerited disparagement of works of real value, so well calculated to elevate art by popularizing the works of its greatest masters, in a form at once cheap and yet most faithful in colour and drawing, Messrs. SAMPSON LOW (specially-appointed Agents of the best Continental producers) have prepared a very carefully-selected list of the best subjects only, which will be forwarded post free to any address.

ALL THE OLEOGRAPHS CAN BE SUPPLIED EITHER

FRAMED OR UNFRAMED.

The Trade supplied on special terms.

LONDON:

SAMPSON LOW, MARSTON, SEARLE, AND RIVINGTON,

CROWN BUILDINGS, 188, FLEET STREET.

"Likely to popularise English art more than anything hitherto attempted .... A valuable repertory of great works of the English school."—*The Spectator.*

New and Enlarged Series of

THE PICTURE GALLERY.

ENCOURAGED by the success which has attended the publication of THE PICTURE GALLERY for the past three years, the Proprietors have resolved to issue a New Series, with Lives of the Great English Artists, illustrated with selections from their most important works. Each part to contain eight pages of Biography and four permanent Photographs.

The Parts already published contain:—

SIR JOSHUA REYNOLDS. The Strawberry Girl; The Hon. Mrs. Lloyd; The Holy Family; Kitty Fisher (with the Doves).

THOMAS GAINSBOROUGH. The Blue Boy; The Market Cart; Mrs. Siddons; The Harvest Waggon.

WILLIAM HOGARTH. His Portrait by Himself; The Rake's Progress—plate I.; The Enraged Musician; Strolling Actresses in a Barn.

BENJAMIN WEST. The Battle of La Hogue; The Death of Nelson; Cromwell Dissolving Parliament; The Landing of King Charles II.

SIR THOMAS LAWRENCE. Pope Pius VII.; Cardinal Gonsalvi; Miss Murray; Miss Selina Meade.

JOHN CONSTABLE. The River Stour; Salisbury Cathedral; The Corn-Field; The Valley Farm.

SIR DAVID WILKIE. Village Politicians; The Blind Fiddler; The Parish Beadle; The Highlander's Home.

GILBERT STUART NEWTON. Captain Macheath; Shylock and Jessica; Lear and Cordelia; Mrs. Lister.

ETTY AND COLLINS. The Combat; Joan of Arc; The Sale of the Pet Lamb; Rustic Civility.

SIR AUGUSTUS WALL CALLCOTT. Anne Page and Slender; Returning from Market; Rotterdam; Trent, in the Tyrol.

CHARLES ROBERT LESLIE. Taming the Shrew; Florizel and Perdita; Who can this be? Who can this be from?

JOSEPH WILLIAM MALLARD TURNER.

THE PICTURE GALLERY *is published monthly, price One Shilling, and may be had at all Booksellers, and at the principal Railway Bookstalls.*

LONDON:
SAMPSON LOW, MARSTON, SEARLE, AND RIVINGTON,
CROWN BUILDINGS, 188, FLEET STREET.

"Sure to succeed."—Athenæum.

Commenced January, 1876.
In Monthly Parts, price Eightenpence.

MEN OF MARK.

A Trustworthy Biography of the Distinguished Men of the Day, with Portraits in Permanent Photography (medallion cabinet size), specially taken for this work.

Parts I. and II. contain Portraits and Memoirs of—

THE RIGHT HON. THE EARL OF DUFFERIN, Governor-General of Canada.
SIR EDWARD CREASY, Professor of Jurisprudence in the four Inns of Court, late Chief Justice of Ceylon.
THE RIGHT HON. SIR RICHARD BAGGALLAY, Judge of the Supreme Court of Appeal, late Attorney-General.
CAPT. BURTON, the Great African traveller.
THE RIGHT HON. SPENCER WALPOLE, M.P. for the University of Cambridge, formerly Secretary of State for the Home Department.
THE RIGHT HON. SIR MICHAEL HICKS-BEACH, M.P., Chief Secretary for Ireland.

The portraits of the following amongst other distinguished men will appear in early succeeding numbers.

LORD LYTTON, VICEROY OF INDIA.

THE LORD BISHOP OF LONDON.	VICE-CHANCELLOR MALINS.
THE DUKE OF ABERCORN, Lord Lieutenant of Ireland.	J. A. FROUDE.
	J. E. MILLAIS, R.A.
SIR GARNET WOLSELEY, K.C.B.	F. LEIGHTON, A.R.A.
CARDINAL MANNING.	SIR W. FERGUSSON, BART.
THE RIGHT HON. THE SPEAKER.	SAMUEL PLIMSOLL, M.P.
THE RT. HON. JOHN BRIGHT, M.P.	ARCHDEACON DENISON.

The portraits are all taken expressly for this work, and cannot be obtained in any other form.

OPINIONS OF THE PRESS.

"The miniatures now before us retain the personal characteristics, the expression peculiar to each face, and the air of the sitter, with *great good fortune*. The book is sure to succeed as a serious companion to 'Vanity Fair.'"—*Athenæum.*

"It contains three splendid photographs, rendered permanent by the Woodbury process, and is got up in faultless style."—*Globe.*

"The portraits are excellently done, and the same may be said of the memoirs."—*Scotsman.*

"We have seen no more beautiful examples of the photographic art than the portraits which commence the series. . . . The plan of the Gallery of Contemporary Portraits is an excellent one."—*Sheffield Daily Telegraph.*

"The specimens in the part are excellent; they present admirable portraiture combined with definiteness absolutely microscopical and a balance of light and shade which bespeak them the work of a genuine artist."—*Brighton Gazette.*

LONDON:
SAMPSON LOW, MARSTON, SEARLE, AND RIVINGTON,
CROWN BUILDINGS, 188, FLEET STREET.

"MESSRS. SAMPSON LOW AND CO. *send us an analysis of the number of books issued during the year* 1875, *as chronicled in the fortnightly list of the* '*Publishers' Circular*,' *in which may be found the full titles of over* 5,400 *publications issued during the past year*."—THE TIMES, January 4, 1876; see also leading article in THE TIMES of January 5, 1876.

Established 1837.

 HE PUBLISHERS' CIRCULAR, and GENERAL RECORD of BRITISH and FOREIGN LITERATURE, is Published by SAMPSON LOW and Co., 188, Fleet Street, London, on the 1st and 15th of each Month. It gives a Transcript of the Title-Page of every Work published in Great Britain, and every work of interest published Abroad. 8s. per annum, including postage.

Publishers are requested to send their ANNOUNCEMENTS of NEW BOOKS in good time for publication on the 1st and 15th of each Month.

N.B. Having a large circulation amongst Literary Men, Publishers, Booksellers, and all connected with Literature, this is one of the best mediums for Announcements of New Publications. Subscribers have the right to advertise for "Books Wanted" which are out of print.

SCALE OF CHARGES FOR ADVERTISEMENTS.

	£	s.	d.
One Page (Demy 8vo.)	3	3	0
Half a Page	1	11	6
Less than Half a Page, per inch	0	10	6
Four Lines	0	2	6
Per line after	0	0	6

New Publications for Review must be addressed to THE EDITOR.

LONDON:
SAMPSON LOW, MARSTON, SEARLE, & RIVINGTON,
CROWN BUILDINGS, 188, FLEET STREET, E.C.

 CHISWICK PRESS:—PRINTED BY WHITTINGHAM AND WILKINS
TOOKS COURT, CHANCERY LANE